Applied economics is both an art and a science. It requires a sound knowledge of economic theory, statistical techniques and data sources, together with an appreciation that behavioural changes can alter apparently established economic relationships. In this book, leading economists illustrate the diversity of the subject, and present a series of studies that demonstrate a range of techniques and their applications to economic policy. It contains chapters which explore approaches to macroeconomic modelling, analyses of corporate performance, new estimates of the evolution of incomes in the UK since the eighteenth century, and assessments of the role of applied economics in guiding macroeconomic policy. All the chapters were specially commissioned to mark the 50th anniversary of the Department of Applied Economics at the University of Cambridge, and the contributions to the book are a fitting tribute to the traditions of work instigated by Sir Richard Stone and carried forward by his successors.

University of Cambridge
Department of Applied Economics

Occasional paper 63

Applied Economics and Public Policy

DAE Occasional papers

Earlier titles in this series and in the DAE Papers in Industrial Relations and Labour series may be obtained from:
The Publications Secretary, Department of Applied Economics,
Sidgwick Avenue, Cambridge, CB3 9DE

Applied Economics and Public Policy

EDITED BY

IAIN BEGG

AND

S. G. B. HENRY

CAMBRIDGE
UNIVERSITY PRESS

CAMBRIDGE
UNIVERSITY PRESS

University Printing House, Cambridge CB2 8BS, United Kingdom

Cambridge University Press is part of the University of Cambridge.

It furthers the University's mission by disseminating knowledge in the pursuit of education, learning and research at the highest international levels of excellence.

www.cambridge.org
Information on this title: www.cambridge.org/9780521624145

© Department of Applied Economics, University of Cambridge 1998

First published 1998

A catalogue record for this publication is available from the British Library

Library of Congress Cataloguing in Publication data

Applied economics and public policy / edited by Iain Begg and S. G. B. Henry.
    p.   cm. – (DAE occasional paper : no. 63)
  Papers presented at a conference on Dec. 15–16, 1995 to mark the
50th anniversary of the founding of the Dept. of Applied Economics,
Cambridge University.
    Includes bibliographical references and index.
    ISBN 0-521 -62414-2 (hardcover)
    1. Economics–Methodology–Congresses. 2. Europe–Economic
conditions–Statistical methods–Congresses. 3. Economic policy–
Methodology–Congresses. 4. University of Cambridge Dept. of
Applied Economics–Congresses. I. Begg, Iain. II. Henry, S. G. B.
III. University of Cambridge. Dept. of Applied Economics.
IV. Series: Occasional papers (University of Cambridge. Dept. of
Applied Economics) : 63.
  HB131.A658   1998
  330.1–dc21   97-44533 CIP

ISBN 978-0-521-62414-5 Hardback

Contents

x   Contents

Figures

Tables

Contributors

Terry Barker	Department of Applied Economics, University of Cambridge and Cambridge Econometrics Ltd
Iain Begg	Business School, South Bank University, London
Andrew Britton	National Institute of Economic and Social Research, London (now at Christchurch Industrial Centre, London)
Andy Cosh	ESRC Centre for Business Research, Judge Institute for Management Studies, and Queen's College, University of Cambridge
Alastair Cunningham	Bank of England, London
Charles Feinstein	All Souls College, Oxford
Wynne Godley	King's College, Cambridge and Jerome Levy Institute, Bard College, Annandale-on-Hudson
Andrew Goudie	Organisation for Economic Cooperation and Development, Paris (now at the Department for International Development, London)
Brian Henry	Centre for Economic Forecasting, London Business School
Alan Hughes	ESRC Centre for Business Research, Department of Applied Economics, University of Cambridge
Timothy Kehoe	Department of Economics, University of Minnesota and Research Department, Federal Reserve Bank of Minneapolis, Minnesota
Kevin Lee	Department of Economics, University of Leicester, Leicester

Hyehoon Lee	Department of Economics, University of Leicester
John Llewellyn	Lehman Brothers, London
Geoff Meeks	Faculty of Economics and Politics, University of Cambridge
David Newbery	Department of Applied Economics, University of Cambridge
Stephen Pudney	Department of Economics, University of Leicester
Ajit Singh	Faculty of Economics and Politics, University of Cambridge
Richard J. Smith	Department of Economics, University of Bristol
Ron Smith	Department of Economics, Birkbeck College, London
Martin Weale	National Institute of Economic and Social Research, London
Peter Westaway	National Institute of Economic and Social Research, London (now at the Bank of England, London)

Foreword

1995 marked the 50th Anniversary of the founding of the Department of Applied Economics, which we celebrated with a two-day conference on 15–16 December in Queens' College. Over 100 former members of the Department and current colleagues attended, many coming from distant parts of the world, to renew long-standing acquaintanceships. The papers presented were fascinating, and speak for themselves in this volume, but the conference was memorable in other ways. Brian Henry demonstrated the newly refurbished Phillips machine in the Meade room. James Meade was unfortunately too ill to attend but was present in spirit on a video (made in 1992) in which he was shown demonstrating the accelerator. It was fascinating to compare the transparency of this early analogue model of the economy with its later and more opaque digital representations discussed in the conference.

The suggestion and initial preparations for the Anniversary Conference came from Iain Begg, who was later joined in this undertaking by the then newly arrived Assistant Director, Brian Henry. The papers recalled past achievements while presenting research at the current frontiers of the subject. We were treated to nostalgia, history of thought and method, and the excitement that good applied economics arouses in those who believe that economics still has a key role to play both in understanding the world and in offering soundly based policy advice.

We are delighted by the support that former alumni and supporters of the Department provided for this conference: Barclays Bank; Terry Barker, still at the Department but in his capacity as Chairman of Cambridge Econometrics; Dermot Glynn (1970–72), now Managing Director at NERA; Fred Hallsworth, of Arthur Anderson; Bill Martin, UBS Philips and Drew; and Roger Witcomb (1976–78), now Finance Director at National Power – all responded to invitations to help financially with the project.

The idea of setting up a Department of Applied Economics, originally floated in 1939, was to provide the empirical research support for the theoretical advances in macroeconomics pioneered in Cambridge by Keynes. The founding of the Department was delayed by the war, but in November 1944 the University set up a Steering Committee, chaired by Keynes, which met and offered the Directorship to Richard Stone as a lifetime appointment. It took the University until May 1945 to approve the creation of the position, and Stone took up his post in July, 1945. It took somewhat longer to settle the details of staffing and funding of the Department. In this, the University was greatly helped by generous donations from the Ford and Rockefeller Foundations, and by 1948 there were six senior research staff and four junior research workers, as well as seven assistant staff.

Stone's international contacts and reputation rapidly made the Department a natural home for a series of distinguished visitors and collaborators. The early reports of the Department list among those who were on the staff or who visited for extended periods: Sydney Afriat, T. W. Anderson, Richard Brumberg, Donald Cochrane, J. S. (Mars) Cramer, Phyllis Deane, James Duesenberry, James Durbin, Mike Farrell, Roy Geary, H. S. Houthakker, Guy Orcutt, Sigbert Prais, Alan Prest, Gerhard Tintner, James Tobin and Geoffrey Watson.

The early reports of the Department set out the objectives very clearly, and they remain valid today. They were:

   (i) To restate economic theories and principles in a form which will allow them to be tested empirically.
  (ii) To collect together such relevant observations as have been made and to make others which are required in order that empirical tests may be applied.
 (iii) To develop the necessary statistical and other tools for the testing of economic hypotheses.
  (iv) Actually to make the test, using either the new tools and data already mentioned or those provided by others working in the same field.

Richard Stone set out his ideas at greater length in 1953 in a memorandum on the value, functions and organisation of a university research institute in applied economics written for Johns Hopkins University. He defended the need to develop and test economic theories using the expanding supply of empirical information, which he argued 'involves the combination of numerous skills and disciplines which are rarely embodied in a single individual'. By then the Department had grown to a research staff of 21 and support staff of 14, but as Stone noted 'there is no reason to suppose that an optimum size has yet been reached'. In practice, with one or two more research staff and rather fewer support staff as capital replaced labour, that remained the equilibrium size of the Department, adequate for 'the diversity of projects which is an essential feature of the kind of institute I am describing'. This volume illustrates that diversity, but also the common attributes of careful research done well.

I became the fourth Director in October 1988, and this anniversary is an appropriate moment to reflect on what has changed, and what has stayed the same, in the purpose and operation of the Department since its founding. The changes are obvious – computers have replaced computors, and our ability to analyse large datasets using sophisticated techniques has been totally transformed. Longer time series from a wider range of countries allow hypotheses to be subjected to more rigorous testing. The old Keynesian macro certainties may have faded as barriers to trade, communications and financial arbitrage have been eroded, but these same changes have increased the prominence of research into microeconomics, which flourishes with better data, better theory, and fewer impediments to market behaviour.

My personal taste in economics is to start where theory and evidence sit most comfortably, at the level of the firm and consumer behaviour, and build up from there to model and understand the interactions of these players with each other and their economic environment, conditioned as that is by institutions and policy interventions. Whether it is privatisation in Britain, or the transition of Eastern Europe, macroeconomic behaviour is profoundly influenced by microeconomic performance, and a proper study of these large questions requires that these interactions be modelled and informed by evidence. As Director, I have therefore endeavoured to build up and maintain our strength in the three branches of the subject – micro, macro, and econometrics, endeavouring to foster links between them. Good examples of this would include the application of microeconometrics to tax reform and the study of transition, or the application of panel data techniques to the study of company finance and macroeconomic performance. In this I am following the spirit of the Stone Growth Project agenda of moving between micro and macro, both based on quantification and estimation. Improved data and techniques together with advances in theory allow us to probe the previously obscure links between micro and macro and give greater coherence to the subject. An increased awareness of the importance of institutions, laws and customs of society, informed by game theory and the recognition that agents interact over time under incomplete information, has made us more receptive to the other social sciences, leading to increased collaboration across subject boundaries.

As we start the next half-century, I am confident that applied economics as a subject is better placed than ever before to investigate large questions, often by answering a set of inter-related smaller questions. By continuing to attract talented economists we shall continue to probe those frontiers of the subject where theory and evidence can be brought to bear on the ever-changing set of economic problems engaging the profession and society.

David M. Newbery
Director, Department of Applied Economics

1 Introduction

Iain Begg and Brian Henry

Applied economics is a dark art. A skilled applied economist has to use the tools of economic theory to articulate the question to be answered, and to identify and analyse the data needed to generate convincing answers. To the extent that it involves increasingly complex statistical and modelling techniques, practitioners of the art need to have a solid grounding in these disciplines. But technique is only part of the armoury of the competent applied economist, especially when the object of the exercise is to interpret potentially capricious behavioural phenomena in a way that provides worthwhile guidance for policy-makers. Good policy advice requires more than clear conceptualisation of the issues and accuracy in calculation, though these are plainly necessary conditions. What ultimately makes the difference is skill in interpretation and the capacity to exercise sound judgement.

Applied Economics is also the name of the Department (the DAE) founded in Cambridge in 1945 at the instigation of Keynes, and which has been at the forefront of so many developments in the subject in its 50 years. Versions of all the chapters in this volume were presented at a conference held in Cambridge in December 1995 to mark the 50th anniversary of the DAE. The event was not just a celebration for past and present members of the DAE, but also provided an opportunity to take stock of the subject. To this end, the papers were specially commissioned from distinguished applied economists who, between them, exemplify some of the most important developments of the subject in the last 50 years.

This volume is, essentially, about the problems in doing applied economics well. The chapters vary in subject and focus, some being largely technical, others concerned principally with interpretation. Although they draw on the traditions of work carried out in the DAE, collectively they present a snapshot of various techniques and applications of applied economics in different contexts. Their common trait is that they illustrate different facets of applied economics or its role in policy advice. Several

1

chapters present new findings which represent technical advances on previous work, while others survey and summarise the experience of individuals who have been involved in bridging the gap between analysis and policy for many years.

This introduction presents a brief overview of the research in applied economics done under the auspices of the DAE. We then reflect on the practice of applied economics, highlighting some of the problems which have arisen, and continue to arise, in producing convincing work. Our focus then shifts to an area of applied economics that has given rise to unfulfilled expectations about what applied economics can deliver: using models to guide policy. Here, we argue that such expectations have, at times, been unrealistic because behaviourial changes have not been adequately incorporated into the models, and also because modelling techniques have often been mis-applied. Finally, we offer some thoughts on the way forward for the subject.

The chapters are grouped into three parts. Part 1 brings together chapters on modelling and forecasting methods, including chapters which illustrate techniques and provide insights into the strengths and weaknesses of alternative methods. Part 2 contains four chapters which exemplify the importance of combining careful data work and the application of sophisticated analytic techniques in shedding light on different issues in applied economics. The final part of the book focuses on the use of methods of applied economics to inform economic policy.

1.1 The DAE contribution to applied economics

The roll-call of former staff of, and visitors to, the DAE testifies to the breadth and quality of the work that it has nurtured. The DAE has embraced a variety of different approaches to applied economics in its history. Some of these have been enduring, the analysis of companies' accounts brought up to date in the chapter by Goudie and Meeks (Chapter 9) being one such. Others have come and gone as the fashions of funding or the priorities of Directors and project leaders have shifted. In the early days, under Sir Richard Stone's Directorship (1945–1955), the DAE achieved a balance between theory and empirical analysis that has rarely been matched. As Smith reports (Chapter 5), the Department was especially prominent in its contributions to econometric methods and their applications. Initially, the focus was on developing the theory of time-series regression methods. Indeed, the DAE can reasonably claim to have spawned 'Durbin–Watson' and 'Cochrane–Orcutt' techniques for handling problems of serially correlated errors, amongst other widely used tools of the trade.

Subsequently, the emphasis shifted to applications of these new methods of analysis, notably with the various attempts to model demand systems. In parallel, considerable efforts were devoted to measurement problems, often involving the simultaneous establishment of new techniques and imaginative approaches to data construction. Dick Stone's Nobel Prize-winning work on national accounts is the most widely-known example, but the DAE was also the source of other highly-regarded research in this mould. During Brian Reddaway's Directorship (1955–1970), the emphasis was more on quantification: combining insights from economic theory with data collection and statistical analysis to answer particular questions. This encompassed seminal work in the quantification of economic history, such as that of Deane and Cole (1962) on measuring British economic growth; and the establishment of the longitudinal database of company accounts that is still in use to this day. The chapters in this volume by Feinstein (Chapter 8); by Cosh, Hughes, Lee and Pudney (Chapter 7); by Cosh, Hughes, Lee and Singh (Chapter 6); and by Cunningham, Smith and Weale (Chapter 3) are all in this tradition of innovation in approaches to measurement and the estimation of apparently simple problems which nonetheless require sophisticated methods of analysis. Major enquiries into the operation of the Selective Employment Tax and the consequences of foreign investment were also carried out in the 1960s.

Wynne Godley's Directorship was identified with the two large modelling groups: the *Growth Project* (CGP) and the *Cambridge Economic Policy Group* (CEPG), both of which gave Cambridge a prominent role in the macroeconomic policy debate. Publication of the *Cambridge Economic Policy Review* became an important media event that engendered strong reactions from the profession and commentators alike. The CGP, inspired by Dick Stone and directed subsequently by Terry Barker, continued to develop increasingly complex multi-sectoral models that provided the only source of consistent industrially disaggregated forecasts for the British economy. The Department's research portfolio also included work in other areas, such as labour markets, company accounts, and urban and regional policy, as well as a long-running economic theory project.

Since David Newbery became Director, the balance has shifted towards applied microeconomics, but there has also been a renewed focus on state-of-the-art econometrics. The DAE has contributed extensively to the debate on privatisation and how to regulate privately-owned utilities with dominant market positions. The econometric work has ranged from the establishment of a large-scale model designed to monitor income distribution to more theoretical work on disaggregation and on techniques for handling complex cross-sectional data. Influential new work over the last few years, on the methodology of modelling structural time-series models with applications to macroeconomic models, returns to earlier DAE interests in macro-modelling and macro-policy advice. A major Economic and Social Research Council (ESRC)-funded project on small businesses paved the way for the recently established ESRC Centre for Business Research which has taken up the DAE tradition of research on industrial and company performance, and linked it with complementary work in law, engineering, geography and management studies.

1.2 Applied economics in practice

What is applied economics? For some, it is deploying economic theory to elucidate a specific problem; others emphasise quantification or the use of econometrics. Samuelson, Koopmans and Stone (1954), quoted by Smith (Chapter 5), suggest that econometrics combines theory, observation and methods of inference, although Smith argues that econometrics is principally about the last of these. This definition does, however, capture much of the essence of applied economics as it has evolved in the DAE, although it would be appropriate to add to this definition a reference to interpretation and application. With this addition, the following definition of the subject matter of applied economics as pursued by the Department to provide quantitative economic analysis is proposed:

applied economics is the bringing together of economic theory, measurement and methods of statistical and econometric analysis, and the interpretation of such analytic work to elucidate economic phenomena and to inform economic policy.

How large a role should intuition have in the process of policy advice? One of the ironies of forecasting is that it is the corrections introduced by the forecasters that, typically, make models tolerably accurate. The chapter by Godley (Chapter 12) makes an eloquent plea for a better understanding of this aspect of applied economics, arguing that models should not be seen as mechanistic tools, but as aids to understanding. The question this raises is that of primacy: is the model the servant of the forecaster, a framework for thinking about how the system works, or is it the function of the operator to tweak the model towards improved performance? In answering this, John Llewellyn brings the perspective of a practitioner who learned his trade as an academic researcher, but has since had to spend many years interpreting the results of research to sceptical and, no doubt, selectively deaf politicians and administrators. Inevitably, the temptation for the decision-maker is to select the attractive option, the one which earns the greatest credit in the short term, even if it has damaging side-effects. Yet, as Llewellyn shows (Chapter 11), the exercise of judgement can be critical in securing acceptance of the results emanating from analytic work.

Striking the correct balance between the mechanics of the subject and the exercise of judgement is, perhaps, the key to applied economics. On the one hand, it is easy to forget that economics is a *social* (or *behavioural*) science, and that the patterns of behaviour which give rise to economic propositions can alter, sometimes radically. Adaptation to inflation (or, now, to greater price stability), as Britton and Westaway point out (Chapter 10), provides a good illustration of this, because such changes can mean that apparently well-established linkages abruptly cease to hold. Consequently, highly sophisticated models employing advanced econometric techniques may have their foundations swept away. This sometimes leads to an even more complex framework being required, for example, in the increasing use of non-linear as opposed to linear models of cyclical behaviour. These developments – where they occur – take considerable time. In the meantime, skilled judgement needs to be deployed in evaluating what may be a changing environment. In his chapter, Llewellyn (Chapter 11) draws attention to several dimensions of the delicate balancing-act that has to be performed.

Data errors, or a failure to appreciate the idiosyncrasies in statistical series, can also lead to misguided conclusions. The careful construction of datasets might appear to be an unglamorous activity, best left to underemployed statisticians. In reality, good preparation is often – as in decorating – the key to convincing applied economics and is one of the key skills that competent practitioners have to develop. An ability instantly to spot rogue figures or to justify entries in tables is, we are told, a defining feature of the applied economists who came under Brian Reddaway's tutelage.

Short-term economic analysis is bedevilled by incomplete, out-of-date, or inaccurate data, and it is not at all uncommon to find that data revisions do as much to change policy prescriptions as genuine movements in critical variables. Yet it is incontrovertible that accurate short-term projections are needed. The methodology proposed by Cunningham, Smith and Weale (Chapter 3) for measuring monthly GDP and for improving the quality of leading indicators creates a tool that complements more formal model-based forecasts. Enhancing the accuracy of data is not, however, an issue germane only to short-term economic analysis. It is also of critical importance in 'quantitative' economic history and in the longitudinal study of corporate performance, two important lines of research in which the DAE has been especially prominent.

Feinstein's fascinating new results on estimates of real incomes are a persuasive reminder of the importance of careful attention to the detail of data. In today's environment, where vast volumes of data can be down loaded *via* the Internet with a few clicks on a mouse, such exercises may seem quaintly obsolete. But the effort needed to render even apparently standardised databases from international agencies such as the Organisation for Economic Co-operation and Development (OECD) or the World Bank usable for research purposes is regularly underestimated, as Summers and Heston would no doubt testify. The value of a database such as the DAE one containing time series of company accounts, therefore, lies not so much in its scale and span as in the considerable efforts that went into scrutinising, standardising and 'sanitising' the data. Three of the papers in the volume draw on this database, extending previous analyses of company performance and the effects of mergers and takeovers. Rigour in accountancy is also central to the estimation of national accounts and the construction of social accounting matrices (SAMs), both fields in which the pioneering work of Dick Stone has been hugely influential. The chapters by Kehoe and Barker (Chapters 4 and 2) derive from and extend this work.

An inventory of research done in the DAE would show the breadth of the fields of enquiry of applied economics and it is clear that the subject has come a long way in the last 50 years. It is, however, important to recognise that good applied economics is often a hard slog. State-of-the-art software packages and ready electronic access to raw data provide today's researchers with tools that their predecessors of ten, let alone 50 years ago would envy. Techniques for analysis, diagnostic tests and the sheer processing power of personal computers have all advanced hugely. Yet it is far from obvious that the quality of economic analysis has advanced commensurately or that applied economics has been able to inform policy advice as effectively as the founders of the DAE hoped. Indeed, in a key field of applied economics – the use of forecasting and macroeconomic models – there has been evident disenchantment with the results. It is instructive to reflect on the reasons for this, and in the next section we look in greater detail at some of the reasons for the comparatively disappointing performance of these tools. In many ways, the evolution of this area of applied economics serves as a benchmark for assessing others.

1.3 The use of models for policy purposes

Structural macro-models have played a significant part in policy debates for decades. But their importance has fluctuated over this time, sometimes considerably so. In the US in particular, much less importance is currently attached to forecasts and policy simulations using large-scale macro-models than was the case in the sixties and seventies. In part, this aversion stems from the joint effects of the Lucas and Sims critiques (Lucas, 1976; Sims, 1980) both of which, though different in their substance, appeared to undermine both the possibility of identifying such macro structures and the use of large-scale models for policy evaluation. Another, often over-looked, factor in this loss of popularity was of a more pragmatic nature: in the early days of macro-modelling there were unduly optimistic expectations about the reliability of large-scale models, views which suffered set-backs with the econometric problems encountered with, for example, the Brookings model. The almost exclusive attention of many large-scale models to the demand side also meant they were ill-equipped to deal with the effects of the oil price shocks at the beginning and at the end of the 1970s. Academic and practical ingredients can thus be discerned here. Alternatives were sought, leading to rich and varied developments in macroeconomic modelling: Real Business Cycle (RBC), Computable General Equilibrium (CGE), and various forms of Vector Autoregressive (VAR) model (e.g. non-structural, structural, or Bayesian) represent just some examples of these developments.

It is an interesting fact that, although similar disputes on modelling methodologies have been (and continue to be) evident in the UK, the prac-tice of macro-modelling here has retained a distinctly structural slant no longer much in evidence in the US, albeit with a modelling sophistication far removed from the models of the 1970s. It may not be possible to account convincingly for this difference between recent US and UK expe-rience, but there seem to be at least two things involved: one financial, the other intellectual. In the US, structural macro-models based more on com-mercial funding have moved towards forecasting, while research using macro-models has declined. In the UK, thanks to continued public funding, the focus has been more on research with potentially a longer-term payoff. Indeed, macro-modelling in the UK has witnessed a burst of activity aimed at absorbing rational expectations, supply-side effects, long-run fiscal solvency rules, and other developments in macroeconomic theory into more structural economic models. There thus appears to have been a robust response to the 'critiques' of both Lucas (1976) and Sims (1980) in UK macroeconomic circles.

Two developments in particular are worth describing more fully. The first development relates to the response to modelling expectations forma-tion. Here, rather than regarding the Lucas Critique – which observed the conflation of dynamics and lags due to expectations formation, thus high-lighting the dependence of a model's marginal properties upon expecta-tions formation – as a barrier to macro policy analysis, there were positive developments in modelling expectations in the UK. As already observed, the leading macro-modellers in the UK actively absorbed rational expecta-tions into equations where an empirical case for this could be established, and dynamic solutions with fully consistent model expectations had become routine by the mid 1980s.

8   Iain Begg and Brian Henry

The second development relates to the issue of identifying structural/behaviourial relationships from econometric analysis. Here, VAR models originally seemed to offer an 'a-theoretic' way of side-stepping the problems relating to identification issues raised in the Cowles Commission simultaneous equation approach (taken as the template for traditional structural models). But since then this debate has moved on, and attention has recently shifted to using identification conditions with more economic content. This movement gained a further impetus with the introduction of cointegration techniques into dynamic modelling, with its explicit identification procedures being proposed by Johansen (1988) for a multivariate dynamic model, in the (potential) presence of multiple co-integrating relationships. More recently, Hashem Pesaran and his colleagues at Cambridge have argued persuasively for the use of economic theoretic restrictions in modelling long-run co-integrating relationships (Pesaran, 1997; Pesaran and Shin, 1995), rather than the 'statistical' identification based on reduced-rank conditions proposed by Johansen. Ironically, these developments, centred on the issue of identification, are illustrative of a convergence of ideas which appears to be taking place between modelling methodologies, whether they are initiated from VARs or structural modelling methods.

Macro-models have continued to be used as test beds for macro-theories, though more evidently in the UK than elsewhere. There are, as Llewellyn reminds us (Chapter 11), at least two roles for models in policy-making (or policy-oriented) organisations: they act as a repository for empirical research results for individual equations or sectors, and they are a means of establishing the implications of shocks, allowing for feedbacks between the principal sectors in the whole economy. They are also used as a tool in producing forecasts, although the tool can only be used with the familiar inputs of residual changes and other judgemental alterations to the conditional dynamic solution to the model itself. It makes sense, therefore, to distinguish the forecast made by the forecasting team from the model forecast. We referred earlier to a feature which emerges very clearly from Llewellyn's account of his work at the OECD, and in the views expressed by Godley on his work with the Cambridge Economic Policy Group and subsequently (Chapter 12), namely that, in this work, the model was never regarded as fixed. The world is complex and changes very often in ways which it is impossible to anticipate, and so no serious macro-economist would sit back and regard an estimated model as 'finished'.

Important and fundamental methodological and modelling issues are, however, provoked by these matters. One is the dual role of these models: they are meant both to represent a complete macro-structure, and to provide useful forecasts. But structures change, sometimes abruptly, and this raised more profound questions about the role of economic theory in models, and the use of models in testing theories. A further, and major, complication is the search for theories which allow for behaviourial change, and the development of techniques for dealing with such change.

The role of theory in models, especially that relevant to what appears to be a changing world, is thus a crucial area for applied economics. Two strands are evident in the debate, and appear in the contributions to this volume. In the first strand, we find developments which link modelling much more closely to the consistent micro-foundations of maximising agents. Two rivals to conventional simultaneous models owe their popularity, to a considerable extent, to their micro-theoretic foundations. CGE models have clear links with the existence theorems in general equilibrium theory and in the computation of general fixed point solutions first introduced by Scarf (1967). RBC models also emphasise neoclassical intertemporal optimising behaviour as the basis on which to account for both growth and business cycles in developed economies. Some have argued that a closer adherence to clear micro-theoretical underpinning is the future for macro-modelling (see Wickens, 1995). There are obviously very important issues raised by these contrasting approaches, involving diverse views on such matters as the efficiency and completeness of markets, expectations formation, and the significance of adjustment costs and inertia.

A model with both a firm theoretical basis and convincing empirical support is the ambition of most modellers of whatever persuasion. The balance between these ambitions differs and, up to now, structural modellers have typically placed most emphasis on econometric criteria in model selection. It is probably more accurate to describe differences in empirical methodologies as being differences in how evidence is used, and in what is regarded as empirical validation of a particular approach. CGE modellers tend to use calibration, and RBC modellers select models on the basis of their ability to reproduce broad time-series properties of the data.

In this context, an issue raised by the forecasting function of models is that of model validation. But the issue is wider than simply judging the veracity of a modelling approach or paradigm by the relative success of its forecasting performance. Even if the way to make that judgment were clear – which it is not – conditioning, the time-series properties of exogenous variables (including policy assumptions and variables), and the time scale chosen for comparisons are all contentious, as Godley points out (Chapter 12). Nonetheless, there is a sense in which forecast failure *should* require the modeller to respecify the model. For example, following financial liberalisation in the UK, a reformulation of forward looking consumption–asset price linkages rightly occurred in many macro-models.[1]

More widely, the issue of the empirical validation of a modelling framework is a continuing one, as illustrated by other papers in this volume. Both Barker (Chapter 2) and Kehoe (Chapter 4) give an assessment of this issue in their comments on CGE models. In the past, these models have often been calibrated and, as noted by Kehoe, this has led some practitioners to recommend they not be used for forecasting at all, but only to provide insights into policy thinking. The parallel of this with the first of the two dual functions of traditional macro models noted earlier is intriguing. However, as Kehoe illustrates in his example of Spain, CGE models may be capable of reasonable conditional forecasting performance.

1.4 The way forward: a research agenda

Several areas of applied economics are revealed by the chapters in this book to be unsatisfactory or in need of fresh thinking. Britton and Westaway (Chapter 10), for example, highlight some of the deficiencies in macroeconomic forecasting models and the compromises they oblige modellers to make. The contrasting approaches of Kehoe and Barker to cross-sectional modelling, similarly, raise questions about how disaggregated modelling is best approached.

A fundamental question confronting the economics profession today is whether applied work has served society well, whether it is delivering policy advice of sufficient quality. In most of the OECD countries (and especially the European ones), slow growth, intractable unemployment and a general feeling of malaise suggest a pervasive failure of economic policy. Is this, as Llewellyn suggests, because too little effort has gone into understanding the supply side? Is it a failure to persuade, possibly born of over-elaboration in empirical methods and inadequate presentation of results? Or is it, less encouragingly, that unrealistic expectations have been engendered about the capacity of economics to 'solve' economic problems once and for all? A more encouraging approach is that – faced with changing behaviour, substantial data deficiencies and alternative economic theories – we must expect that robust empirical results will be extremely difficult to come by. The potential for economic behaviour to change over time, by itself, suggests that our knowledge needs to evolve quickly enough to keep pace. Offsetting, to some extent, the negative evidence of forecast failure – to anticipate the recession of the early 1990s both in the US and the UK, for example – there are some positive signs. The greater emphasis on economic theory in model building, already alluded to, and evidenced in this volume, is a helpful development, as is the convergence in some areas on the need to test these theories in empirical models. In this context, the traditional segmentation of economics into macro and micro has long been problematic, with a tendency for each to work from a highly stylised and often obsolete variant of the other. The chapter by Goudie and Meeks (Chapter 9) is an interesting attempt to escape the straitjacket by combining macroeconomics as embodied in the Cambridge Econometrics model of the economy with company data to assess how macroeconomic policy affected company failure in the early 1980s. The advantage of this approach is that it allows the effects on company performance of what were profound changes in macroeconomic conditions to be modelled explicitly.

Such innovation in approach, combined with advances in the tools of the trade, opens up new opportunities for research in applied economics. Raw computing power and data handling facilities have ceased to be the constraints they were in the early days of the DAE; econometric methods have reached new levels of sophistication; the availability of data is greater than ever before; and statistical series are long enough to allow more complex experimentation. The chapters in this volume point to some of the emerging directions for applied economics; the DAE will, no doubt, help to develop others.

The DAE, in our view, has exemplified the best in applied economics, because it has fostered research which has brought together the differing talents of theorists, data experts and policy advisers. A combination of these ingredients is needed for worthwhile work, yet it is often conspicuous by its absence. In the DAE, as the work in this volume testifies, standards have been and remain high, and the output impressive. It is a proud tradition and one which we firmly expect to continue.

Note

1 It should be clear that it is forecasts from models which are meant here. Indeed, real-time forecasts from a model may be the only genuine (*ex ante*) test we have of a model.

Part One

Modelling and forecasting methods

2 Large-scale energy–environment–economy modelling of the European Union

Terry Barker

2.1 Introduction

The meteorological experts of the Intergovernmental Panel on Climate, a United Nations body charged with assessing the problem of global warming, have concluded that the atmosphere is heating up and that human activity is responsible (*Financial Times*, 1 December 1995). If greenhouse gas (GG) emissions go on rising, there will be an increasing risk of catastrophic climate change (Cline, 1992), e.g. an average temperature rise of 6°C over the next 200 years, rising sea levels caused by the melting ice caps, and more extreme events due to the increased latent energy in the atmosphere.

The emissions are an unwanted byproduct of economic activity, such as the burning of fossil fuels for heat, light and power, and the clearing of forests. However, energy can be produced from a variety of sources, some with very low carbon contents, and used in a variety of ways, offering the possibility of even lower levels of emissions. Consumption can also be much less carbon-intensive than at present. In general, there are substantial opportunities for emissions to respond to relative prices (Barker, Ekins and Johnstone (eds), 1995), so that fiscal policy could make a major contribution to reducing emissions, with benefit to the economy and the environment, e.g. through carbon tax revenues being recycled *via* reductions in employment taxes (Barker, 1995) and by the reduction in fossil fuel use being associated with the reduction in other pollution, such as sulphur dioxide, low-level ozone, noise and dust (Ekins, 1996).

The pervasive use of fossil fuels in economic activity, and the absence of a cost-effective end-of-pipe technology to remove the CO_2 arising, mean that fiscal policies are more suited to GG abatement than regulation. Large-scale models have great potential to inform the policy-making process for three reasons: the economy-wide nature of the problem; the availability of a range of fiscal options for tackling it (carbon/energy tax, road fuel duties, energy-saving R&D and other expenditure); and the need to assess the effects of the policies on competitiveness. This has been recognised in the research funding of large-scale energy–environment–economy (E3) models since 1990 by many national and international organisations.[1]

Most of the research effort has gone into the development of Computable General Equilibrium (CGE) models, and this methodology dominates the field.[2] The other approaches in E3 modelling are CGE-energy-engineering systems (e.g. Barns, Edmonds and Reilly, 1992; Manne and Rutherford, 1994) and econometric models (the model described below, OPEC's World Energy Model, and the London Business School world model). This chapter is not a review of these models, several of which are under construction, but a classification of them and an assessment of the strengths and weaknesses of each approach. The chapter puts the econometric approach in context.

2.2 Approaches to large-scale E3 modelling

2.2.1 Definitions

Econometric models will be defined as those based directly on formal methods of statistical inference involving cross-section and/or time-series data to estimate the parameters of the model. This definition is assumed to exclude simple input–output models and CGE models which use one observation of a matrix of flows to derive a set of parameters. It excludes CGE models which incorporate parameters based on expert views or literature surveys without embedding these priors into a formal estimation system; and it excludes those CGE models which use data, where time-series are available, to make projections into the future without consideration of their time-series properties. Large-scale economic and econometric models are those with hundreds if not thousands of stochastic equations; most aggregate macroeconometric models have fewer equations and for the most part they are more concerned with short-term forecasting than long-run analysis, but their long-run properties have come under increasing scrutiny in recent years.[3]

2.2.2 Model taxonomy

The chapter is concerned with economy-wide large-scale E3 models. Research involving such models and their use is proceeding at a rapid pace and the models which have been developed and published fall into the following groups:[4]

- static applied general equilibrium models
- dynamic applied general equilibrium models
- multisectoral dynamic econometric models
- operational multi-model systems.

Static applied computable general equilibrium models

CGE models stem from economic theory going back to Walras and developed by Arrow and Debreu (1954); they have been applied by calibrating them on input–output tables following the work of Leontief; Whalley (1991) provides a survey. These models began as a means of measuring the effects of tariff and tax policy (Evans, 1972; Shoven and Whalley, 1984), but have been developed into global E3 modelling, most notably in the OECD GREEN model (Burniaux *et al.*, 1992). GREEN, which includes Western Europe as a world region, has been applied to a range of questions concerning the implementation of carbon and energy taxes in different world areas, together with different schemes for distributing the revenues (Nicoletti and Oliveira-Martins, 1992, 1995; Oliveira-Martins *et al.*, 1992). Since it is perhaps the most developed global E3 model, with many publications available describing and applying the model, it is used below as the primary example of CGE modelling.

Dynamic applied general equilibrium models

One of the leading US modelling programmes on E3 policies builds on Jorgenson's Dynamic General Equilibrium Model (DGEM) (Jorgenson and Wilcoxen, 1990, 1992, 1993). The model combines the CGE approach with time-series econometric estimation of important sets of relationships (e.g. production functions). A more recent development in this direction is the G-CUBED multi-country model (McKibbin and Wilcoxen, 1992; McKibbin, 1992), a model combining dynamic optimisation with econometric estimation of consumption and production functions, although this published version of the model was estimated on input–output tables and trade data for one year, 1987.

GEM-E3 is an integrated E3 CGE model of European economies constructed under the JOULE II/SOLFEGE programme (Capros, 1992). GEM-E3 is a set of large national general equilibrium models with trade treated by means of general equilibrium market clearing, rather than by estimated time-series econometric equations. The national models will be calibrated on input–output tables and linked to a set of partial equilibrium energy models PRIMES. GEM-E3 is under construction and it is not clear to what extent it will be a dynamic or static CGE.

Multisectoral dynamic econometric models

These models also use input–output tables, but combine them with the time-series analysis of macroeconometric models. The Cambridge Growth Project model, MDM (Barker and Peterson (eds), 1987) has become the Cambridge Econometrics E3 model of the UK, designed with the objective of assessing the feasibility of substantial reductions in UK CO_2 emissions (Barker, 1995). Models in the same tradition for national economies have been built by the INFORUM group of modellers (Almon, 1991), by the Norwegian Central Bureau of Statistics in its MODAG model (Cappelen, 1991) and by the Netherlands Central Plan Bureau, amongst others.

These are however national models. E3ME (Barker, Gardiner and Dieppe, 1995) is a dynamic regional econometric E3 model capable of long-term projections incorporating changes in relative prices and forward-looking expectations. WARM (Carraro, 1992) is another model sharing these features. However, WARM is based on the theory of the individual firm and agent, assuming representative agents, with equations estimated on industry and country data treated as panel data. WARM, unlike the other models in this group, does not include gross output and does not use input–output tables.

Operational multi-model systems

The integrated modelling approach is distinguished from the multi-model approach of the Data Resources Incorporated (DRI) suite of models used to assess the EC tax (DRI, 1991 and 1992), or the HERMES-MIDAS system (European Commission, 1993; Laroui and Velthuijsen, 1992). The term multi-model is used to describe systems of models, in this case those used to analyse the effects of carbon taxes and related policies at the European level.

2.2.3 Large-scale UK modelling in the DAE

For many years this activity was almost synonymous with that of the Cambridge Growth Project, founded by Richard Stone and Alan Brown in 1960. Stone and his colleagues proposed to investigate the possibilities of faster growth in the British economy by means of a large-scale econometric model using the latest computing techniques available at the time and based on earlier work in the DAE by Stone and his colleagues on the National Accounts in the 1940s, and input–output tables and consumer demand systems in the 1950s. The project they founded was to last 27 years until 1987, but this is not the place for a history of the Cambridge Growth Project. A surprisingly small proportion of the research went directly into model construction and application, perhaps 10–20% of the resources. Most effort went into data issues and the applied econometrics of different aspects of UK economic behaviour: consumer demand, production structure, foreign trade, the public company and policy formulation.

In 1961 and 1962, when Stone and Brown published details of their proposed new disaggregated economic model in several papers (Stone, 1961, 1962; Stone and Brown 1962a) including the first volume of the series 'A Programme for Growth' (Stone and Brown, 1962b), one important feature was the linking of a demand system and an input–output table.[5] Stone and Brown provided a bridge between the time-series econometric analysis of consumer demand and the cross-section analysis of industrial demand represented by the input-output table. The value of the input-output table (especially when incorporated into the wider coverage of a social accounting matrix) in providing a disaggregated framework for the National Accounts was earlier recommended in the UN's *System of National Accounts* prepared under Stone's leadership.

The work on the static model was consolidated in Barker (ed.) (1976), just at the time that, at the behest of the UK Treasury, members of the project set up Cambridge Econometrics (CE) to provide a commercial service using the project's model. This required the development of MDM, a dynamic version of the model (Barker, 1977) which would in principle, and eventually in practice, allow industrial forecasts to be made alongside projections of alternative scenarios. Members of the project were able to use the data and forecasts provided by CE in their research, removing a huge burden of work in data collection and in the preparation of a standard view to compare scenarios. The last version of the succession of dynamic models (MDM6) built by the project was published in 1987 (Barker and Peterson). When ESRC funding was ended in that same year, responsibility for model estimation and validation passed to CE, but research involving the model continued in the DAE with its extension to become an E3 model in 1993. MDM has also become a UK regional model and is used by CE as the basis of its industrial, E3 and regional services. MDM and E3ME, described in this chapter, are in a direct line of succession from the original Rocket (Stone and Brown, 1962b, p. 302).

The econometric work in the DAE put measurement on a par with theory in large-scale modelling: great effort went into both the construction of social accounting matrices and the preparation of disaggregated, consistent time-series data; and formal methods of statistical inference were used to interpret the data and estimate the models. From the early 1970s to 1982, the DAE also housed the Cambridge Economic Policy Group, who constructed a small model of the UK economy (Coutts,

1976). Their model was built to embody and promote a particular view of the way the economy works and the group and the model became closely associated with a particular policy recommendation, import controls. The Growth Project's models were also based on a world view, but one in which disaggregation was important for its own sake, to represent industrial structure and consumer demand, and one in which more emphasis was placed on techniques of statistical inference.

2.2.4 The conception, design and development of E3ME

Purpose

E3ME (a general Energy–Environment–Economy Model for Europe) is a general model for Europe designed to address issues that link developments and policies in the areas of energy, the environment and the economy (see Barker, 1995; Barker, Gardiner and Dieppe, 1995). The European economy is becoming more and more integrated; at the same time, the relationship between economic activity, energy use and the environment is of pressing concern in the environmental policy debate.

Design

The guiding principles of the model are such that it is

- at a *European* rather than at a national level, with the national economies being treated as regions of Europe
- dealing with energy, the environment, population and the economy in *one modelling framework* and allowing short-term deviations to occur while convergence to a long-run outcome takes place
- designed from the outset to address issues of central importance for *economic, energy and environmental policy* at the European level
- capable of providing *short-term and long-term economic and industrial forecasts* for business and government
- capable of analysing *long-term structural change* in energy demand and supply and in the economy
- focused on the contribution of *research and development*, and associated technological innovation, on the dynamics of growth and change.

Modelling a Europe of regions

Although it makes sense to model the European economy as a single entity, there are large differences in the constituent regions' economic efficiency and well-being. The most extreme of these are between the traditional agricultural economies of the peripheral southern Mediterranean (Portugal, Greece, southern Italy) and those of the developed core. Notable also are the differences between the eastern and western *Länder* of a united Germany. These differences have implications for migration, regional transfers of funds and economic development. Any model which ignored them would have limited policy relevance. The application of the subsidiarity principle within the European Union (EU) also implies that many functions of government will continue to operate at the level of the national state, or indeed at a more local level. Finally, accession of new members (Austria, Sweden, Finland) and the need for an integrated treatment of other important European economies (Norway, Switzerland) mean that the national dimension of economic development is likely to continue to be of central concern.

A single European market characterised by regional/national differences is matched in modelling terms by a general model dividing Europe into regions, consisting of each of the member states with Germany divided into east and west and Italy divided into north and south. These regions have quite different characteristics for the modelling of energy policy. The industrialised centre tends to lead in terms of energy efficiency. The agricultural south is in the process of rapid development and urbanisation, with an expectation that fuel use will rise rapidly, while the new market conditions in eastern Germany make for major problems of transformation of its energy market, with a change to much higher relative prices of energy and accelerated replacement of its capital stock. Equally, sectoral detail is important because of the different energy characteristics of each sector.

The E3ME model therefore reflects the characteristics of Europe rather than the US, or other national industrialised economies, in that the EU is a union of member states with great diversity in language, law, tradition, culture and taste. The model treats member states as distinct economic entities (or in the case of Italy and Germany each as two regions of the same economy) interacting with one another; but at the same time it is one model giving the benefits of common classifications, definitions and methodology, and with equation estimates and results capable of being aggregated at the European level. In this it differs from the DRI collection of EU models (DRI, 1992, 1994) and some state-of-the-art US models, e.g. Jorgenson's Dynamic GEM (Jorgenson and Wilcoxen, 1992).

It is also in a new generation of models, looking to the problems of the next 20 to 30 years, and taking advantage of the increasing power of desktop computing and new software for portability and presentation. As an energy–economy model of European states, it is a successor to the EXPLOR models of the 1970s and the HERMES models (European

Table 2.1. *Classifications in E3ME*

RZ	Regions	14
A	World areas	14
Y	Industries	32
K	Investment sectors	33
V	Investment assets	8
C	Consumer expenditure	28
H	Institutional sector	7
R	Receipts and payments	34
T	Commodity taxes	17
FU	Fuel users	17
J	Fuel types	11
EM	Environmental emissions	10

Commission, 1993) of the 1980s and 1990s, but adopts a single model framework to limit (if not remove) the problems of linkage, and uses new econometric techniques which allow for long-run relationships to be distinguished from short-term dynamics. To the author's knowledge, there are no other E3 integrated models for Europe at this level of detail, capable of addressing both cyclical and long-term problems.

The construction of a general E3 model is very ambitious in relation to the available data and the resources required. It has required a radical approach (by macroeconometric standards) to the estimation and solution of the model in order to take advantage of consistent disaggregation across regions using panel-data techniques. The organisation of the work of constructing and updating the model has also changed radically compared to earlier projects. In earlier European modelling (e.g. for HERMES) national teams worked on own-country models; in E3ME different groups have worked in different areas (e.g. consumption) on many European economies, and the model has been pan-European from day one. However, this has not meant that the special features of member-state economies have been ignored: national expertise is still required to validate equations and results.

Table 2.1 lists the number of regions, sectors, fuels and other items in several of the sets or classifications distinguished in the model. For various reasons, in version 1.1 of the model no estimates have been made for eastern Germany, north/south Italy and Greece; furthermore, two of the 32 industrial sectors are inoperative (recycling and unallocated) in terms of model estimation.

Table 2.2. *Average goodness of fit in E3ME*

Function name		Dynamic equations		
		No. of est. equations	RSQ (IV)* (unadjusted)	RSQ (IV)** (adjusted)
BFR0	Aggregate energy demand	185	0.42	0.28
BFRC	Coal demand	115	0.42	0.24
BFRO	Heavy fuel oil demand	144	0.45	0.33
BFRG	Natural gas demand	105	0.53	0.42
BFRE	Electricity demand	146	0.32	0.17
BRSC	Aggregate consumption	9	0.71	0.71
BCR	Disaggregate consumption	234	0.39	0.30
BKR	Industrial investment	247	0.36	0.26
BQRX	Export volume	270	0.44	0.28
BQRM	Import volume	291	0.43	0.29
BYRH	Hours worked	296	0.20	0.10
BYRE	Industrial employment	285	0.42	0.25
BPYR	Industrial prices	274	0.58	0.46
BPQX	Export prices	270	0.61	0.53
BPQM	Import prices	277	0.64	0.56
BYRW	Industrial average earnings	332	0.91	0.89
BLRP	Participation rate	32	0.33	0.22
BRRI	Residual income	9	0.34	0.17
BRDW	Investment in dwellings	11	0.57	0.43

Notes:
* RSQ=Generalised R^2 for IV.
** RSQ=Generalised R^2 for IV adjusted for degrees of freedom (Pesaran and Smith, 1994).

Table 2.2 gives a count of the estimated stochastic equations in each of the main sets of equations in the model. There are 3,532 equations in 19 such sets, each set with its own specification, with most estimated on panel data of sectors and regions; however, each sector/region equation is estimated independently with no cross-industry or cross-region restrictions. At an early stage in the research, it was found that such restrictions were not justified. The table gives two averaged estimates of goodness of fit for the estimated dynamic equations. The first is the Generalised R^2 for the instrumental variable estimates, as proposed by Pesaran and Smith (1994), calculated by Ordinary Least Squares (OLS) of the dependent variable on the predicted variables from the regression of each of the variables on the instruments; and the second is the Generalised R^2 adjusted for degrees of freedom.

These results come at a stage before the construction and testing of the model have been completed. The employment, wage and price relationships have been finished (Barker and Gardiner, 1996), but in other areas, for example consumption (Bracke and Brechet, 1994), the research of the team has not been fully incorporated into the model. The estimated equations are a starting point for further research, and the goodness-of-fit statistics are one criterion for deciding whether an improvement has been made.

2.3 The roles of theory and data

CGE models are quantitative expressions of theory and there is not much else to be said; they stand or fall according to the plausibility or otherwise of the theory. The role of theory in econometric models is more complicated: some time-series models rely entirely on statistical methods with no input from economic theory; others are built to test it. The first *Report* of the DAE takes the purpose of applied economics to be the testing of theory; but this is immediately qualified by the observation that theory is not much use when it comes to questions of timing or adjustment, or in the specification of functional forms. A feature of the development of econometric modelling is the exploration of alternative functional forms for consumer demand in the work of Deaton (1975) and the creation of new theory to explain the facts, for example those underlying the wage bargaining models of Lee and Pesaran (1993).

2.3.1 The treatment of time

Since economic modellers cannot normally rewrite or relive history, models which are intended to guide policy must be forward looking. This immediately raises a problem for modelling because much of economic theory describing behaviour by consumers, producers, traders and investors, is a-temporal. Agents are usually assumed to be in equilibrium and there is not much explanation as to how or at what speed they move from one equilibrium to another. In such theory, history is usually of no consequence. The problem was recognised by Marshall in his distinction between the short period, during which the capital stock was fixed, and the long period, when it can change. This is a fundamental problem when it comes to representing economic change in an estimated model because all observations have dates attached and these observations are not likely to be of the equilibria of the theory.

Econometric modelling

Econometric modellers have re-interpreted the theory so that equations can be estimated on time-series data. This has been a continuing process since Tinbergen first estimated a macroeconomic model for the Netherlands in the 1930s. Three developments have helped in interpreting that data, identifying long-term behaviour and improving forecasting performance: the technique of cointegration which helps to reduce the effects of spurious temporal association (Engle and Granger, 1987, 1991); the error-correction method of Hendry and others (Hendry, Pagan and Sargan, 1984; Hendry, 1994) which allows the separation of a long-term relationship from a short-term adjustment; and the use of calibration in forecasting with macroeconomic modelling (Hendry and Clements, 1994; Kim and Pagan, 1995).

Large-scale modellers, econometric or otherwise, face the same problem. Johansen's MSG model (Johansen, 1960) and the Growth Project steady-state model (Brown, 1965) coped with it by estimating equations on annual data and ignoring any short-term influences in the specification or removing them in the solution. Because they have ignored or smoothed out short-term fluctuations, such models cannot represent the short-term year-to-year fluctuations in the economy, but since they are estimated, it is a short step to include short-term variables in the equations and model solution and to make them dynamic. It was however 16 years before the Growth Project Model became dynamic (Barker, 1977) and even later before the Norwegian Central Bureau of Statistics developed a dynamic companion (MODAG) for MSG. The combination of cointegration, error correction, flexible software and modern PC computer power now allows the large-scale estimation of sets of equations in which each equation contains an explicit representation of both short-term and long-term behaviour.

CGE modelling

CGE modellers have sought to get round the problem of dynamics by assuming that the base year used to calibrate the model is in equilibrium. There may be a choice of base years, or the modeller may wish to check that the assumption is reasonable. However, in order to measure the 'equilibrium' state of an economy, a substantial exercise would be required to analyse the economy over as many trade cycles as possible, so that the short-run effects can be separated from the long-run ones.

Another difficulty of assuming equilibrium is not in measurement but in theory: what if some markets are in equilibrium and others are not? At any time in an economy there is ample evidence of some markets being in a state of adjustment, the evidence taking the form of rationing, queues, unexpected stockbuilding and unforeseen events. The UK housing market in 1995 was in the process of adjustment to the collapse of house prices in 1989, with large numbers of houseowners discouraged from moving by 'negative equity', i.e. their home loan being greater than the market value of the house. If just one market is out of equilibrium, the whole system will be out of equilibrium. In order to get round these further problems, the assumption has to be extended to assert that the economy is in equilibrium *in all markets all the time*. The trade cycle has then to be explained as an evolution of sequential equilibria.[6]

Jorgenson estimates his CGE model on time-series data as an econometric model, but GREEN and GEM-E3 are calibrated on one year's data. In using these two CGE models for projections over the next 30 years, the whole process of economic change must be introduced by the model-builder without formal reference to the history of change. The model-builder is also basing the model and its results on a particular view of the economic system.

2.3.2 Statistical methods and tests in an econometric model

Statistical inference also includes the identification of the influence of different independent variables in an equation, a task made more difficult in a simultaneous system with many equations and endogenous variables. The OLS regression technique identifies these influences, but the estimates are biased if some of the explanatory variables are endogenous in the whole system of equations. Many econometric models use OLS on the assumption that the bias is not serious, but it remains a potential problem especially in wage–price equations where there is a very close relationship between two sets of variables. E3ME uses the technique of instrumental variables for estimation, and tests the results to check whether the instruments are truly exogenous. This is made possible by the use of the software package MREG, written and maintained by Peterson (1995), which can estimate the whole model and calculate a battery of test statistics and aggregations in about 90 minutes on a desk-top personal computer. Table 2.3 gives a count of the stochastic equations passing and failing four of these tests. They are discussed briefly below, and accompany the usual tests on properties of the data and the standard errors of the parameters. The point of listing them is that they help in the choice of alternative specifications in each area in the model.

Testing for cointegration in the long-run equations

This is the ADF test on the long-run residuals with four lags. The test has a null hypothesis that a unit root exists, so a value of greater than three is

Table 2.3. *Diagnostic statistics from E3ME estimation*

Function name		No. of equations	Coint. equations	Wu–Hausman	LM test failures	Restriction failures
BFR0	Aggregate energy demand	185	27	1	19	0
BFRC	Coal demand	115	15	0	13	1
BFRO	Heavy fuel oil demand	144	30	3	14	0
BFRG	Natural gas demand	105	19	0	7	3
BFRE	Electricity demand	146	26	0	8	2
BRSC	Aggregate consumption	9	5	0	0	0
BCR	Disaggregate consumption	234	75	5	17	3
BKR	Industrial investment	247	47	1	21	9
BQRX	Export volume	270	40	1	17	9
BQRM	Import volume	291	53	0	17	19
BYRH	Hours worked	296	56	2	22	10
BYRE	Industrial employment	285	75	4	15	1
BPYR	Industrial prices	274	51	6	19	27
BPQX	Export prices	270	40	0	17	9
BPQM	Import prices	277	34	0	24	10
BYRW	Industrial average earnings	332	64	0	29	24
BLRP	Participation rate	32	11	0	4	0
BRRI	Residual income	9	0	0	0	0
BRDW	Investment in dwellings	11	2	0	0	1
	Total	3532	670	23	263	128

usually sufficient to indicate stationarity, and thus a cointegrating relationship. Choosing the number of lags to include, i.e. the order of the ADF test, is somewhat arbitrary but useful in removing problems caused by serial correlation and to cater for multi-period shocks. About 20% of the long-run equations are significantly cointegrating on this test; it is assumed that the remainder can be treated as such, even though they do not pass the test.

Test for exogeneity in the long-run equations

The Wu-Hausman test of exogeneity is a test to check that the instruments in an instrumental variable regression are not correlated with the residuals. The test is a Chi-squared test with the null hypothesis that the regressors are independent, i.e. that there is no correlation, so a significant test indicates the existence of simultaneity. A very small number of equations fail the test.

Testing for error autocorrelation in the dynamic equations

The Lagrange Multiplier (LM) statistic tests for general forms of autocorrelation with lagged dependent variables on the RHS of an equation. The test is distributed as a Chi-squared order 1 with the null hypothesis that there is no serial correlation, i.e. a significant test indicates the existence of 1st-order serial correlation. About 8% of the equations fail the test.

Testing for the validity of the restrictions on the dynamic equations

The Wald test on the combined restrictions tests for the validity of the restrictions, with a significant test indicating that the restrictions are not valid. Very few of the equations, about 3%, fail the test.

2.3.3 Calibration in CGE models

The treatment of data in CGE models is quite different. The database of GREEN is one set of cross-section information for a base year, usually 1985, including input–output tables and data from social accounting matrices (Burniaux et al., 1992, pp. 49–51). Although some parameters such as input–output coefficients can be calculated directly for the base year, most are imposed by the model-builder or come with the GAMS software used to build and solve the models. To quote the builders of GREEN: 'It is common practice in (CGE) modelling to fix a number of "key" parameters on the basis of empirical evidence or the modeller's priors, while other parameters are adjusted in order to reproduce the benchmark-year data set under the assumption that the economy is in a steady-state equilibrium in that particular period' (p. 51). The 'empirical evidence' used by CGE modellers is not normally based on measurement of the economies as defined by the cross-section data used in the models, with its particular industrial classification and price base, but on literature searches relating to supply and demand elasticities or values adopted by other CGE modellers. In order to make long-term projections, GREEN is calibrated on exogenous growth rates in GDP, population and neutral technical progress in energy use.

The calibration of a large-scale CGE is a huge task and has to be done with care and some precision to allow the model to be solved, but it is far removed from the methods of statistical inference developed in econometrics. The method as practised for large and small macroeconomic and simulation models is discussed by Kim and Pagan (1995). There is no doubt that the technique has a role to play in macroeconometric models when the data are sparse or unavailable (Hendry and Clements, 1994). However, the approach as adopted in some CGE models is, firstly, casual in its measurement of parameters and, secondly, uninformed in that the time-series data which are usually available are also usually not utilised in the modelling process and in that the approach does not build on earlier work: in particular, it ignores the advances made in econometric methods over the last 20 years.

2.4 Equilibrium and the model solution

2.4.1 The long run

Since CGE models assume equilibrium *ab initio*, their long-run properties are decided by assumption, even though the models are used to generate policy results for actions to be taken at different times in the future. The dates that are attached to the CGE projections are those in the exogenous assumptions; each solution is a 'long-run' solution. In econometric model-building, however, equilibria can be defined for different long-run solutions, depending on what variables are made endogenous in the solution.[7] Since the models are based on time-series analysis, they can give some information about the time lags involved in adjustment. For example, Britton and Westaway (1992) report that the NIESR model has a short-run equilibrium for output and relative prices within about three years, but that full stock equilibrium takes several decades to achieve. The long time of adjustment is not surprising given the long life of much capital stock and institutional behaviour. Transport infrastructure, which helps to determine the scale of GG emissions, is very long-lived indeed, and affects where people live and work, the available means of transport and the cost of transport.

2.4.2 Optimising behaviour

CGE and engineering models usually assume that the economy is operating at maximum efficiency and delivering maximum welfare. As a practical necessity in order to solve the models, it is assumed that the welfare in
an economy is identified with individual private consumers' utility (often
measured by total private consumption) and that this is maximised. To
solve the models as a sequence of equilibria into the future, given that
certain actions taken at one time will affect consumption at another, the
total discounted present value of utility (or consumption) over all the time
periods is maximised.

These assumptions are seldom questioned and no evidence is presented
to justify them, yet they determine the models' results and policy
recommendations. They are, to say the least, an oversimplification of the
way the political process decides priorities. It is easy to think of other
maxima, e.g. the growth rate or the sum of private and public consumption, but this exercise brings home that the model-builder is adopting a
simplified social welfare function. In effect, the models are answering the
question: if the world behaves *as if* private consumption were maximised,
then given all the assumptions, should the carbon tax be set at this particular rate?

The econometric models do not in general assume that a social welfare
function exists or that such welfare should be maximised. Constituent
parts of the model may well assume maximising behaviour, e.g. trade
unions maximising the real wages of their members (Lee and Pesaran,
1993), but no overall maximum is required to solve the model. The model
produces outcomes for income, employment, emissions, and other variables depending on its specification and the user is left to judge the social
value of the policy being modelled.

2.4.3 Environmental externalities

The issue of interest, however, is abatement of global warming. The
problem is partly that the carrying capacity of the global atmosphere is
common property, and those responsible for GG emissions reduce that
capacity without bearing the cost. If the externality is acknowledged, the
CGE equilibrium prices should be adjusted, so that all markets clear at the
new set of prices, depending on GG emissions. This then would be the
undistorted equilibrium at which welfare is maximised.

However, this is not the procedure actually followed. The initial equilibrium, without effects of externalities, is used as a standard or reference
point to compare with the position after a change, e.g. after the imposition

of a carbon tax. The method is well illustrated in an initial paper reporting results of the GREEN model (Burniaux *et al.*, 1992): the paper reports that OECD welfare is reduced by the imposition of a carbon tax, but the model assumes that the base line does not include distortions. The double dividend from E3 policies comes about in CGE models as a correction of two distortions in the economy, one coming from the charges for use of some environmental services, e.g. use of the atmosphere to discharge exhaust gases, and the other from the removal of taxes on beneficial activities, e.g. the provision of employment. The two dividends are measured against a theoretical optimum usually achieved in the models by summing consumption or 'utility' linked to consumption, variously including current private and/or public consumption or future consumption.

Goulder (1994) follows this line of reasoning, but it is flawed because the theoretical optimum should *already* include the effect of the externality, global warming, on all the markets in the economy as well as the effect of removing all distorting taxes: the environmental dividend is then the difference between this optimum and the distorted solution excluding the externality; and the employment dividend is the difference between the optimum and the solution with the distorting labour tax. A further objection to the method is that the optimum usually omits some costs which are central to the case for environmental tax reform: the social costs of unemployment and the external costs of private consumption such as local air pollution. It also usually omits consideration of equity.

In contrast, in the framework adopted in most time-series econometric models there is no overall optimum in this sense; the environmental dividend in these models comes from the reduction of CO_2 and associated reduction in other emissions; and the economic dividend comes from the extra employment from the tax shift. The extra employment can mean lower short-term unemployment with the long-term level unaffected or it can also mean a higher non-inflationary level of full employment. The opportunity of a double, or triple, dividend depends on the exact assumptions adopted in the models, most notably the treatment of investment and technical progress, of taxation, and of involuntary unemployment.

2.4.4 Technology and production

CGE models also usually assume that there are no effects of the tax in stimulating energy-saving R&D which in turn stimulates long-term growth. Changes in the energy efficiency of technology are usually introduced in the models by means of an exogenous trend. However, such an endogenous effect has been found to be central in the LBS projections of the effect of a carbon tax on energy saving in the world economy

(Mabey, 1995). Following the treatment proposed and tested by Lee, Pesaran and Pierse (1990) for employment demand, E3ME includes R&D-enhanced accumulated gross investment in energy, employment and trade equations, so that technology effects are pervasive in the model results.

2.5 Aggregation and model size

Aggregation is a pervasive and unresolved problem in econometrics (Barker and Pesaran, 1990); and econometric models usually become large-scale when they are disaggregated. This section considers questions of the size, rather than the complexity, of models; model complexity is considered in the next section. Here the question is: how far should a model of a given complexity be disaggregated?

2.5.1 Small versus large models

The appropriate size of an econometric model depends on the questions being asked and the availability of data. If the policy issue is that of the best mix of fiscal and other policies to reduce greenhouse gas emissions in Europe, then the model is bound to be large-scale. Factors important in determining the appropriate size of a model are as follows.

Policy applications
Important policy decisions are taken at national level, so national economies must be distinguished (i.e. at least 12 or more countries).

Carbon content of fuels
The main GG emission problem in Europe is CO_2 from combustion of fossil fuels. However, the main fuels concerned, gas, oil and coal, have substantially different carbon contents per unit of heat released. The model should include several fuels and fuel users. In fact, the data are available for 10 energy carriers (electricity is not strictly a fuel) and 17 fuel users, and it is convenient to include these classifications as they stand.

Different industrial structures
There is then the question of how to compare economies with different industrial structures, from Finland in the north with her timber, paper and pulp to Portugal in the south with her wine and tourists. Clearly, the more disaggregated the industrial sector, the more relevant detail can be captured in the model. With the requirement of having the main energy carriers, and the collection of data by EUROSTAT at a 25–NACE level, and

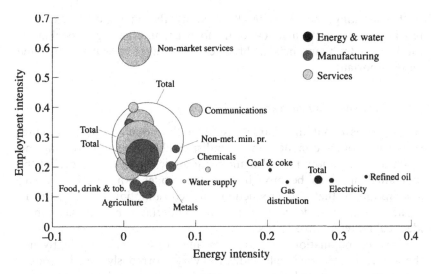

Figure 2.1 Production characteristics of EU industries, 1991
Note: Size of bubbles is proportional to numbers employed.

additional sectors for recycling and unallocated, these add up to 32 industrial sectors.

Production characteristics

Finally, the production characteristics of industries, their energy- and labour-intensities, can differ by an order of magnitude. Figure 2.1 illustrates this characteristic by showing the energy and employment intensities for 25 EU industrial sectors.[8] These large differences imply that structural shifts in consumption and production can have a substantial impacts on energy use and GG emissions. The disaggregation allows these to be taken into account.

2.5.2 *The forecasting properties of large* versus *small models*

Large models have occasionally been drastically cut in size: the Treasury model was slimmed down in the late 1980s. The reasons are to cut out dead wood, to reduce resources in estimation and solution, and to understand and manage the model more easily. These are good reasons, but a smaller model is not necessarily less complex and the forecasting performance of the model may deteriorate. There is not much evidence on this question. Schink (1975) compares the *ex post* forecasts of a small and a large version of the Brookings model of the US economy: the small model performed relatively better in the first year of the forecast, and the large model in the third and later years, presumably because changes in structure become more important.

2.5.3 The assumption of representative agents

Assumptions about the characteristics of the populations being represented in economic models are an indispensable means of avoiding too much disaggregation; they also allow economic theory at the level of the individual agent to be brought into the model. An especially useful assumption is that the production and consumption activities in an economy can be modelled as if they were undertaken by a population of identical representative agents.

However, populations of industries and consumers are patently not those of identical individuals. Industries vary enormously in their production characteristics and in their organisation, with some being dominated by a few companies and some, particularly energy industries, being subject to stringent regulation. Consumers can also differ markedly from each other according to social group, family type, and lifestyle. Large-scale pollution is highly specific to certain productive activities and certain consumer lifestyles, which can be much more polluting than others. Thus the assumption of representative agents, introduced to keep the model small, may rule out of consideration important effects, as industrial structures and patterns of consumer spending respond to relative price shifts. The consumers who pay pollution taxes are not identical as a group to the workers (and consumers) who benefit from the recycling of the revenues through reductions in employment taxes. Granger (1990) is strongly critical of the assumption after conducting tests on models of consumer behaviour, stating that it can lead to a badly mis-specified macro-relationship: successful aggregation depends on the existence of common factors in the movement of the explanatory variables, such as income.

If the assumption of representative agents is dropped, as in most macro-econometric models, then the connection with micro-theory is usually lost, and the aggregation problem changes. Macro-models assume that their equations can represent the changing underlying structures of each aggregate variable, usually as regular time trends. This can lead to serious bias in the estimation of the aggregate response (e.g. Lee, Pesaran and Pierse, 1990, find an elasticity of -0.6 for UK labour demand response to real wage rates, compared to a response estimated from aggregate equations of unity). Disaggregation helps to reduce the risk of bias in estimation and the effects of structural change in forecasting and analysis.

2.5.4 Averaging across countries and panel data techniques

Disaggregation brings another benefit, the ability to compare estimates across sectors and regions. This is especially valuable for establishing the credibility of a parameter, because it allows an interpretation to be made of differences between parameters. For example, in modelling the European labour market, a much higher value than average was found for the external effects on Irish wage rates, confirming the integration of the Irish and UK labour markets (Barker and Gardiner, 1996).

Use of panel data also increases the information available to estimate parameters, especially those such as the long-run response to real energy prices, which are difficult to estimate on time-series data alone (Baltagi and Griffin, 1983). Pesaran and Smith (1995) recommend that, when large panel datasets are available, regressions should be estimated for individual relations and then averaged over groups. They report that they have found that the homogeneity hypothesis (that the slope equations are the same across groups) is regularly rejected (p. 43). This was apparent in the estimation of the equations of E3ME, and industrial and other sectoral responses have been allowed to vary across regions, but formal tests have not yet been done to reject such homogeneity.

2.5.5 Model size and software problems

Estimation and solution

There is a cost in constructing large-scale models in that the software for estimating and solving the models is not as advanced as in the case of small models. E3ME has to be estimated using one software package (MREG: Peterson, 1995) and solved using another (IDIOM: Cambridge Econometrics, 1995). This opens up the possibility of differences in definition and specification between the two packages, a possibility which is removed if the software allows just one definition of the equations to be estimated and solved, as in facilities provided in the packages TROLL or MODLER.

Single equations versus equation sets

However, the combined estimation/solution packages have one feature which is very limiting for large-scale models: the basis of operation for the time-series analysis is the single equation. In contrast, a feature of IDIOM, and for CGE models, the GAMS software, is that the software recognises and works with matrices – in the case of IDIOM, matrices of up to three dimensions, with each dimension being defined on up to 102 different sets or classifications, 12 of which were presented in Table 2.1 above. This is a very powerful way of allowing for disaggregation, but at the same time keeping the structure of the model consistent and coherent. One of these classifications is the time period of the solution, allowing some key variables, e.g. oil prices, to be defined over the whole solution period, and so incorporating forward-looking expectations.

One consequence of working in several dimensions is that the models can become unmanageably huge. The main ways of reducing the size are, first, holding in store only the current year's values for all the time-series variables and explicitly defining lagged and other transformations as extra variables and, second, only defining those variables on intersections between dimensions that are of interest.

2.6 Model complexity, integration and linkage

Model complexity is different from model size: a small model of just one variable can have a chaotic solution and a three-equation model can embody the main features of the operation of an industrial economy; and a large-scale model such as the basic input–output model can be linear with a simple, deterministic solution. There is a related issue, that of the value of an integrated E3 model, as opposed to the use of a suite of different models. What are the problems of linkage between different models used for the same analysis? What is the case for having one model of the EU rather than a set of country models?

2.6.1 Simple versus complex models

There are several reasons why a simple model is to be preferred to a complex one. First, there is the philosophical point of Occam's Razor, that a simpler postulate is always to be preferred to the more complex one in any explanation. This is related to the fact that complex models are much more difficult to understand and therefore less accessible and less useful for teaching and exposition. Second, one of the purposes of many models is to provide explanations for events and effects of policy changes; the easier it is to understand the model, the better.

When the main purpose of the model is to quantify and bolster a belief in the way the economy works, this argument goes further: all detail and complexity outwith the area of interest are not just redundant, they are confusing and potentially damaging. Models built over the period 1975–1985 by the LBS, the Cambridge Economic Policy Group and Minford's Liverpool project all had this purpose (Kenway, 1994). Further variables would have increased complexity and distracted from the objective, e.g. the inclusion of tariffs in the LBS model would not have helped the objective of quantifying international monetarism.

2.6.2 Integrated models versus multi-model systems

In principle, linked models such as the HERMES-MIDAS system could be estimated and solved consistently for all the economies involved. However, in practice, this often proves difficult, if not impossible, and considerable resources have to go into linking. In E3ME any linkage problems are not obvious to the user because there is only one model. However, there are costs to such a unified approach: the general nature of the model means that country-specific detail may be lost. A model could include a facility to introduce condensed forms of country models to help to reduce this loss; in addition, more emphasis could be placed on validation of equations and results by country experts.

Even if the consistency problem in linkage can be solved by successive iterative solutions of the component models, as reported in the DRI study (1991, 1992), there remains a more basic problem with the multi-model approach if it attempts to combine macroeconomic models with detailed industry or energy models. This problem is that the system cannot adequately tackle the simulation of 'bottom-up' policies. Normally, these systems are first solved at the macroeconomic level, then the results for the macroeconomic variables are disaggregated by the industry model. However, if the policy is directed at the level of industrial variables, it is very difficult (without substantial intervention by the model-operator) to ensure that the implicit results for macroeconomic variables from the industry model are consistent with the explicit results from the macro-model. As an example, it is probably very difficult to use a macro-industry two-model system to simulate the effect of exempting selective energy-intensive industries from the carbon/energy tax.

2.6.3 National models versus regionalised EU models

The regionalised modelling approach has the advantage that parameters estimated for different sectors and different regions can be readily compared. The approach is well illustrated in the estimation of a wage equation for some 20 UK industrial sectors by Lee and Pesaran (1993); in E3ME, the corresponding equation is estimated for 30 industries and 14 regions.

These advantages also come with costs. It is particularly difficult to obtain consistent time series of the disaggregated data required by the model. Experience with the initial version of the model also suggests that, for at least some of the national economies, a national model would be more capable of representing E3 interactions because it can adopt more appropriate industrial detail, a more recent price base, and a tailored approach to country-specific behaviour. However, the results of such models are difficult to compare precisely because their design and data characteristics are not consistent.

2.7 Conclusions

This chapter has traced the evolution of the econometric approach to large-scale modelling in the DAE from the Stone–Brown static model of the 1960s, designed to support policies to raise long-term growth in Britain, to a regionalised energy–environment–economy model, designed for European greenhouse gas abatement policies. The main characteristics of the approach can be summarised as follows. First, the industrial sector is disaggregated so that there can be a dialogue between the model-builder and industrial experts in the construction and use of the model and its results. Second, the models are based on both theory and measurement using formal methods of statistical inference, which were OLS and system estimators in the DAE and are now instrumental variables, cointegration and error correction. The emphasis is not on testing theory, but on using theory to explain economic structure and change. Third, the models are always forward-looking in that the parameters are not seen as immutable, but liable to change as technology and tastes change; the detail is partly to accommodate that change in a consistent and sensible manner. Finally, the modelling is always to inform a specific policy issue; the design of the model, the questions it is to address, are always seen as the starting point in new model development. The models were not built to test economic theory, but to explore policy choices and inform industrial planning.

The approach requires substantial resources, particularly those associated with the database. It has been followed independently by Almon and his colleagues and in a number of government economic institutes, foremost being the Norwegian Central Bureau of Statistics and the Netherlands Central Planning Bureau (1990), perhaps reflecting the national reputation of early econometric modellers such as Frisch and Tinbergen.

However, most national econometric modelling is overwhelmingly dominated by macro-models, which seem to be getting smaller and less structural, whilst the prevailing best-practice in policy modelling appears to be general equilibrium. These are surprising trends given that data on disaggregated economic behaviour are becoming more abundant and the means of analysing them more available in terms of user-friendly econometric software and powerful low-cost computer hardware.

In this chapter, the econometric approach is contrasted with the general equilibrium approach. In the econometric approach, the models are based on time-series data, with the specification of the equations informed more or less by theory. In the CGE approach, the purpose of measurement is to quantify the theory and there is no attempt to explain the facts. The main value of the CGE models seems to be that they provide results which conform to general equilibrium theory in all its manifestations. There is no possibility of falsifying such models, since they always fit the data. Worse still, there is a danger that results from the models, derived entirely from assumptions but apparently based on facts, will be taken as hard evidence for or against particular action. Builders of some econometric models can be accused of promoting their model results along these lines, but at least their method permits in principle that the results can be discredited by appeal to the data.

Notes

1 The results reported in this chapter rely on the contributions of those involved in the E3 Model for Europe (E3ME) project, especially who have worked on the data and the estimation of the model, Alistair Dieppe, Ben Gardiner and Peter Madsen. I am also grateful to Kevin Lee of the University of Leicester for discussions on econometric practice. The views represented in this paper are those of the author and are not necessarily those of any of the institutions supporting the research. Readers should note that the data on which the results in the paper are based are in the process of validation, so all the results must be considered as preliminary and indicative. The E3ME project has been supported by the Commission of the European Communities, Directorate-General XII for Science, Research and Development, under the EC Non-Nuclear Energy Programme: JOULE-II Area I: Analysis of Strategies and Modelling (SOLFEGE), Contact No. JOU2-CT92-0203, managed by Pierre Valette. This support is gratefully acknowledged.

2 The US EPA has funded Jorgenson's DGEM model, the OECD has constructed its world GREEN model and DG XII, the Directorate responsible for the EC's R&D expenditures, has funded several models, including GEM-E3 and E3ME in two programmes, JOULE II (just completed), and JOULE III (just starting). The UK Global Environmental Change Programme of the ESRC funded a project in the DAE in 1992 and 1993 which extended Cambridge Econometrics' MDM model to become an E3 model for the UK and a project at the LBS to extend the LBS–NIESR world model to include energy and CO_2 emissions, EGEM (Mabey, 1995). All these models except E3ME, MDM and EGEM are CGE.

3 The 'long-run' solution is the equilibrium or steady-state solution allowing

wealth and capital stocks to change, so a 'short-term' model can have a 'long-run' solution (Britton and Westaway, 1992). The long-run solution may not be an equilibrium one. The long term is usually understood to refer to a period of more than 5 or so years into the future (Kenway, 1994, pp. 138–9).

4 This brief review concentrates on E3 modelling; for a survey of the economics of CO_2 abatement policies, see (Mors, 1991); for a survey of the modelling and estimation of the economic costs of abatement, see (Boero, Clarke and Winters, 1991; and Hoeller, Dean and Hayafuji, 1992); and for a review of the role of input–output in E3 modelling, see (Pearson, 1989).

5 This was not the first such empirical synthesis: Leif Johansen's *A Multi-sectoral Study of Economic Growth* (MSG) published in 1960 linked an input–output table for Norway in 1950 with a Cobb–Douglas production function and a demand system; the book had been completed in 1959 while he was a Visiting Scholar in the DAE.

6 The controversy surrounding the estimation and analysis of the real business cycle is explored in the *Economic Journal*, Vol. 105, No. 433, pp. 1594–1648, November 1995.

7 The long-run properties of several macroeconometric models are reported in Hargreaves (ed., 1992); and those of the UK NIESR's model are discussed by Britton and Westaway (1992). The long-run properties of disaggregated models such as the Cambridge Growth Project's dynamic model and E3ME can in principle be developed in the same way (Barker, 1976).

8 Energy is measured by the value of energy inputs, employment is measured by wage and salary costs and output is measured as gross industrial output; all these measures are in current prices in 1991. The size of the bubbles in Figure 2.1 is proportional to numbers employed (both part-time and full-time) in 1991. The industrial data are aggregated across the EU, except those for Greece which were unavailable. The provision of energy services is of course beneficial in most instances; however, the burning of fossil fuels to produce energy has external costs in the form of unwanted emissions into the atmosphere. In general, the use of energy is closely associated with such pollution.

3   Measurement errors and data estimation: the quantification of survey data

Alastair W. F. Cunningham, Richard J. Smith and Martin R. Weale

3.1 Introduction

The seminal paper by Stone, Champernowne and Meade (1942) analysed systematically the appropriate attribution of measurement error when estimating National Accounts data from disparate sources. Since its inception, the Department of Applied Economics (DAE) has been intimately concerned with problems of data estimation. More recently, an important component of the research programme at the DAE has been the estimation of *expectations* data and associated questions; see *inter alia* Lee (1994, 1995) and Pesaran (1984, 1987a). Research into the problem of estimating National Accounts data has also enjoyed a resurgence; see Weale (1992), Sefton and Weale (1995) and Smith, Weale and Satchell (1997).

This chapter conducts a re-examination and re-assessment of the use of macroeconomic survey data. Survey data on individual economic agents in conjunction with macroeconomic information offer the possibility of providing a rapid assessment of the current state of the economy and a tool for predicting the likely movement of the economy. Retrospective survey data may be available before the relevant macroeconomic data are published. Hence, together with other prior information, these data, if reliable, may be used to provide estimators for current but unavailable macroeconomic variables. Prospective survey data offer the possibility of the estimation of the expectations of macroeconomic variables. Therefore, these data, in conjunction with model-based forecasts, may prove useful as indicators of the likely future state of the economy.

The type of survey data typically available involves *qualitative* rather than *quantitative* responses. Moreover, these data are usually in aggregate form rather than at the individual microeconomic level. The question of how to integrate this information together with other macroeconomic data has been a topic of extensive research. Two main strands for the econometric analysis of macroeconomic survey data have emerged. The first, the

41

probability method, was initiated by Theil (1952) and applied to UK data by Carlson and Parkin (1975). The second are *regression*-based approaches; see *inter alia* Pesaran (1984). Other authors, including Pesaran (1987a), Pesaran and Wright (1992) and Lee (1994, 1995), have looked at a range of associated questions including the examination of whether expectations are rational or whether time-varying models should be adopted. An extensive review of these approaches and various applications is presented in Pesaran (1987a, Chapter 8, pp. 207–44).

The econometric methods adopted in this chapter are similar in spirit to the probability method. We extend this earlier work to take into account more fully the implied theoretical properties of the survey data. We conduct a preliminary examination of the applicability of these methods to the growth in UK manufacturing output using the retrospective survey data from the CBI *Quarterly Industrial Trends Survey* to estimate the current growth rate in manufacturing output which may be unavailable in published form.

The survey data to be analysed here are briefly introduced in section 3.2. The theoretical framework underpinning the econometric methods we used is presented in section 3.3. Section 3.4 discusses alternative estimation methods for the quantification of qualitative survey data together with an account of the theoretical basis of the regression approach. Section 3.5 applies these methods to the retrospective qualitative data and compares the data estimates for the growth rate in UK manufacturing output with the actual outcomes. Section 3.6 draws some conclusions.

3.2 The survey structure

The survey under consideration, the CBI's *Quarterly Industrial Trends Survey*, asks respondents two questions of interest; *viz.*

- 'Has your output risen, fallen, or stayed the same during the last four months?'
- 'Do you expect your output to rise, fall or stay the same during the next four months?'.

Respondents can answer 'not applicable' instead of giving one of the three answers indicated by these questions. The number of relevant non-responses is very small and, hence, is ignored in our later analysis.

The survey questionnaire is sent to manufacturing firms. Therefore, the survey responses should be compared with the data on manufacturing output provided by the Office for National Statistics (ONS). The results of the survey are presented as the proportion of respondents falling into each of the four categories. In many cases, the econometric literature has been concerned simply with the balance, that is, the proportion expecting a rise less the proportion expecting a fall. Our point of departure from this earlier literature is that we treat the proportions individually rather than amalgamating them as a balance.

For these data to be useful at a macroeconomic level, these proportions need to be straightforwardly related to the actual changes in output which not only manufacturing firms but, more importantly, the economy are experiencing. The next section sets out a theoretical model describing such linkages.

3.3 An econometric model of survey information

3.3.1 The model

We consider N_t economic agents and assume that the individual-specific random variable y_{it} is related to the economy-wide variable x_t by the formulation

$$y_{it} = x_t + \eta_{it} + \epsilon_{it}, \tag{3.3.1}$$

$i = 1, \ldots, N_t$, $t = 1, \ldots, T$. In (3.3.1), the random variable η_{it} represents information private to agent i at time t which is not observed by the econometrician; for example, η_{it} might consist of information which is persistent for agent i over time representing slowly varying aspects of the firm and/or industry together with additional information which is both individual- and time-specific, reflecting particular transient influences. The random variable ϵ_{it} is a shock unanticipated by agent i in period t and thus is not observed by both the individual agent and the econometrician. In our application, x_t is the macroeconomic growth rate indicating the state of the macro-economy, η_{it} is the divergence of the firm-specific growth rate from the economy-wide rate x_t anticipated by firm i and ϵ_{it} is that part of the actual firm-specific growth rate y_{it} unanticipated by firm i at time t.

At the beginning of period t, agent i makes a prediction, y_{it}^*, of y_{it} based on information available at a macro-economic level to all agents, the information set Ω_{t-1}, together with the agent-specific information η_{it}. We denote the relevant individual-specific information set by Ω_{t-1}^i, $i = 1, \ldots, N_t$. If this prediction is formed rationally,

$$y_{it}^* = E\{y_{it} | \Omega_{t-1}^i\} = x_t^* + \eta_{it}$$

where $x_t^* = E\{x_t | \Omega_{t-1}\}$ is the economy-wide rational expectation prediction of x_t, that is, the prediction which would be made by an econometrician who did not have access to the private information η_{it} available to the individual agent i, $i = 1, \ldots, N_t$. Consequently, we may write

$$x_t = x_t^* + \zeta_t, \tag{3.3.2}$$

where ζ_t is macroeconomic shock, unanticipated by both agents and the econometrician, $t = 1, \ldots, T$. After substitution into (3.3.1), we obtain the random effects formulation

$$y_{it} = x_t^* + \eta_{it} + \zeta_t + \epsilon_{it},$$

$i = 1, \ldots, N_t, t = 1, \ldots, T$.

At this point, we emphasise that the unanticipated macroeconomic shock ζ_t is uncorrelated with the information sets Ω_{t-1} *and* Ω_{t-1}^i; in particular, $E\{\zeta_t | \Omega_{t-1}^i\} = 0$ and thus ζ_t is uncorrelated with η_{it} the private information of agent i at time t, $i = 1, \ldots, N_t, t = 1, \ldots, T$.

3.3.2 The observation rules

At the microeconomic level, each agent i provides two pieces of categorical information on the individual-specific random variable y_{it} in time period t; *viz.* for $i = 1, \ldots, N_t, t = 1, \ldots, T$,

- a prediction of y_{it} made at the beginning of period t
- the actual outcome y_{it} in period t.

The categorical prediction concerns the *expected* value of y_{it} given information available to agent i at the *beginning* of period t, namely Ω_{t-1}^i; that is, it concerns y_{it}^*. This prediction is denoted by the discrete random variable $y_{it,j}^p$ defined as $y_{it,j}^p = 1$ if $c_{j-1}^p < y_{it}^* \leq c_j^p$ and 0 otherwise, $j = 1, 2, 3$, where we adopt the convention $c_0^p = -\infty$ and $c_3^p = \infty$.

Similarly, the second categorical information concerns the actual outcome, y_{it}, and is defined *via* the discrete random variable $y_{it,j}^r = 1$ if $c_{j-1}^r < y_{it} \leq c_j^r$ and 0 otherwise, $j = 1, 2, 3$, where again we adopt the convention $c_0^r = -\infty$ and $c_3^r = \infty$.

Note that we have assumed that the intervals (c_{j-1}^p, c_j^p) and (c_{j-1}^r, c_j^r), $j = 1, 2, 3$, are invariant both with respect to individuals, $i = 1, \ldots, N_t$, and time, $t = 1, \ldots, T$. However, we do allow the intervals to differ in width between prospective and retrospective surveys in order to reflect the difference in confidence or uncertainty between the two cases. We have restricted the number of categories to be equal in both cases, reflecting the survey data addressed in this paper.

Defined in terms of the error terms in (3.3.1), the observation rules become respectively

- *prospective information*

$$y_{it,j}^p = 1, \text{ if } c_{j-1}^p - x_t^* < \eta_{it} \leq c_j^p - x_t^*, \tag{3.3.3}$$

$j=1,2,3;$

• *retrospective information*

$$y^r_{it,j}=1, \text{ if } c^r_{j-1}-x_t<\eta_{it}+\epsilon_{it}\le c^r_j-x_t, \tag{3.3.4}$$

$j=1,2,3;$

with 0 observed otherwise in both cases, $i=1,...,N_t$, $t=1,...,T$.

3.4 Estimation

3.4.1 Prospective survey information

Firstly, consider the predicted categorical observations, $y^p_{it,j}$, $i=1,...,N_t$, $j=1,2,3$, $t=1,...,T$. The use of these observations is of particular interest if one is concerned with information on the expected movement in the economy. In order to give a probabilistic foundation to the observation rule (3.3.3), let the scaled error terms $\{\sigma_p\eta_{it}\}$, where $\sigma_p>0$, possess a common and known *cumulative distribution function* (c.d.f.) $F_\eta(.)$, $i=1,...,N_t$, which is parameter free and is assumed time-invariant. Then,

$$P\{y^p_{it,j}=1|x^*_t\}=F_\eta(\mu^p_j-\sigma_p x^*_t)-F_\eta(\mu^p_{j-1}-\sigma_p x^*_t),$$

$j=1,2,3$, where $\mu^p_j=\sigma_p c^p_j, j=1,2,3, i=1,...,N_t$.

The error term ζ_t of (3.3.2) is an unanticipated macroeconomic innovation and uncorrelated with $\{\eta_{it}\}^{N_t}_{i=1}$; see subsection 3.3.1. Hence, the category totals $N^p_{tj}=\Sigma^{N_t}_{i=1}y^p_{it,j}, j=1,2,3$, which are formed using the agent-specific information sets Ω^i_{t-1}, $i=1,...,N_t$, cf. (3.3.3), are uncorrelated with the macroeconomic shock ζ_t also. We strengthen this implication by assuming that ζ_t is conditionally *independent* of the category totals $N^p_{tj}, j=1,2,3, t=1, ..., T$. Therefore, given knowledge of $F_\eta(.)$ and assuming that observations are independently and identically distributed, $t=1, ..., T$, consistent $(N_t\to\infty)$ estimation of x^*_t, which may be regarded as a time-varying intercept, $t=1,...,T$, together with the time-invariant intercepts μ^p_1, μ^p_2 and the scale parameter σ_p, may be achieved by the method of maximum likelihood (ML) using the log-likelihood function

$$-\frac{T}{2}\ln2\pi-\frac{T}{2}\ln\sigma^2_\zeta-\frac{1}{2\sigma^2_\zeta}\sum^T_{t=1}(x_t-x^*_t)^2$$

$$+\sum^T_{t=1}(N^p_{t1}\ln F_{\eta1,t}+N^p_{t3}\ln F_{\eta3,t}+(N_t-N^p_{t1}+N^p_{t3})\ln(1-F_{\eta1,t}-F_{\eta3,t})),$$

where $F_{\eta1,t}=F_\eta(\mu^p_1-\sigma_p x^*_t)$, $F_{\eta3,t}=1-F_\eta(\mu^p_2-\sigma_p x^*_t)$ and $\sigma^2_\zeta=var\{\zeta_t\}$, $t=1,...,T$. Note that the consistency $(N_t\to\infty)$ property of the ML estimator for x_t^*, $t=1, ..., T$, is unaffected if we relax the assumption of independence of observations over time.

We may also describe various regression-based approaches. Define the prospective survey *aggregate* proportions by

$$P_{t,j}^p = N_t^{-1} \sum_{i=1}^{N_t} y_{it,j}^p, j=1,2,3, t=1, ..., T.$$

As $E\{y_{it,j}^p|x_t^*\} = F_\eta(\mu_j^p - \sigma_p x_t^*) - F_\eta(\mu_{j-1}^p - \sigma_p x_t^*)$, $E\{P_{t,j}^p|x_t^*\} = F_\eta(\mu_j^p - \sigma_p x_t^*)$ $-F_\eta(\mu_{j-1}^p - \sigma_p x_t^*)$, $j=1,2,3$, $t=1, ..., T$. If we further assume that the c.d.f. $F_\eta(.)$ is *symmetric*, then $E\{P_{t,1}^p|x_t^*\} = F_\eta(\mu_1^p - \sigma_p x_t^*)$ and $E\{P_{t,3}^p|x_t^*\}$ $=F_\eta[-(\mu_2^p - \sigma_p x_t^*)]$, $t=1, ..., T$. Hence, we may define the *non-linear* regressions

$$P_{t,1}^p = F_\eta(\mu_1^p - \sigma_p x_t^*) + \xi_{t,1}^p,$$
$$P_{t,3}^p = F_\eta[-(\mu_2^p - \sigma_p x_t^*)] + \xi_{t,3}^p, \tag{3.4.1}$$

where $(\xi_{t,1}^p, \xi_{t,3}^p)$ are multinomial conditional on x_t^* with mean 0 and variance matrix

$$\begin{pmatrix} N_t^{-1} F_{\eta1,t}(1-F_{\eta1,t}) & -N_t^{-1} F_{\eta1,t} F_{\eta3,t} \\ -N_t^{-1} F_{\eta1,t} F_{\eta3,t} & N_t^{-1} F_{\eta3,t}(1-F_{\eta3,t}) \end{pmatrix}, \tag{3.4.2}$$

or as $N_t \to \infty$

$$N_t^{1/2} \begin{pmatrix} \xi_{t,1}^p \\ \xi_{t,3}^p \end{pmatrix} \to^L N\left(\begin{pmatrix} 0 \\ 0 \end{pmatrix}, \begin{pmatrix} F_{\eta1,t}(1-F_{\eta1,t}) & -F_{\eta1,t} F_{\eta3,t} \\ -F_{\eta1,t} F_{\eta3,t} & F_{\eta3,t}(1-F_{\eta3,t}) \end{pmatrix} \right),$$

$t=1, ..., T$.

Taken together with (3.4.2), the regression formulation (3.4.1) emphasises the moment information available for estimation. That is, the error terms ζ_t and $(\xi_{t,1}^p, \xi_{t,3}^p)$ have mean zero conditional on x_t^* and, thus, are uncorrelated with measurable functions of x_t^*, $t=1, ..., T$. These conditional moments may then be used to implement generalised method of moments (GMM) or, equivalently, instrumental variable (IV) estimation of x_t^*, $t=1, ..., T$, together with the time-invariant intercepts μ_1^p, μ_2^p and the scale parameter σ_p; see Hansen (1982). Note that restricting ourselves to categories $j=1$ and $j=3$ results in no loss of information as $\Sigma_{j=1}^3 P_{t,j}^p = 1$. Unfortunately, although we can consistently ($N_t \to \infty$) estimate the components of (3.4.2) using the aggregate proportions, because we do not have additional independent estimators for (3.4.2), for example, standard error estimators for the aggregate proportions $P_{t,j}^p$, $j=1,2,3$, the multinomial variance structure (3.4.2) is not available to use for more efficient estimation of x_t^*, $t=1, ..., T$.

The GMM estimation procedure outlined above results in a number of non-linear equations for solution. However, this difficulty may be circumvented and GMM estimation rendered considerably simplified if we use the additional information that the aggregate proportions $P^p_{t,j}, j=1,2,3$, are conditionally uncorrelated with ζ_t, $t=1,...,T$. In particular, this assumption implies that measurable functions of the observable x_t are uncorrelated with the errors $(\xi^p_{t,1}, \xi^p_{t,3})$, $t=1,...,T$. Hence, the resultant GMM estimating equations will be linear in x^*_t, $t=1,...,T$, and the time-invariant intercepts μ^p_1, μ^p_2 and the scale parameter σ_p.

The non-linear regression method outlined above may be simplified further. If $\{\eta_{it}\}^{N_t}_{i=1}$ are independently distributed across individuals, $i=1,...,N_t$, then, as $N_t \to \infty$

$$P^p_{t,j} \to^P F_\eta(\mu^p_j - \sigma_p x^*_t) - F_\eta(\mu^p_{j-1} - \sigma_p x^*_t),$$

$j=1,2,3$; see Amemiya (1985, Section 9.2.5, pp. 275–8). In particular, under symmetry, $P^p_{t,1} \to^P F_\eta(\mu^p_1 - \sigma_p x^*_t)$ and $P^p_{t,3} \to^P F_\eta[-(\mu^p_2 - \sigma_p x^*_t)]$. Hence, using the inverse probability integral transform $F^{-1}_\eta(.)$, we may create the *asymptotic* $(N_t \to \infty)$ linear regression models from (3.4.1)

$$F^{-1}_\eta(P^p_{t,1}) = \mu^p_1 - \sigma_p x^*_t + u^p_{t,1},$$
$$F^{-1}_\eta(P^p_{t,3}) = -\mu^p_2 + \sigma_p x^*_t + u^p_{t,3}, \qquad (3.4.3)$$

where the error terms $(u^p_{t,1}, u^p_{t,3})$ are asymptotically normally distributed with multinomial variance matrix; that is

$$N^{1/2}_t \begin{pmatrix} u^p_{t,1} \\ u^p_{t,3} \end{pmatrix} \to^L N\left(\begin{pmatrix} 0 \\ 0 \end{pmatrix}, \begin{pmatrix} f^{-2}_{\eta 1,t} F_{\eta 1,t}(1-F_{\eta 1,t}) & -f^{-1}_{\eta 1,t} f^{-1}_{\eta 3,t} F_{\eta 1,t} F_{\eta 3,t} \\ -f^{-1}_{\eta 1,t} f^{-1}_{\eta 3,t} F_{\eta 1,t} F_{\eta 3,t} & f^{-2}_{\eta 3,t} F_{\eta 3,t}(1-F_{\eta 3,t}) \end{pmatrix} \right),$$

$$(3.4.4)$$

where $f_{\eta 1,t} = f_\eta(\mu^p_1 - \sigma_p x^*_t)$, $f_{\eta 3,t} = f_\eta[-(\mu^p_2 - \sigma_p x^*_t)]$, $t=1,...,T$, and $f_\eta(z) = dF_\eta(z)/dz$ is the common *density* function of $\{\eta_{it}\}^{N_t}_{i=1}$; see Amemiya (1985, Section 9.2.5, pp. 275–8). If $\{x^*_t\}^T_{t=1}$ were observed and the observations $\{P^p_{t,1}, P^p_{t,3}\}^T_{t=1}$ were independently and identically distributed, then generalised least squares (*minimum chi-squared*) estimation of (3.4.3) is asymptotically equivalent to ML estimation; see Amemiya (*ibid.*). GMM estimation as described above for (3.4.1) may be applied to (3.4.3) together with (3.4.2).

3.4.2 Retrospective survey information

Essentially one may proceed with a similar analysis to that given immediately above. However, as this survey information concerns the actual outcome itself, cf. (3.4.4), one may replace x^*_t by x_t, $t=1,...,T$, for example, in (3.4.1) and (3.4.3).

Estimation
The appropriate log-likelihood function is given, cf. (3.4.4), by

$$\sum_{t=1}^{T} (N_{t1}^r \ln F_{\eta\epsilon 1,t} + N_{t3}^r \ln F_{\eta\epsilon 3,t} + (N_t - N_{t1}^r - N_{t3}^r) \ln(1 - F_{\eta\epsilon 1,t} - F_{\eta\epsilon 3,t})),$$

where the category totals $N_{tj}^r = \Sigma_{i=1}^{N_t} y_{it,j}^r$, $j=1,2,3$, $F_{\eta\epsilon 1,t} = F_{\eta\epsilon}(\mu_1^r - \sigma_r x_t)$, $F_{\eta\epsilon 3,t} = F_{\eta\epsilon}[-(\mu_2^r - \sigma_r x_t)]$, $t=1, ..., T$, $\mu_j^r = \sigma_r c_j^r$, $j=0,1,2,3$, and $F_{\eta\epsilon}(.)$ is the common *symmetric* cumulative distribution function of the scaled error terms $\{\sigma_r(\eta_{it} + \epsilon_{it})\}_{i=1}^{N_t}$, $\sigma_r > 0$.

Define the *retrospective* survey aggregate proportions

$$P_{t,j}^r = N_t^{-1} \sum_{i=1}^{N_t} y_{it,j}^r,$$

$j=1,2,3$. Hence, the *non-linear* regressions corresponding to (3.4.1) are

$$P_{t,1}^r = F_{\eta\epsilon}(\mu_1^r - \sigma_r x_t) + \xi_{t,1}^r,$$
$$P_{t,3}^r = F_{\eta\epsilon}[-(\mu_2^r - \sigma_r x_t)] + \xi_{t,3}^r, \qquad (3.4.5)$$

where $(\xi_{t,1}^r, \xi_{t,3}^r)$ are multinomial conditional on x_t with mean $\mathbf{0}$ and variance matrix

$$\begin{pmatrix} N_t^{-1} F_{\eta\epsilon 1,t}(1 - F_{\eta\epsilon 1,t}) & -N_t^{-1} F_{\eta\epsilon 1,t} F_{\eta\epsilon 3,t} \\ -N_t^{-1} F_{\eta\epsilon 1,t} F_{\eta\epsilon 3,t} & N_t^{-1} F_{\eta\epsilon 3,t}(1 - F_{\eta\epsilon 3,t}) \end{pmatrix}, \qquad (3.4.6)$$

or as $N_t \to \infty$

$$N_t^{1/2} \begin{pmatrix} \xi_{t,1}^r \\ \xi_{t,3}^r \end{pmatrix} \to^L N\left(\begin{pmatrix} 0 \\ 0 \end{pmatrix}, \begin{pmatrix} F_{\eta\epsilon 1,t}(1 - F_{\eta\epsilon 1,t}) & -F_{\eta\epsilon 1,t} F_{\eta\epsilon 3,t} \\ -F_{\eta\epsilon 1,t} F_{\eta\epsilon 3,t} & F_{\eta\epsilon 3,t}(1 - F_{\eta\epsilon 3,t}) \end{pmatrix} \right),$$

$t=1, ..., T$. The *asymptotic* $(N_t \to \infty)$ linear regression models are given by

$$F_{\eta\epsilon}^{-1}(P_{t,1}^r) = \mu_1^r - \sigma_r x_t + u_{t,1}^r,$$
$$F_{\eta\epsilon}^{-1}(P_{t,3}^r) = -\mu_2^r + \sigma_r x_t + u_{t,3}^r, \qquad (3.4.7)$$

$t=1, ..., T$. The error terms $(u_{t,1}^r, u_{t,3}^r)$ are asymptotically normal with multinomial variance structure; that is,

$$N_t^{1/2} \begin{pmatrix} u_{t,1}^r \\ u_{t,3}^r \end{pmatrix} \to^L N(\mathbf{0}, \mathbf{V}_t),$$

$$\mathbf{V}_t = \begin{pmatrix} f_{\eta\epsilon 1,t}^{-2} F_{\eta\epsilon 1,t}(1 - F_{\eta\epsilon 1,t}) & -f_{\eta\epsilon 1,t}^{-1} f_{\eta\epsilon 3,t}^{-1} F_{\eta\epsilon 1,t} F_{\eta\epsilon 3,t} \\ -f_{\eta\epsilon 1,t}^{-1} f_{\eta\epsilon 3,t}^{-1} F_{\eta\epsilon 1,t} F_{\eta\epsilon 3,t} & f_{\eta\epsilon 3,t}^{-2} F_{\eta\epsilon 3,t}(1 - F_{\eta\epsilon 3,t}) \end{pmatrix} \qquad (3.4.8)$$

where $f_{\eta\epsilon 1,t} = f_{\eta\epsilon}(\mu_1^r - \sigma_r x_t)$, $f_{\eta\epsilon 3,t} = f_{\eta\epsilon}[-(\mu_2^r - \sigma_r x_t)]$, $t=1, ..., T$, and $f_{\eta\epsilon}(z) = dF_{\eta\epsilon}(z)/dz$ is the common density function. For this case, given that x_t, $t=1, ..., T$, is observable, generalised least squares (GLS) estimation of (3.4.5) and (3.4.7) is feasible and asymptotically efficient utilising the multinomial structure of the variance matrices (3.4.6) and (3.4.8). The restriction linking the coefficients of x_t in the two equations is easily testable by standard methods.

Estimation of the underlying data

Suppose now that the aggregate proportions for period $T+1$, $(P^r_{T+1,1}, P^r_{T+1,3})$, are available. Given the estimators from the sample, $t=1, \ldots, T$, of the intercept terms μ^r_1, μ^r_2, and σ^r denoted by $\hat{\mu}^r_1$, $\hat{\mu}^r_2$ and $\hat{\sigma}^r$ respectively, it then becomes possible to produce an estimator of x_{T+1} which may pre-date those published by official statistical organisations such as the ONS. In particular, we may invert the relations linking x_{T+1} to the observed proportions $P^r_{T+1,1}$ and $P^r_{T+1,3}$. The estimators are given from (3.4.5) by

$$\hat{x}_{T+1,1} = \hat{\sigma}^{-1}_r [\hat{\mu}^r_1 - F^{-1}_{\eta\epsilon}(P^r_{T+1,1})], \hat{x}_{t,3} = \hat{\sigma}^{-1}_r [\hat{\mu}^r_2 + F^{-1}_{\eta\epsilon}(P^r_{T+1,3})]. \qquad (3.4.9)$$

As $N_{T+1} \to \infty$, from above, $P^r_{T+1,1} \to^P F_{\eta\epsilon}(\mu^r_1 - \sigma_r x_{T+1})$ and $P^r_{T+1,3} \to^P F_{\eta\epsilon}[-(\mu^r_2 - \sigma_r x_{T+1})]$ conditional on x_{T+1}. Moreover, under our assumptions, $\hat{\mu}^r_1$, $\hat{\mu}^r_2$ and $\hat{\sigma}_r$ are consistent estimators for μ^r_1, μ^r_2 and σ_r respectively. Therefore, the estimators $\hat{x}_{T+1,1}$ and $\hat{x}_{T+1,3}$ are both consistent ($N_t \to \infty$, $t=1, \ldots, T+1$) estimators for x_{T+1}. Within-sample predictors, which are useful as a basis for a mis-specification test of the approach of this paper and its associated assumptions, may be provided for x_t, $t=1, \ldots, T$, by a suitable adaptation of (3.4.9).

The estimators $\hat{x}_{T+1,1}$ and $\hat{x}_{T+1,3}$ of (3.4.9) are *unbalanced*; that is, although consistent estimators for x_{T+1}, they are likely to differ in finite samples. A standard method for their reconciliation is to use the least squares method due to Stone, Champernowne and Meade (1942); see also Weale (1992). Other regression-based techniques are described by Smith, Weale and Satchell (1997); see also Sefton and Weale (1995). We assume that $N_{t+1}/N_t \to 1$ as $N_t \to \infty$, $t=1, \ldots, T$. Consider a first-order Taylor series expansion of (3.4.9) for the predictors $\hat{x}_{t,1}$ and $\hat{x}_{t,3}$ about μ^r_1, μ^r_2 and σ_r which as $(u^r_{t,1}, u^r_{t,3}) \to^P \mathbf{0}'$ $(N_t \to \infty)$ yields from (3.4.7)

$$N^{1/2}_t \begin{pmatrix} \hat{x}_{t,1} - x_t \\ \hat{x}_{t,3} - x_t \end{pmatrix} = \sigma^{-1}_r N^{1/2}_t \begin{pmatrix} u^r_{t,1} \\ u^r_{t,3} \end{pmatrix} + \sigma^{-1}_r \mathbf{X}^*_t N^{1/2}_t \begin{pmatrix} \hat{\mu}^r_1 - \mu^r_1 \\ \hat{\mu}^r_2 - \mu^r_2 \\ \hat{\sigma}_r - \sigma_r \end{pmatrix} + o_p(1),$$

where

$$\mathbf{X}^*_t = \begin{pmatrix} 1 & 0 & -x_t \\ 0 & 1 & -x_t \end{pmatrix},$$

$t=1, \ldots, T+1$. Now, assuming that observations are independent over time,

$$N^{1/2}_{T+1} \begin{pmatrix} \hat{x}_{T+1,1} - x_{T+1} \\ \hat{x}_{T+1,3} - x_{T+1} \end{pmatrix} \to^L N(\mathbf{0}, \mathbf{\Omega}_{T+1}),$$

where

$$\Omega_{T+1} = \sigma_r^{-2} \left[V_{T+1} + X_{T+1}^* \left(\sum_{t=1}^{T} X_t' V_t^{-1} X_t \right)^{-1} X_{T+1}^{*\prime} \right],$$

$$X_t = \begin{pmatrix} 1 & 0 & -x_t \\ 0 & -1 & x_t \end{pmatrix},$$

and V_t is defined in (3.4.8), $t = 1, \ldots, T+1$. A consistent estimator $\hat{\Omega}_{T+1}$ for Ω_{T+1} may be constructed using either of the estimators (3.4.9) together with the sample proportions $(P_{T+1,1}^r, P_{T+1,3}^r)$, $t = 1, \ldots, T$, and the estimators $\hat{\mu}_1^r$, $\hat{\mu}_2^r$ and $\hat{\sigma}_r$. Therefore, the reconciled estimator is given by

$$\begin{pmatrix} \hat{x}_{T+1} \\ \hat{x}_{T+1} \end{pmatrix} = \left(I_2 - \hat{\Omega}_{T+1} A' (A \hat{\Omega}_{T+1} A')^{-1} A \right) \begin{pmatrix} \hat{x}_{T+1,1} \\ \hat{x}_{T+1,3} \end{pmatrix}, \tag{3.4.10}$$

where $A = (1, -1)$ and the reconciled estimator $\hat{x}_{T+1}$ is asymptotically efficient ($N_t \to \infty$, $t = 1, \ldots, T+1$); cf. Stone, Champernowne and Meade (1942). Therefore, from above

$$N_{T+1}^{1/2} \begin{pmatrix} \hat{x}_{T+1} - x_{T+1} \\ \hat{x}_{T+1} - x_{T+1} \end{pmatrix} \to^L N(0, \Omega_{T+1} - \Omega_{T+1} A' (A \Omega_{T+1} A')^{-1} A \Omega_{T+1}).$$

To combine the within-sample predictors efficiently, by a similar analysis

$$N_t^{1/2} \begin{pmatrix} \hat{x}_{t,1} - x_t \\ \hat{x}_{t,3} - x_t \end{pmatrix} \to^L N(0, \Sigma_t),$$

where Σ_t is given in

$$\sigma_r^2 \Sigma_t = V_t + X_t^* \left(\sum_{t=1}^{T} X_t' V_t^{-1} X_t \right)^{-1} X_t^{*\prime} + X_t^* \left(\sum_{t=1}^{T} X_t' V_t^{-1} X_t \right)^{-1} X_t'$$

$$+ X_t \left(\sum_{t=1}^{T} X_t' V_t^{-1} X_t \right)^{-1} X_t^{*\prime}.$$

A consistent estimator $\hat{\Sigma}_t$ for Σ_t may be obtained as above, $t = 1, \ldots, T$. Therefore, the balanced estimator is given by

$$\begin{pmatrix} \hat{x}_t \\ \hat{x}_t \end{pmatrix} = \left(I_2 - \hat{\Sigma}_t A' (A \hat{\Sigma}_t A')^{-1} A \right) \begin{pmatrix} \hat{x}_{t,1} \\ \hat{x}_{t,3} \end{pmatrix}, \tag{3.4.11}$$

and

$$N_t^{1/2} \begin{pmatrix} \hat{x}_t - x_t \\ \hat{x}_t - x_t \end{pmatrix} \to^L N(0, \Sigma_t - \Sigma_t A' (A \Sigma_t A')^{-1} A \Sigma_t),$$

$t = 1, \ldots, T$.

3.4.3 Choices of distribution function

We now turn to consider choices of the c.d.f. $F_\eta(.)$. We deal with the prospective data only; more or less identical comments may be made for the retrospective data.

One choice is to allow the $\{\eta_{it}\}_{i=1}^{Nt}$ to be identically distributed as *logistic* random variables which results in using the *log-odds* ratios as dependent variables in (3.4.1) and (3.4.5); *viz.*

$$F_\eta^{-1}(P_{t,1}^p)=\ln\left(\frac{P_{t,1}^p}{1-P_{t,1}^p}\right),\ F_\eta^{-1}(P_{t,3}^p)=\ln\left(\frac{P_{t,3}^p}{1-P_{t,3}^p}\right),$$

$t=1,\ldots,T$. If observations are such as to render the error terms $(u_{t,1}^p,u_{t,3}^p)$ close to their mean of zero, then the results are likely to be similar to those based on the normal c.d.f. and other similarly shaped distribution functions rendering mis-specification due to the choice of $F_\eta(.)$ rather small.

Alternatively, choosing $F_\eta(.)$ to be uniform reproduces a *linear probability* model for the proportions $P_{t,1}^p$ and $P_{t,3}^p$; *viz.*

$$P_{t,1}^p=\mu_1^p-\sigma_p x_t^*+\xi_{t,1}^p,$$
$$P_{t,3}^p=-\mu_2^p+\sigma_p x_t^*+\xi_{t,3}^p, \tag{3.4.12}$$

$t=1,\ldots,T$. As is well-known, the linear probability approach (3.4.12) has the disadvantage of *not* contraining the predicted values of $P_{t,1}^p$ and $P_{t,3}^p$ to lie in the unit interval [0,1].

3.4.4 Regression approaches to transforming survey responses

Regression methods offer an alternative method of using survey responses to estimate the quantitative data. For example, Pesaran (1984) regressed the actual variable of interest (the inflation rate in his case rather than output growth) on the proportions predicting rises or falls; that is, the prospective data survey, which yields a regression model of the form

$$x_t=\beta_0^p+\beta_1^p P_{t,1}^p+\beta_3^p P_{t,3}^p+u_t^p, \tag{3.4.13}$$

where the expectation x_t^* has been substituted from (3.3.2), $t=1,\ldots,T$. Similarly, the retrospective survey would naturally use the actual data x_t:

$$x_t=\beta_0^r+\beta_1^r P_{t,1}^r+\beta_3^r P_{t,3}^r+u_t^r, \tag{3.4.14}$$

$t=1,\ldots,T$.

Apart from problems induced by sources of error associated with the surveys and the way that they have been conducted which have been also ignored in our analysis, the regression models (3.4.13) and (3.4.14) are entirely *ad hoc*. Essentially they are concerned with *best linear unbiased* predictors for x_t using the *current* information in the respective aggregate proportions $\{P_{t,j}^p\}_{j=1}^3$ and $\{P_{t,j}^r\}_{j=1}^3$; cf. Smith, Weale and Satchell (1997). Depending on the time-series properties of the actual data, in particular, if substantial serial correlation is present which may manifest itself in the error terms u_t^p and u_t^r, $t=1, ..., T$, then *lagged* and, possibly, *future* proportions may be informative for prediction; see Smith, Weale and Satchell (1997). The hypotheses $\beta_1^p+\beta_3^p=0$ and $\beta_1^r+\beta_3^r=0$ in (3.4.13) and (3.4.14) respectively are of some interest because if acceptable they imply that we may work with the respective balances $(P_{t,1}^p - P_{t,3}^p)$ and $(P_{t,1}^r - P_{t,3}^r)$.

More natural regression models considered by Pesaran (1984), which assume that the above restrictions are valid, are the *inverse* regressions

$$(P_{t,1}^p - P_{t,3}^p)=\gamma_0^p+\gamma_1^p x_t+v_t^p, \tag{3.4.15}$$

and

$$(P_{t,1}^r - P_{t,3}^r)=\gamma_0^r+\gamma_1^r x_t+v_t^r, \tag{3.4.16}$$

$t=1, ..., T$. The second regression (3.4.16) for the retrospective survey data at least appears to place any measurement error where it belongs; that is, in the survey rather than the actual data. The regression (3.4.16) would be relevant if one wished to calibrate the link between the retrospective survey and the measured out-turn and has been given a formal microeconometric foundation under rather special circumstances as the difference of the two linear probability regressions (3.4.12) for the retrospective data. Regression (3.4.15) is clearly less appropriate. In particular, (3.4.15) may be obtained as the difference of the two linear probability equations (3.4.12) *after* the substitution of x_t for x_t^* which destroys the multinomial variance structure of the error terms and renders the resultant composite error term correlated with x_t, $t=1, ..., T$. Similar to above, both regression models may be interpreted as *ad hoc*; cf. (3.4.13) and (3.4.14).

3.5 An application to UK manufacturing output: 1977Q1–1995Q4

This section applies the methods outlined earlier to UK manufacturing output for the period 1977Q1 to 1995Q4. In particular, we conduct a preliminary examination of the *retrospective* data from the CBI *Quarterly Industrial Trends Survey* over this period as a possible early source of information on UK manufacturing growth over this period.

We consider the following regression models developed from (3.4.5) and (3.4.7) respectively for the retrospective aggregate proportions giving a rise (category 1) $P_{t,1}^r$ and a fall (category 3) $P_{t,3}^r$ in production at the individual firm level; *viz.* the *linear probability* model (3.4.12)

Table 3.1. *Retrospective survey (unrestricted)*

		Linear probability		Logistic	
		estimate	standard error	estimate	standard error
Rise (1)	β_{10}	24.25	0.9543	-1.213	0.05556
	β_{11}	214.6	56.91	13.70	3.354
Fall (3)	β_{30}	22.89	1.105	-1.311	0.06208
	β_{31}	-312.63	66.72	-16.76	1.92

$$P^r_{t,1}=\beta_{10}+\beta_{11}x_t+\xi^r_{t,1},\ P^r_{t,3}=\beta_{30}+\beta_{31}x_t+\xi^r_{t,3}, \qquad (3.5.1)$$

and the *logistic* model

$$\ln\left(\frac{P^r_{t,1}}{1-P^r_{t,1}}\right)=\beta_{10}+\beta_{11}x_t+u^r_{t,1}, \ln\left(\frac{P^r_{t,3}}{1-P^r_{t,3}}\right)=\beta_{30}+\beta_{31}x_t+u^r_{t,3}, \quad (3.5.2)$$

where x_t is the economy-wide growth rate in UK manufacturing output, $t=1,...,T$.

The results are presented in Table 3.1. In both cases, a Wald test was performed for the restriction, $\beta_{11}+\beta_{31}=0$ which reflects the assumption of *symmetry* for the c.d.f. $F_{\eta\epsilon}(.)$; cf. (3.4.5) and (3.4.7). For the linear probability model (3.5.1), the test statistic value was 8.01 which strongly rejects the symmetry restriction at the 0.05 level [$\chi^2_1(0.95)=3.84$] whilst for the logistic model (3.5.2) the test statistic value was 4.07 which is also significant at the 0.05 but not at the 0.025 level [$\chi^2_1(0.975)=5.02$].

Although Table 3.1 indicates that the above regression models are misspecified *vis-à-vis* the micro-econometric foundations outlined in section 3.3, these regressions still have validity as *ad hoc* specifications. Therefore, it is worthwhile to see what light (if any) these regressions cast on the ability of the method described in sub-section 3.4.2 to provide a rapid assessment of the state of the economy. Figure 3.1 compares the unbalanced estimates (3.4.9) of the growth rate in UK manufacturing production obtained using the linear probability model (3.5.1). Figure 3.2 gives the balanced *within* sample estimate (3.4.11) whereas Figure 3.3 compares the balanced one-step ahead estimate (3.4.10) with (3.4.11). Note that these reconciled estimates utilise properties deduced from the assumed microeconometric structure of section 3.3. In particular, the weights used in combining the unbalanced estimates are based on the multinomial variance structure for the regression errors; cf. sub-section 3.4.2.

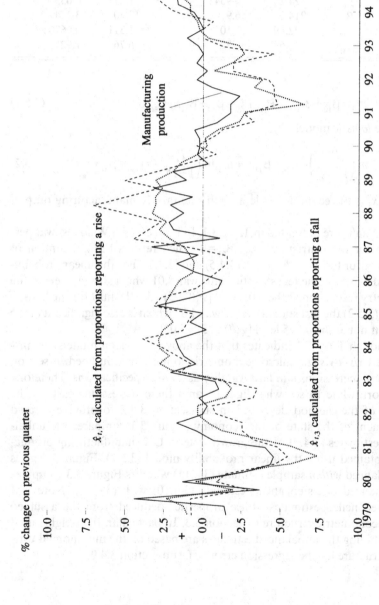

Figure 3.1 Unbalanced estimates of output growth from a retrospective survey: linear

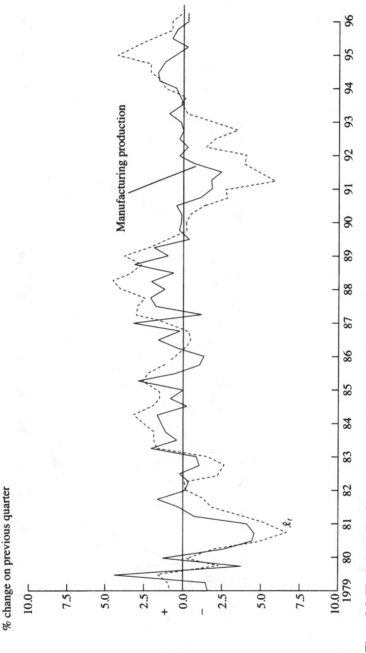

% change on previous quarter

Manufacturing production

$\hat{y}_t$

Figure 3.2 The balanced estimate compared with the out-turn: retrospective linear

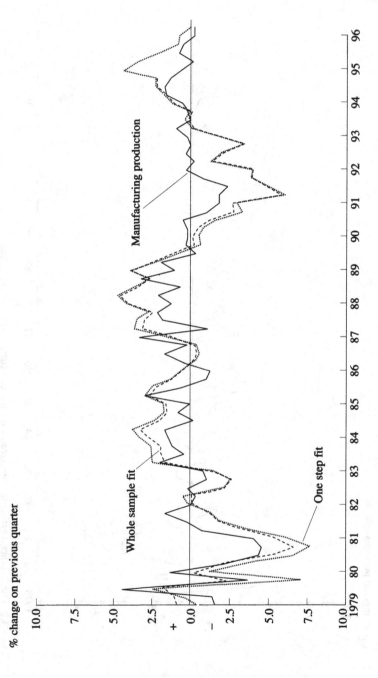

Figure 3.3 One-step and whole-sample: retrospective linear

Figure 3.1 shows that the unbalanced estimates obtained from the rises and falls do not differ widely from each other. However, in particular periods, they are markedly different from the realised UK manufacturing output growth rate, in particular, in the early eighties and nineties, as is emphasised by Figure 3.2. As can be seen from Figure 3.3, there are only marginal differences between the balanced one-step ahead estimate (3.4.10) and the within-sample estimate (3.4.11) with a very close correspondence nearer the end of the sample as should be expected. Overall then, it appears from these figures that the balanced estimates, within-sample and one-step ahead, provide rather poor information regarding the state of the economy.

3.6 Evaluation and future research

As reported in the preliminary investigation of section 3.5 of the retrospective data on manufacturing output from the CBI *Quarterly Industrial Trends Survey*, the balanced estimates, within-sample and one-step ahead, give a poor (in absolute terms) approximation to the realised values of the growth in UK manufacturing output. Hence, these estimates, and, more particularly, the underlying econometric model, cannot be recommended as a means for providing a rapid assessment of the state of the economy. However, these preliminary results, in particular, the rejection of the symmetry restriction, indicate that the linear probability model is unsatisfactory, with the logistic model marginally more satisfactory on this account. Although not presented here, confidence intervals based on standard errors estimated as indicated in sub-section 3.4.2 may be associated with the balanced estimates. These estimated standard errors, although time-varying, are all in the region of 0.2% for both linear probability and logistic formulations, which confirms that both models are unsatisfactory for data estimation purposes.

A major problem ignored in the above analysis is that observations may be correlated across time. This difficulty has also not concerned some other authors. For example, Pesaran and Wright (1992) simply state that they do not concern themselves with this issue whereas Pesaran (1987) discusses this issue in greater detail but regards it as evidence for the presence of irrationality. Serial correlation does not in itself necessarily invalidate the above econometric analysis. However, the estimators would be rendered inefficient and the estimated standard errors invalid. (See Smith, Weale and Satchell, 1997 for a discussion of this point.) In particular, the growth rate of manufacturing output shows some evidence of serial correlation. Moreover, the retrospective survey responses display stronger serial correlation properties than the growth series.

Table 3.2. *Markov matrices for boom/recession transition*

	Output data		Retrospective survey data		Prospective survey data	
	boom	recession	boom	recession	boom	recession
Boom	0.60	0.50	0.85	0.14	0.86	0.15
Recession	0.40	0.50	0.15	0.86	0.14	0.85

To shed some light on these phenomena, Table 3.2 presents Markov matrices for two categorical states: 'boom', if the balance of survey responses and if the growth rate are above average over the sample period, and 'recession' if *vice versa*. It is evident that the survey responses display stronger state persistence than the actual manufacturing output growth series. Such time-series properties in the survey and actual data should be fully accommodated in any theoretical econometric model. This aspect is currently under investigation by the authors. Initial attempts to deal with the serial correlation issue have included lagged dependent variable terms in (3.4.1) and (3.4.2) in an attempt to deal with the serial correlation in the error terms evident when they are omitted. However, such an approach is not entirely satisfactory because the micro-econometric foundations for such an approach are unclear, rendering the procedure *ad hoc*; cf. the regression methods of sub-section 3.4.4. Moreover, the symmetry restriction appears unacceptable in both linear probability and logistic model specifications, indicating that the choice of a symmetric distribution may be inappropriate.

As mentioned above, an additional feature of some concern is the assumption of symmetry made in the choice of the linear probability and logistic specifications which is rejected by the data in both cases. Experiments with alternative asymmetric distributional specifications are in progress. Moreover, suitable diagnostic tests for distributional and other potential forms of misspecification are also the subject of current research.

Note

This version is a revision of a paper presented at the Department of Applied Economics 50th Anniversary Conference, Queen's College, Cambridge. The authors are grateful to William Peterson for his helpful comments on the earlier version.

4 Social accounting matrices and applied general equilibrium models

Timothy J. Kehoe

4.1 Introduction

The use of social accounting matrices (SAMs) to record all of the transactions that take place in a national economy during one year has a distinguished ancestry. This ancestry can be traced back at least as far as Quesnay's (1759) *Tableau économique*. (See Studenski, 1958 and Stone's 1986 Nobel Memorial Lecture for histories of social accounting.) In the twentieth century, social accounting has been heavily influenced by the work on national income accounts by Kuznets (1937) and that on input–output matrices by Leontief (1941). The development of SAMs as they are used today began with the work by Meade and Stone (1941) for the Economic Section of the British Cabinet Office, which developed the first logically complete set of double-entry national income accounts. Subsequent work by Stone (1947) resulted in the conventions for social accounting embodied in the United Nations' (1953, 1968) system of national accounts and currently used throughout the world.

The development of social accounting went hand-in-hand with the development of planning models that used these data. Indeed, Meade and Stone's (1941) original work was meant to provide data to aid in implementing Keynes's (1940) proposals for funding Britain's war effort during the Second World War. Stone's later work on social accounting in Britain provided data for the Cambridge Growth Model at the Department of Applied Economics. Indeed, in the hands of some users, SAMs have become economic models in and of themselves, with spread-sheet type relationships between entries. The volume edited by Pyatt and Round (1985) contains a number of illustrative examples of this sort of modelling.

An even more popular – but closely related – use of SAMs has been to provide databases for constructing applied general equilibrium (GE) models. Like social accounting, applied GE modelling has a long and distinguished – and sometimes overlapping – ancestry. Numerical applications of general equilibrium narrowly defined began with the work of Harberger (1962) and Johansen (1960). Harberger used a model with two production sectors, one corporate and the other noncorporate, calibrated to US data from the 1950s, to calculate the incidence of the US corporate income tax. Johansen used a model with 19 production sectors, calibrated to Norwegian data from 1950, to identify the sources of economic growth in Norway over the period 1948–53.

Work on applied GE models received a crucial stimulus from the research of Scarf (Scarf, 1967; Scarf and Hansen, 1973) on the computation of economic equilibria. Scarf developed an algorithm for calculating an equilibrium of a multisectoral GE model. Refinements of this algorithm are still used by some modellers. Probably the most significant consequences of Scarf's work, however, were to establish a close connection between applied GE research and the theoretical research of such economists as Arrow and Debreu (1954) and McKenzie (1951) on existence of equilibrium in very general models and to inspire a generation of Yale graduate students to enter the applied GE field. (Arrow and Kehoe, 1994 discuss Scarf's contributions to applied GE modelling.)

Two of Scarf's most prominent students are Shoven and Whalley (1972), who developed a calibrated, multisectoral general equilibrium framework to analyse the welfare impact of government tax policy. Shoven and Whalley (1984, 1992) provide surveys of this work and the large literature that has followed it. Early models in the Shoven–Whalley tradition were explicitly static, studying the determination of equilibrium in a single period. Later models studied the evolution of capital stocks over time in a framework where the people in the model either solve static problems (as in Johansen's model) or, what is almost the same, where people have myopic expectations, that is, they expect current relative prices to persist in the future; see Fullerton, Shoven, and Whalley (1983) for an example of the latter approach. Ballard and Goulder (1985) developed a perfect foresight version of the Fullerton–Shoven–Whalley model.

Researchers working in the Shoven–Whalley tradition have stressed developing theoretical underpinnings for applied GE models and producing results that are meant to be compared with those of simpler theoretical frameworks. They have spent little effort in comparing their results with outcomes of policy changes in the world. Whalley (1986, 1988), for example, contends that these models are not intended to forecast the values of economic variables, but rather to provide useful insights that may help policymakers to undertake more informed, and presumably more desirable, policy actions. This line of thought has led Whalley to suggest that the concept of positive economics should be perhaps altogether abandoned in applied GE modelling. As we shall see, however, applied GE models can be used to make conditional forecasts with some accuracy.

Several other groups of researchers began using static applied GE models to do policy analysis after Shoven and Whalley (1972). One such group centred around the World Bank and focused on developing countries; a survey of its work is presented by Dervis, de Melo, and Robinson (1982). Another group has come to prominence doing policy analysis in Australia; a summary of early work by this group is given by Dixon et al. (1982); a more recent survey is presented by Dixon et al. (1992).

There is a large and expanding literature on multisectoral applied GE models. A recent search of the EconLit database produced references to more than 200 books and journal articles on this subject. Prominent contributors – besides those mentioned above – include Ginsburgh and Waelbroeck (eds) (1981), Jorgenson (1984), and Manne (ed.) (1985). There have also been numerous collected volumes of papers on this subject: Scarf and Shoven (eds) (1984); Piggott and Whalley (eds) (1985, 1991); Srinivasan and Whalley (eds) (1986); Bergman, Jorgenson, and Zalai (eds) (1900); Don, van de Klundent, and van Sinderen (eds) (1991); and Mercenier and Srinivasan (eds) (1994).

This paper illustrates the use of SAMs in applied GE modelling. We first present an aggregated SAM for the Spanish economy in 1980, based on a disaggregated matrix constructed by Kehoe, Manresa, Polo, and Sancho (1988). Using this matrix, we calibrate a simple applied GE model. The idea is to construct artificial people – households, government, and foreign sectors – who make the same transactions in the equilibrium of the model economy as are observed in the SAM. This calibration procedure can be augmented, or partially substituted for, by statistical estimation of key parameters.

We show the usefulness of such an applied GE model by presenting the comparative statics exercise of Kehoe, Manresa, Noyola, Polo, and Sancho (1988) that analyses the economic impact of the policy changes that accompanied Spain's 1986 entry into the then European Community (EC). We also present results obtained by Kehoe, Polo, and Sancho (1995), who find that the results of the model were remarkably accurate in predicting the change in relevant economic variables that occurred in Spain in 1986. This is especially true if we account for two other major shocks – a fall in international petroleum prices and a bad harvest – that hit the Spanish economy in 1986.

Table 4.1. *Sectors in the aggregated 1980 social accounting matrix for Spain*

Producer goods		
1	Primaries	(1–2ᵃ)
2	Manufacturing	(3–7)
3	Construction and services	(8–12)
Consumer goods		
4	Food and beverages	(17–18)
5	Clothing, housing and household articles	(19–21)
6	Services	(22–25)
Factors of production		
7	Labour	(26–27)
8	Capital	(28)
Institutions		
9	Low-income households	(I, III, V, VII)
10	High-income households	(II, IV, VI, VIII)
11	Government	(13, IX)
11a	Direct taxes	
11b	Indirect taxes and tariffs	
Capital account		
12	Investment	(14)
Foreign sector		
13	Rest of the world	(15–16, X–XI)

Note:
ᵃ Corresponding sectors in Kehoe, Manresa, Polo, and Sancho (1988).

4.2 An aggregated Spanish SAM

Tables 4.1 and 4.2 present an aggregated SAM for Spain in 1980. It is based on a matrix constructed by Kehoe, Manresa, Polo, and Sancho (1988) that has a much higher degree of disaggregation and precision. The inter-industry transactions have been aggregated under the categories of three industrial sectors: primaries, manufactures, and services. These sectors are highly aggregated. The manufacturing sector, for example, lumps together such diverse goods as machinery, transportation equipment, and processed foods. The model actually used to analyse the impact on different industrial sectors of policies that accompanied Spain's entry into the EC has a finer disaggregation, as shown in Tables 4.5 and 4.6.

Table 4.2. *Aggregated 1980 social accounting matrix for Spain (in trillion 1980 pesetas[a])*

		Expenditures													
		1	2	3	4	5	6	7	8	9	10	11	12	13	Total
	1	2	1	1	1	1	0						0	0	6
	2	1	4	1	1	1	1						1	2	12
	3	0	1	3	1	2	3					2	2	0	14
R	4									2	1				3
E	5									2	2				4
C	6									2	2				4
E	7	1	2	3											6
I	8	1	1	5											7
P	9							4	2			1		0	7
T	10							2	5			0		0	7
S	11	0	1	1	0	0	0			0	1				3
	11a									0	1				1
	11b	0	1	1	0	0	0								2
	12									1	1	0		1	3
	13	1	2	0											3
Total		6	12	14	3	4	4	6	7	7	7	3	3	3	

Note:
[a] US trillions, British/Spanish billions; 0 represents a non-zero number that has been rounded down to zero.
Source: Kehoe, Manresa, Polo, and Sancho (1988).

All quantities in Table 4.2 are expressed in trillions of 1980 Spanish pesetas (that is, US trillions, British/Spanish billions). In 1980, the exchange rates between pesetas and US dollars averaged about 72 pesetas per dollar; that between pesetas and pounds sterling averaged about 167 pesetas per pound. The 1980 Spanish gross domestic product (GDP) of 15 trillion pesetas reported in Tables 4.2 and 4.4, for example, corresponds to 208 billion US dollars or 90 billion pounds sterling.

In a SAM, the label on a column indicates who made an expenditure, and the label on a row indicates who received it. Reading down the second column of Table 4.2, for example, we see that in 1980 producers of manufacturing goods in Spain purchased 1 trillion pesetas of intermediate inputs from producers of primaries and paid 2 trillion pesetas for labour inputs. Reading across the second row, we see that producers of services purchased 1 trillion pesetas of manufactures and that 2 trillion pesetas of manufactures were exported. The rows and columns of the matrix in Table 4.2 are ordered so that the transactions break down into blocks: producer goods, consumer goods, factors of production, institutions, the capital account, and the foreign sector.

It is worth making three observations about this SAM: first, the matrix disaggregates households using data from the Spanish household income and expenditure survey. As explained by Stone (1985), this sort of dis- aggregation of consumers requires a different disaggregation of consumer goods than that used for inter-industry transactions – consumers report on their purchases of food, for example, not on the complex combination of agriculture, food products, commercial services, and transportation ser- vices that are embodied in that food. The second 3×3 matrix on the top of the SAM in Table 4.2 shows this combination. Consumer purchases of 4 trillion pesetas of clothing, housing, and household articles, for example, translate into purchases of 1 trillion pesetas of primaries, 1 trillion pesetas of manufactures, and 2 trillion pesetas of services. Second, the SAM reported in Table 4.2 includes an input–output matrix as a collection of sub-matrices. That input–output matrix is reported in Table 4.3. Third, the transactions reported in the SAM are also consistent with the figures in the national income and product accounts presented in Table 4.4, which records the Spanish GDP in 1980 as being 15 trillion pesetas.

4.3 A simple applied GE model

We construct an applied GE model by inventing artificial households, pro- ducers, a government, and foreigners who make the same transactions in the base case equilibrium of the computer economy as do their counter- parts in the world. With a large amount of data (for example, a time series of SAMs), we could use statistical estimation techniques to find the para- meters that characterise the people in the artificial economy (see Jorgenson, 1984).

A more common method for constructing an applied GE model is to calibrate its parameters (see Mansur and Whalley, 1984). Using simple functional forms, we work backward from the data in Table 4.2 to con- struct economic agents whose transactions duplicate those observed. As we explain later, statistical estimates of key parameters can easily be incor- porated into this calibration procedure.

To understand the uses of this sort of model and the procedure used to calibrate it, consider a highly simplified model in which there are four con- sumers: a representative low-income household, a representative high- income household, the government, and the rest of the world. In this economy, eight goods are produced: primaries, manufactures, services,

Table 4.3. *1980 aggregated input–output matrix for Spain (in trillion 1980 pesetas)*

	Intermediate inputs			Final demand				Total demand
Receipts	primaries	manufactures	services	private consumption	investment	government consumption	exports	
Intermediate inputs								
primaries	2	1	1	2	0		0	6
manufactures	1	4	1	3	1		2	12
services	0	1	3	6	2	2	0	14
imports	1	2	0		2			3
Components of the value added								
labour	1	2	3					6
capital	1	1	5					7
indirect taxes and tariffs	0	1	1					2
Total production	6	12	14	11	3	2	2	50

Table 4.4. *1980 national income and product accounts for Spain (in trillion 1980 pesetas)*

Expenditures		Income	
Private consumption	11	Wages and salaries	6
Private investment	2	Other factor payments	7
Government consumption	2	Indirect taxes and tariffs	2
Government investment	1		
Exports	2		
less Imports	−3		
Gross domestic product	15	Gross domestic product	15

Government accounts		Foreign accounts	
Government consumption	2	Imports	3
Government investment	1	*less* Exports	−2
Government transfers	1		
less Indirect taxes and tariffs	−2		
less Direct taxes	−1		
Government deficit	1	Trade deficit	1

food, housing, consumer services, an investment good, and an export/import good. Each of these goods is produced using intermediate inputs of the other goods; the two factors of production, labour and capital; and the import good.

We assume that a consumer solves a utility maximisation problem of the form

$$\max u_i(c_1^i, \ldots, c_8^i)$$

subject to

$$\sum_{j=1}^{8} p_j c_j^i \leq I^i$$

In the utility function c_j^i is the purchase of good j by consumer i. The SAM tells us that consumers 1 and 2 make purchases of the consumer goods 4, 5, and 6 and the investment good 7. The government makes the purchases of good 3, services, and good 7, investment. The rest of the world purchases good 7, investment (this is the capital flow compensating for the Spanish trade deficit), and good 8, exports. In the budget constraint p_j is the price of good j and the I^i is the income of consumer i. Consumers 1 and 2 have after-tax income from selling the services of their labour and capital and from transfers they receive from the government,

$$I^i = (1-\tau_i)(w\bar{\ell}^i + r\bar{k}^i) + T^i.$$

Here w and r are the wage rate and capital rental rate, $\bar{\ell}^i$ and $\bar{k}^i$ are the consumer's endowments of labour and capital, τ_i is the direct tax rate, and T^i is the transfer payment. The government receives income from taxes and, if it runs a deficit, from selling bonds that are a perfect substitute for the investment good. The rest of the world receives income from selling imports and, if there is a trade surplus, from selling the investment good.

We put purchases of the investment good into the utility functions to account for the savings observed in the data. In a dynamic model, consumers save so that they can enjoy future consumption, and purchases of the investment good in one period augment the capital stock in the next. In this type of static model, however, investment is treated as another final demand for goods, like consumption. A simple form for the utility function is linear in logarithms:

$$u_i(c_1^i, \ldots, c_8^i) = \sum_{j=1}^{8} \theta_j^i \log c_j^i.$$

Hence, the numbers θ_j^i are non-negative parameters, the calibration of which we describe later.

We assume that domestic output of each of the eight produced goods has a constant-returns production function that combines intermediate inputs in fixed proportions and labour and capital with substitution possibilities governed by a Cobb–Douglas production function of the form $\beta k^\alpha \ell^{1-\alpha}$. Subsequently, we explain how this domestic output combines with inputs. The general form of the domestic production function is

$$y_{jd} = \min(x_{1j}/a_{1j}, \ldots, x_{8j}/a_{8j}, \beta_j k_j^{\alpha_j} \ell_j^{1-\alpha_j}).$$

Here, x_{ij} is the intermediate input of good i used in the production of good j; a_{ij} is the amount of good i required to produce one unit of good j; and a_{ij}, β_j, and α_j are parameters to be calibrated.

Not every good is used in the production of every other good. We handle this problem by dropping the corresponding entry from the production function, rather than by adopting complicated conventions about dividing by zero and so on. The production function for manufactures, for example, is

$$y_{2d} = \min(x_{12}/a_{12}, x_{22}/a_{22}, x_{32}/a_{32}, \beta_2 k_2^{\alpha_2} \ell_2^{1-\alpha_2}).$$

Both x_{42} and x_{72}, for example, are omitted here because Table 4.2 shows that neither the food nor the investment good is used in the production of manufactures. Similarly, the production function for food is

$$y_{6d}=\min(x_{14}/a_{14},x_{24}/a_{24},x_{34}/a_{34}).$$

Both k_4 and ℓ_4 are omitted here because, in keeping with the accounting conventions used in Table 4.2, we consider food to be produced by selling a combination of the producer goods rather than by any process that involves labour and capital directly: commercial mark-ups, transportation costs, and so on, are already included in the intermediate input of services in the food column.

We assume that producers minimise costs and earn zero after-tax profits. Since this assumption implies that producers never waste inputs, we can write the domestic production function for manufactures, for example, as

$$y_{2d}=x_{12}/a_{12}=x_{22}/a_{22}=x_{32}/a_{32}=\beta_2 k_2^{\alpha_2}\ell_2^{1-\alpha_2}.$$

Cost minimisation further implies that k_2, ℓ_2 solve

$$\min w\ell_2+rk_2$$

subject to

$$\beta_2 k_2^{\alpha_2}\ell_2^{1-\alpha_2}\geq y_{2d}.$$

Again, w is the wage rate, and r is the capital rental rate. Our assumption that after-tax profits equal zero is

$$(1-t_2)p_2 y_{2d}-\sum_{i=1}^{8}p_i a_{i2}y_2-w\ell_2-rk_2=0.$$

Here, t_2 is the indirect tax rate on sales of manufactures.

In our model, as in many applied GE models, we distinguish goods by industry and by country of origin. Thus, for example, a Spanish-produced car is a different good from a German-produced car – a close but imperfect substitute. This specification, named the Armington (1969) specification after the economist who invented it, has three advantages over obvious alternatives for matching the model to data on trade flows. One is that it accounts for the large amount of cross-hauling present in the data, where a country both imports and exports goods of the same product category. In a model where goods are homogeneous, there is no reason for cross-hauling. Another advantage of this specification is that it explains the empirical observation that even at a very disaggregated level, most countries produce goods in all product categories. In models where goods are not distinguished by country of origin and produced goods exceed factors of production, countries typically specialise in the production of a limited number of goods. Still another advantage of the Armington specification is that it allows for differing degrees of substitution among domestic and imported goods across different products and allows for changes in the relative prices of different imported goods. Empirical studies indicate that both of these phenomena are found in time-series data (see, for example, Shiells, Stern, and Deardorff, 1986). Neither is possible in a model that aggregates all imports together or in a model that treats domestic and imported goods as perfect substitutes.

To implement the Armington specification we need a SAM in which imports are classified by the sector that produces them, the sector of origin, and not by the sector that purchases them, the sector of destination. SAMs can be arranged according to either convention: the SAM in Table 4.2 follows the sector of origin convention; thus, the 2 in column 2, row 13 indicates that Spain imported 2 trillion pesetas of manufactures in 1980, not that the Spanish manufacturing sector purchased 2 trillion pesetas of imported goods of all sorts. To keep things simple, we assume that domestic output is combined with imports to produce a composite good according to a Cobb–Douglas Armington aggregator. Later, we explain how this can be generalised. The composite manufactured good is the Cobb–Douglas aggregate

$$y_2 = \gamma_2 y_{2d}^{\delta_2} x_{28}^{1-\delta_2}$$

Here, y_2 is the aggregate of manufactures, y_{2d} is domestic output specified above, and x_{28} is imports of manufactures. We can think of imports as being produced by an international trade activity that uses exports as inputs:

$$y_8 = \min[x_{18}/a_{18}, x_{28}/a_{28}].$$

We require that this activity make zero profits, thus determining the relative price of imports. As explained below, however, we do not require balanced trade.

The behaviour of the government and the rest of the world needs to be carefully specified. The government, for example, derives income from direct and indirect taxes. (In the disaggregated model it also receives tariff revenues and capital income although these are so small that they have been rounded to zero here.) It uses this income to purchase government services and investment and to make transfers to consumers. We specify these transfers as fixed in terms of a relevant consumer price index:

$$T^i = \left(\sum_{j=1}^{8} \theta_j p_j \right) \overline{T^i}$$

where $\theta_j = (\theta_j^1 I^1 + \theta_j^2 I^2)/(I^1 + I^2)$ is the total consumption share of good j and $\overline{T}^i$ is a constant. (In the more detailed model actually used for policy evaluation in Spain, transfers are modelled in far more detail, including health benefits that depend on the price of medical services and unemployment benefits that depend on an endogenously determined unemployment rate.)

The difference between total revenues and expenditures determines the public surplus or deficit. The model satisfies the macroeconomic identity that private saving is equal to private investment plus the government deficit minus the trade deficit with the rest of the world.

The model allows some flexibility in choosing the variables that are exogenous and endogenous. The government deficit, for example, can be endogenous or exogenous. In the first case, the activity level of the government is fixed, while in the second the activity level is endogenous. This flexibility allows us to answer two different questions: What would be the government deficit when the government activity level is arbitrarily fixed? and, What would be the variation needed in the government activity level to achieve a given government deficit target?

We also have the option of making exports to the rest of the world exogenous or endogenous. If exports are exogenously fixed, for example, then, since imports are endogenously determined, so is the trade deficit. In contrast, if the trade deficit is arbitrarily fixed, then exports are endogenous. We, therefore, have two options: to make the government deficit endogenous or exogenous, and to make the trade deficit endogenous or exogenous. There are potentially, therefore, four different macroeconomic closure rules. There are additional possibilities for macroeconomic closure that involve making investment exogenous; we do not consider such closure rules here.

All these elements of the model economy are linked by the concept of equilibrium. An equilibrium is specified by listing values for all of the endogenous variables in the model: a price for each of the produced goods $\hat{p}_j$, a price for domestic production of each of the goods $\hat{p}_{jd}$, a level of consumption for each good by each consumer $\hat{c}_j^i$, a wage rate $\hat{w}$, a capital rental rate $\hat{r}$, a production plan for each of the produced goods $(\hat{y}_j, \hat{x}_{1j}, ..., \hat{x}_{8j}, \hat{k}_j, \hat{l}_j)$, a level of government tax receipts $\hat{R}$, transfer payments to consumers $\hat{T}^i$, a government deficit $\hat{GD}$, and a trade deficit $\hat{TD}$. To be an equilibrium, such a list must satisfy the following properties:

- The consumption vector $(\hat{c}_1^i, ..., \hat{c}_8^i)$ solves the utility-maximisation problem of consumer i
- The production plan $(\hat{y}_j, \hat{x}_{1j}, ..., x_{8j}, \hat{k}_j, \hat{\ell}_j)$ minimises costs subject to the feasibility constraints and earns zero after-tax profits
- Supply equals demand in the market for each produced good:

$$\hat{y}_j = \sum_{i=1}^{4} \hat{c}_j^i + \sum_{\ell=1}^{8} \hat{x}_{j\ell}$$

for $j = 1, \ldots, 8$

- Supply equals demand in each factor market:

$$l^{-1} + l^{-2} = \sum_{j=1}^{8} \hat{\ell}_j$$

$$k^{-1} + k^{-2} = \sum_{j=1}^{8} \hat{k}_j$$

- The tax receipts equal total taxes paid:

$$\hat{R} = \sum_{j=1}^{2} \tau_i(\hat{w}\overline{\ell}^i + \hat{r}\hat{k}^i) + \sum_{j=1}^{8} t_j\hat{p}_j\hat{y}_j$$

- Transfer payments are fixed in real terms:

$$\hat{T}_i = \left(\sum_{j=1}^{8} \theta_j\hat{p}_j\right)\overline{T}^i$$

- The government satisfies its budget constraint:

$$\hat{p}_3\hat{c}_3^3 + \hat{p}_7^3\hat{c}_7^3 + \hat{T}^1 + \hat{T}^2 = \hat{R} + \hat{GD}$$

If the government deficit is fixed in real terms – $\hat{GD} = (\sum_{j=1}^{8} \theta_j^3\hat{p}_j)\hat{GD}$ – then government spending $\hat{c}_3^3$, $\hat{c}_7^3$ varies endogenously. If government spending is fixed – $\hat{c}_3^3 = \overline{c}_3^3$ and $\hat{c}_7^3 = \overline{c}_7^3$ – then the government deficit varies endogenously

- The rest of the world satisfies its budget constraint:

$$\hat{TD} = \hat{p}_7\hat{c}_7^4 = \hat{p}_8\left(\hat{y}_8 - \sum_{j=1}^{8} \hat{x}_{8j}\right)$$

If the trade deficit is fixed – $\hat{c}_7^4 = \overline{c}_7^4$ – then exports $\hat{y}_8$ vary. If exports are fixed – $\hat{y}_8 = \overline{y}_8$ – then the trade deficit $\hat{c}_7^4$ varies endogenously.

4.4 Calibration and simulation

We calibrate the parameters of the model economy so that the equilibrium reproduces the transactions observed in the SAM. We start with the households. Table 4.2 reports that the high-income household, for example, receives a factor income of 7 (trillion pesetas) – 2 in wages and salaries from selling labour services and 5 from other factor payments. As is standard practice in this sort of work, we aggregate these other factors into a single factor called capital. Table 4.2 also reports that this consumer pays 1 in direct taxes, leaving a disposable income of 6. Of this disposable income, 5 is spent on consumption and the residual, 1, is saved. This consumer receives no significant transfers from the government, although the representative low-income household does.

If we use calculus to solve the consumer's problem, we obtain

$$c_j^2 = \theta_j^2 (1 - \tau_2)(w\bar{\ell}^2 + r\bar{k}^2)/p_j.$$

(We have normalised the parameters θ_j^2 to sum to one.) We could think of each of the goods as being measured in some type of natural unit: primaries in terms of litres, for example, or labour services in terms of hours. Let us choose different physical units for the goods, such that one unit of each good is worth 1 trillion 1980 pesetas. This choice of units is already implicit in the construction of Table 4.2, where, for example, grapes and oranges have been aggregated into the primaries good. One advantage of these units is that we can calibrate the prices p_j, the wage w, and the capital rental rate r all to equal one in the base case equilibrium. (Think of these variables as price indices, which are naturally set equal to one in the base case.)

The calibration is now straightforward. Since we know that labour income is 2, we calibrate $\bar{\ell}^2 = 2$; since we know that capital income is 5, we calibrate $\bar{k}^2 = 5$; and since we know that direct tax payment on private income of 7 is 1, we calibrate $\tau_2 = 1/7$. Of the total after-tax income of $6 = (1 - \tau_2)(w\bar{\ell}^2 + r\bar{k}^2)$, we know that 1 is spent on food. We therefore calibrate $\theta_1^2 = 1/6$, for example. Similarly, we calibrate $\theta_3^2 = 2/6$ to get the consumer to spend 2 on housing in the base case equilibrium and $\theta_7^2 = 1/6$ to get the consumer to save 1.

The calibration of the unit input requirements a_{ij} in the production functions is equally easy. Since we know that 1 unit of primaries is required to produce 10 units of domestic production manufactures, we calibrate $a_{12} = 1/10$. Calibrating the Cobb–Douglas function that describes how labour and capital are combined to produce value added is slightly more complicated. If we choose inputs of labour and capital to minimise costs, we know that the ratio of the marginal products should equal the factor price ratio:

$$(1 - \alpha_2)k_2/(\alpha_2 \ell_2) = w/r.$$

Since we want $k_2 = 1$ and $\ell_2 = 2$ in the base case equilibrium and we have chosen units so that $w = r = 1$, we calibrate $\alpha_2 = 1/3$. Inserting this value for α_2 into the Cobb–Douglas production function along with the observed values of labour, capital, and output, we obtain

$$\beta_2 = y_{2d}/(k_2^{\alpha_2}\ell_2^{1-\alpha_2}) = 10(2)^{-2/3}.$$

Since producers of manufactures pay indirect taxes of 1 on total sales of 10, we calibrate the indirect tax rate $t_2 = 1/10$.

We calibrate the Armington aggregator for manufactures using the same procedure. The condition that the ratio of marginal products should equal the price ratio,

$$(1-\delta_2)y_{2d}/(\delta_2 x_{28}) = p_8/p_{2d}$$

implies that $\delta_2 = 10/12$. Inserting this value of δ_2 and the observed values of y_{2d} and x_{28} into the Armington aggregator, we obtain

$$\gamma_2 = y_2/(y_{2d}^{\delta_2} x_{28}^{1-\delta_2}) = 12(10)^{-10/12}(2)^{-2/12}.$$

We can calibrate the production functions for other sectors similarly. The domestic production function for primaries, for example, is

$$y_{1d} = (5/2)x_{11} = 5x_{21} = (5/2)k_1^{1/2}\ell_1^{1/2}$$

The Armington aggregator is

$$y_1 = 6(5)^{-5/6}y_{1d}^{5/6}x_{18}^{1/6}.$$

The production function for housing is simply

$$y_5 = 4x_{15} = 4x_{25} = 2x_{35}.$$

If we calibrate the model as above, we can use it to evaluate a change in government policy. We simply change a tax parameter, say t_2, and then calculate the new equilibrium. In general, the values of all of the endogenous variables change, and reporting on how some of them change is informative. When we report on the prices of produced goods and factors, we need to be explicit about the normalisation. Like any general equilibrium model, this model allows for an arbitrary choice of a numeraire, that is, the unit in terms of which all values are expressed. (Looking at the definition of equilibrium, we see that multiplying $\hat{p}_j$, $\hat{p}_{jd}$, $\hat{w}$, $\hat{r}$, $\hat{R}$, $\hat{T}^i$, $\hat{GD}$, and $\hat{TD}$ by the same positive constant still results in an equilibrium.) A typical practice is to normalise prices so that a certain price index remains constant. We could, for example, normalise prices according to a price index based on consumption weights,

$$\sum_{j=1}^{8} \theta_j p_j = 1.$$

Changes in the wage rate would then be termed changes in the real wage rate.

One of the most interesting results to report is how consumer welfare changes. Since utility is expressed in no natural units, economists often choose to measure welfare using an index based on income. A common measure of welfare is how much income the consumer would need, when faced with the base case prices, to achieve the same level of utility as in the simulation. Changes in this measure of welfare are called the equivalent variation.

In calibrating both the consumer and the producers in our simple model, we have used either Cobb–Douglas or fixed-proportion functions, and therefore all elasticities of substitution are equal to one or infinity. (The utility function is the logarithm of a Cobb–Douglas function.) If information is available on elasticities of substitution in consumption or production, however, it can easily be incorporated into the calibration procedure. Suppose, for example, that we have information from econometric estimates that the elasticity of substitution in consumption for high-income households is $\frac{1}{2}$. Then we need to calibrate the constant elasticity of substitution utility function

$$u_2(c_1^2, \ldots, c_8^2) = \sigma_2 \sum_{j=1}^{8} \theta_j^2 ((c_j^2)^{1-1/\sigma_2} - 1)/(1-\sigma_2)$$

where $\sigma_2 = \frac{1}{2}$ is the elasticity of substitution. Again, we calibrate by working backward from the solution to the utility-maximisation problem,

$$c_j^2 = (\theta_j^2)^{\sigma_2}(1-\tau_2)(w\bar{\ell}^2 + r\bar{k}^2)/\left(p_j^{\sigma_2} \sum_{\ell=1}^{8} (\theta_\ell^2)^{\sigma_2} p_\ell^{1-\sigma_2}\right).$$

We obtain, for example, the parameter for food $\theta_1^2 = 1/10$ and the parameter for housing $\theta_2^2 = 4/10$.

Similarly, suppose that we have evidence that the elasticity of substitution between domestic manufactures and imported manufactures in the Armington aggregator is $\frac{3}{2}$:

$$y_2 = \gamma_2 [\delta_2 y_{2d}^{1-1/\rho_2} + (1-\delta_2) x_{28}^{1-1/\rho_2}]^{\rho_2/(\rho_2-1)}.$$

Solving the problem of minimising $p_{2d} y_{2d} + p_8 x_{28}$ subject to obtaining total output of y_2 and inserting $\rho_2 = \frac{3}{2}$, $y_2 = 12$, $y_{2d} = 10$, $x_{28} = 2$, and $p_{2d} = p_8 = 1$, we can calibrate $\delta_2 = 5^{2/3}/(1+5^{2/3})$ and $\gamma_2 = (1+5^{2/3})^3/36$.

Even if we allow for more flexible functional forms, the model that we have described is highly simplified. In practice, applied GE models allow more disaggregation, more institutional details, and some market imperfections. Models used in policy analysis typically include many more production sectors. Factors of production may also be disaggregated. For example, labour might be broken down by skill level. Unfortunately, data restrictions usually prevent any simple breakdown of the aggregate capital input. In models that focus on public finance issues, more detail usually goes into specifying government tax, transfer, and subsidy systems.

A market imperfection often built into a static applied GE model is in the labour market. The real wage, specified in terms of an index of other prices, is typically modelled as being downwardly rigid. Changes in the demand for labour result in varying rates of unemployment. If demand for labour rises so much that full employment occurs, the real wage then rises so that supply is equal to demand (see Kehoe and Serra-Puche, 1983). Another possibility is to fix the return to capital. Then the interpretation involves not unemployment of capital but rather international capital flows. If demand for capital rises, an inflow from the rest of the world occurs. If demand for capital falls, an outflow occurs.

The simple model that we have described has constant returns in production and perfect competition among producers. This was the dominant model in early applied GE analyses of trade policy (see, for example, Srinivasan and Whalley (eds), 1986). Over the past decade, however, there has been a trend toward incorporating such phenomena as increasing returns, imperfect competition and product differentiation in applied work on trade policy.

The first applied GE model to incorporate increasing returns and imperfect competition was developed by Harris (1984) to analyse the impact on Canada of the then-proposed US–Canada Free Trade Agreement. Harris (1984) and Cox and Harris (1985) show that by incorporating increasing returns and imperfect competition into some industrial sectors of an applied GE model, they can capture the gains from specialisation and access to larger markets for a relatively small economy like Canada. This research played an important role in the political debate in Canada leading up to approval of the agreement. Such models also played an important role in the political debate leading up to the approval of the North American Free Trade Agreement (see Kehoe and Kehoe (eds) 1995 for a survey).

4.5 The applied GE model of Spain

In 1985–86, a team at the Universitat Autònoma de Barcelona constructed a disaggregated SAM of the Spanish economy and used it to calibrate an applied GE model of the Spanish economy. This model was used to analyse the impact on the Spanish economy of the fiscal reform implemented on 1 January 1986, to accompany Spain's entry into the European Community. The principal ingredient of these reforms was the introduction of a value-added tax (VAT) on consumption to replace a complex range of indirect taxes, including a turnover tax applied at every stage of the production process. The results obtained in this analysis have been issued as working papers or published in a variety of outlets (see Kehoe *et al.*, 1985a, 1986a, 1986b; Kehoe, Manresa, Noyola, Polo, and Sancho 1988; Kehoe *et al.*, 1989).

Using recently published data, Kehoe, Polo and Sancho (1995) compare the results generated by the model to the changes that actually occurred in Spain during the period 1985–86. They find that the model performed well in predicting the changes that actually occurred. This is particularly true when they incorporate two major exogenous shocks that hit the Spanish economy in 1986: a sharp fall in the price of petroleum imports and a decline in productivity in the agricultural sector due mostly to weather conditions. The major difference between the simple applied GE model presented in the previous section and that used to analyse the 1986 policy changes is the level of disaggregation: the disaggregated model has 12 production sectors, rather than 3, and 9 consumption goods, rather than 3. Furthermore, there are 3 factors of production, rather than 2; labour is broken down by two skill levels. (All these sectors are listed in Table 4.5.) In addition, the institutions are disaggregated: there are 8 representative households, rather than 2, and the rest of the world has been disaggregated into the rest of the EC and the non-EC rest of the world (see Table 4.6).

The other significant difference between the simple model and that used to analyse the 1986 policy changes is the modelling of the labour market. Labour demand is determined by producers to minimise costs and to meet demand for goods. Unemployment arises when the induced demand for labour is not enough to hire all labour supplied by workers. We assume that workers, or unions, fix the real wage and that all labour available is supplied at this wage, although not all is demanded. The real wage fixed depends on the unemployment rate, so that, in equilibrium, the following condition is satisfied in each of the two labour markets:

$$\omega_i = [(1-u_i)/(1-\bar{u}_i)]^{1/\beta}.$$

Here ω_i is the real wage, the nominal wage divided by an appropriate consumer price index, for either unskilled labour or skilled labour; u_i is the unemployment rate in the corresponding labour market; $\bar{u}_i$ is the corresponding benchmark unemployment rate; and β is a non-negative parameter that measures the sensitivity of real wages to unemployment. (There is, of course, another interpretation of this specification in terms of an elastic supply of labour.)

In the simulation results reported in the next section, β is chosen to be 1.5, following Andrés et al. (1988). Sensitivity analysis by Kehoe, Polo and Sancho (1995) shows that the central results of the simulation of the 1986 policy changes are not sensitive to this choice, as opposed to the choices of fixing a real wage index and letting unemployment vary or of fixing unemployment and letting wages vary. They also show that the results are not very sensitive to the choice of the macroeconomic closure rule discussed previously.

Table 4.5. *List of sectors in disaggregated 1980 social accounting matrix for Spain*

Model	Input–output table[a]
Production goods	
1 Agriculture	1–4
2 Energy	5–9
3 Basic industry	10–23
4 Machinery	24–29, 31–34
5 Automobile industry	30
6 Food products	35–49
7 Other manufacturing	50–62
8 Construction	63
9 Commerce	64–66
10 Transportation	67–73
11 Services	74–81, 85(1/2)
12 Government services	82–84, 85(1/2)
Non-consumption demand	
13 Government consumption	88
14 Investment and inventory accumulation	90–91
15 Exports to the European community	93
16 Exports to the rest of the world	93

Model	Consumer expenditure survey[b]
Consumption goods	
17 Food and nonalcoholic beverages	111–121
18 Tobacco and alcoholic beverages	131, 141, 142
19 Clothing	211–222
20 Housing	311–342
21 Household articles	411–461
22 Medical services	511–551
23 Transportation	611–642
24 Recreational services	711–741
25 Other services	811–924
Factors of production	
26 Unskilled labour	
27 Skilled labour	
28 Capital and other factors	

Notes:
[a] Corresponding categories in *Contabilidad Nacional de España, Base 1980, Cuentas Nacionales y Tabla Input–Output*, Instituto Nacional de Estadística, 1986.
[b] Corresponding categories in *Encuesta de Presupuestos Familiares, 1980–81*, Instituto Nacional de Estadística, 1988.

Table 4.6. *List of institutions in disaggregated 1980 social accounting matrix for Spain*

Age of household head	1980 income	Education of household head
Households		
I 24 years or less	less than 700,000 pesetas	
II 24 years or less	more than 700,000 pesetas	
III between 25 and 65 years	less than 1,000,000 pesetas	no higher
IV between 25 and 65 years	more than 1,000,000 pesetas	no higher
V between 25 and 65 years	less than 1,000,000 pesetas	some higher
VI between 25 and 65 years	more than 1,000,000 pesetas	some higher
VII 66 years or more	less than 700,000 pesetas	
VIII 66 years or more	more than 700,000 pesetas	
Other institutions		
IX Government		
X Rest of European Community		
XI Rest of world		

4.6 Comparisons with actual data, 1985–86

Spain's 1986 entry into the European Community was accompanied by two major government policy reforms. The first, and most significant, policy reform introduced a consumption value added tax to replace the previous indirect tax system. The second policy reform reduced trade barriers against imports from other EC countries. In contrast with the fiscal policy reform, which took place immediately, the trade policy reform was scheduled to be phased in gradually over six years. The part of the reform that took place in 1986 mostly involved changes in tariff rates. Kehoe *et al.* (1985a, 1986a, 1986b, 1989) and Kehoe, Manresa, Noyola *et al.* (1988) incorporate the tax and tariff parameters that correspond to both these policy reforms into the model described in the previous section. It should be stressed, however, that the parameter changes involved in the tax reform are far larger than those involved in the trade reform.

In this section we confront the results generated by the model with the data that describe the changes that actually took place in the Spanish economy during the period 1985–86. It is changes over a time horizon of one or two years that Kehoe, Polo and Sancho (1995) argue that this type of model can capture. On one hand, it can be argued that this time horizon is long enough so that there can be enough gestation or depreciation of capital stocks in each sector to justify assuming mobility of capital, at least as long as changes in capital utilisation by sector are less than, say, 10%. On the other hand, it can be argued that this time horizon is short enough to justify ignoring secular trends and the intersectoral impact of changes in the growth rate.

As we have mentioned, the model was not designed to predict changes in inflation or in the growth rate. Consequently, in reporting both the simulation results and the actual data, we deflate by an appropriate price or output index. In the case of consumer prices and industrial activity levels, this procedure produces changes whose weighted average is zero. Dividing consumer prices by a consumer price index based on consumption expenditure shares by sector, for example, produces changes that sum to zero when weighted by these expenditure shares. Similarly, we obtain changes in industrial activity levels that sum to zero when weighted by value added shares by sector. In the case of producer prices, however, prices are normalised using the consumer price index rather than by a producer price index. Although this treatment of producer prices is somewhat asymmetric, it is useful because it makes it easy to compare the changes in the relative prices of consumer goods and producer goods. The change in the producer price index relative to that in the consumer price index can be recovered by summing the changes in producer prices weighted by value of production shares by sector. In all three cases, the weights used in the different indices are taken from the 1980 SAM constructed by Kehoe, Manresa, Polo and Sancho (1988) that provides the database for the model. Since the model has been calibrated to a different year than the year in which the tax reform took place, the choice of weights is somewhat arbitrary. Fortunately, calculations not reported here indicate that the results are not sensitive to this choice.

Tables 4.7–4.10 present the actual changes that occurred in the Spanish economy over the period 1985–86 in terms of consumer prices, producer prices, activity levels, and macroeconomic aggregates. Because of limited data on the changes that actually took place in 1986, we report changes in producer prices and activity levels for only a sub-set of producer prices and activity levels. Examining the actual changes that took place over 1985–86, we see a substantial increase in indirect tax rates. This increase manifests itself in the sharp decline in the relative prices of producer goods, reported in the first column of Table 4.8, compared to those of consumer goods, reported in the first column of Table 4.7. This change in relative prices is to be expected since the VAT largely exempts producer goods from taxes. The increase in indirect taxes can also be seen in the changes in macroeconomic variables reported in the second column of Table 4.10, where indirect tax revenues increase as a percentage of GDP and private consumption falls.

Table 4.7. *Spanish model results (consumer prices) (percentage change[a])*

	Actual 1986/1985[b]	Model policy only	Model shocks only[c]	Model policy and shocks
17 Food and nonalcoholic beverages	1.8	−2.3	4.0	1.7
18 Tobacco and alcoholic beverages	3.9	2.5	3.1	5.8
19 Clothing	2.1	5.6	0.9	6.6
20 Housing	−3.2	−2.2	−2.7	−4.8
21 Household articles	0.1	2.2	0.7	2.9
22 Medical services	−0.7	−4.8	0.6	−4.2
23 Transportation	−4.0	2.6	−8.8	−6.2
24 Recreation	−1.4	−1.3	1.4	0.1
25 Other services	2.9	1.1	1.7	2.8
Change in consumer price index	8.4	0.0	0.0	0.0
Weighted correlation with 1986/1985[d]	1.000	−0.079	0.872	0.936
Prediction R^2 for 1986/1985[e]	1.000	−0.995	0.226	0.657

Notes:
[a] Change in sectoral price index deflated by the consumer price index. The weights used are the consumption shares (1) 0.2540, (2) 0.0242, (3) 0.0800, (4) 0.1636, (5) 0.0772, (6) 0.0376, (7) 0.1342, (8) 0.0675, and (9) 0.1617.
[b] Actual data are derived from *Indice de Precios de Consumo, Boletin Trimestral*, Octubre–Diciembre 1987 and Octubre–Diciembre 1987. See Kehoe, Polo and Sancho (1995) for details.
[c] The input requirements of all inputs in the agricultural sector, except imports, are divided by 0.9227. The price of energy imports is multiplied by 0.5240.
[d] Weighted correlation coefficients with actual changes 1986/1985. The weights are the same as those in note (a).
[e] Weighted R^2 in predicting actual changes 1986/1985. The weights are the same as those in note (a).

We also see in Table 4.10 that tariff revenue falls in 1986 as a percentage of GDP. The results presented in the second columns of Tables 4.7 and 4.8 and the fourth column of Table 4.10 show that these patterns are captured by the model when it simulates the policy changes that took place in 1986.

Comparing the first column in Table 4.7 with the second column, we see that the model does poorly in tracking the changes that actually took place in two large sectors, food and transportation. The reasons for this should be readily apparent to observers of the Spanish economy. In 1986, food prices rose sharply because of a poor harvest, and petrol prices fell sharply because of both an appreciation of the peseta against the dollar and a fall in the dollar price of oil. The final column of Table 4.7 reports the results of a simulation where we take these two exogenous shocks into account in the simplest possible ways: we reduce the ratio of output to inputs in the agricultural production sector by 7.73%. This number is the reduction in the ratio of an index of output to an index of intermediate inputs in agriculture from 1985 to 1986, taken from the *Anuario de Estadística Agraria, 1987*. We also reduce the price of energy by 47.60%. This number is the fall in the price index of energy imports from 1985 to 1986, taken from the *Boletín Trimestral de Coyuntura, Septimbre 1990* (see Kehoe, Polo and Sancho, 1995 for details).

In comparing the results of the model with the data we report two measures of goodness of prediction, each of which implicitly compares the match between the model prediction and the actual change with the match between the prediction of no change and the actual change. The first is the weighted correlation coefficient:

$$r = \sum_{i=1}^{n} \alpha_i^2 y_i \hat{y}_i \Bigg/ \left(\sum_{i=1}^{n} \alpha_i^2 y_i^2 \sum_{i=1}^{n} \alpha_i^2 \hat{y}_i^2 \right)^{1/2}.$$

Here α_i is the weight measuring the relative size of sector i; y_i is the actual change in sector i; and $\hat{y}_i$ is the predicted change. A high correlation coefficient rewards predictions that have the right signs and relative magnitudes. It does not take into account the absolute magnitudes of changes. The second measure of goodness of prediction that we report is the weighted prediction R^2:

$$R^2 = 1 - \sum_{i=1}^{n} \alpha_i^2 (y_i - \hat{y}_i)^2 \Bigg/ \left(\sum_{i=1}^{n} \alpha_i^2 y_i^2 \right)$$

A high R^2 rewards small weighted mean squared errors in prediction. Although this measure has the advantage of taking into account absolute magnitudes of changes, it has the disadvantages of being asymmetric in y_i and $\hat{y}_i$ and of heavily penalising predictions that are correct in signs and relative magnitude but too large. (The R^2 reported in the tables can be thought of as that obtained from the regression:

$$(\alpha_i y_i) = a + b(\alpha_i \hat{y}_i) + u_i$$

where a is constrained to be 0 and b is constrained to be 1.)

Once the exogenous shocks are incorporated into the model, it performs very well in accounting for the changes that actually took place in consumer prices. The correlation of the changes in the first column with those in the fifth, weighted in each case by 1980 consumption shares, is 0.936. The prediction R^2 is 0.657; in other words, by simulating the introduction of the VAT and the shocks to agricultural productivity and oil prices, the model is able to account for almost two-thirds of the variation in relative prices that actually took place. It is important to notice that a substantial amount of variation did, in fact, take place.

Table 4.8. *Spanish model results (industrial prices) (percentage change[a])*

	Actual 1986/1985[b]	Model policy only	Model shocks only[c]	Model policy and shocks
1 Agriculture	−0.3	−6.0	8.0	1.6
2 Energy	−17.9	−7.5	−32.8	−37.8
3 Basic industry	−8.5	−6.2	−3.1	−9.1
4 Machinery	−3.1	−6.5	−0.1	−6.6
5 Automobiles	−1.2	−3.9	0.0	−3.9
6 Food processing	−4.1	−6.4	4.0	−2.7
7 Other manufacturing	−4.3	−5.7	0.5	−5.1
8 Construction	−0.6	−6.1	0.0	−6.0
Change in consumer price index	8.4	0.0	0.0	0.0
Change in industrial price index	2.1	−6.3	−3.9	−9.7
Weighted correlation with 1986/1985[d]	1.000	0.794	0.840	0.960
Prediction R^2 for 1986/1985[c]	1.000	0.627	0.146	0.046

Notes:

[a] Change in sectoral price index deflated by the consumer price index.

[b] Actual data are derived from *Boletín Trimestral de Coyuntura*, Septiembre 1990. See Kehoe, Polo, and Sancho (1995) for details.

[c] See Table 4.3, note (c).

[d] Weighted (uncentred) correlation coefficient with actual changes 1986/1985. The weights used are value of total production shares, (1) 0.1110, (2) 0.1487, (3) 0.1695, (4) 0.1281, (5) 0.0443, (6) 0.1447, (7) 0.1326, and (8) 0.1211.

[e] Weighted R^2 in predicting actual changes 1986/1985. The weights are the same as those in note (a).

A comparison of the final three columns of Table 4.7 shows that accounting for both the policy changes and the exogenous shocks that occurred in 1986 is essential for the model to obtain these results. Incorporating the exogenous shocks separately produces changes in relative prices that have a lower weighted correlation coefficient with the changes that actually took place in 1986, 0.872, and a substantially lower prediction R^2, 0.226.

The performance of the model in tracking producer prices and activity levels, reported in Tables 4.8 and 4.9 is not as impressive as that for consumer prices. The model without adjustments underestimates the relative changes in producer prices that took place; the model with adjustments overestimates them. In both cases, however, the relative changes are in the right direction, causing the weighted correlation coefficients to be fairly high, 0.794 and 0.960. The model also does a fair, but not impressive, job in tracking changes in production, failing notably in the case of basic

Table 4.9. *Spanish model results (industrial activity levels)*
(percentage change[a])

	Actual 1986/1985[b]	Model policy only	Model shocks only[c]	Model policy and shocks
2 Energy	−2.7	−2.3	3.1	0.4
3 Basic industry	−4.5	1.4	−0.6	0.8
4 Machinery	5.8	4.0	−1.0	3.1
5 Automobiles	5.5	1.2	2.6	3.7
6 Food processing	−4.2	−2.3	−1.3	−3.8
7 Other manufacturing	1.9	−2.4	−0.3	−2.8
Industrial output index	3.5	−0.2	2.0	1.8
Weighted correlation with 1986/1985[b]	1.000	0.443	−0.193	0.389
Prediction R^2 for 1986/1985[e]	1.000	0.155	−0.225	0.104

Notes:
[a] Change in sectoral industrial production index deflated by industrial output index. The weights used are the value added shares (2) 0.1506, (3) 0.2108, (4) 0.2172, (5) 0.0511, (6) 0.1431, and (7) 0.2271.
[b,c] See notes (b) and (c) to Table 4.3.
[d] Weighted correlation coefficient with actual changes 1986/1985. The weights are the same as those in note (a).
[e] Weighted R^2 in predicting actual changes 1986/1985. The weights are the same as those in note (a).

industry. The decline in basic industry in Spain seems to be part of a secular trend that has occurred throughout the 1980s but is not accounted for in the model.

The performance of the model in tracking major macroeconomic variables, reported in Table 4.10, is, at first glance, spectacular. Much of the model's success in this direction, however, can be accounted for by simply remembering that the model predicted that the tax reform would result in a substantial increase in indirect taxes paid by consumers. It is worth pointing out that in 1985 this prediction of the model was controversial and was treated with considerable scepticism by a number of policy-makers.

4.7 Concluding remarks

A major challenge is to use the shortcomings of this model to develop a new version of the model more suitable for prediction. One obvious direction to take is to incorporate secular trends and to account for more

Table 4.10. Spanish model results (major macroeconomic variables) (change from benchmark)

Variable	Benchmark 1985[a]	Actual 1986–85	Benchmark 1980	Model – 1980 policy only	Model – 1980 shocks only[b]	Model – 1980 policy and shocks
Unemployment	21.94	-0.46	11.53	1.92	-2.06	0.08
Wages and salaries[c]	46.23	0.53	51.18	-0.87	-0.03	-0.90
Business income	46.79	-1.27	44.26	-1.64	0.45	-1.25
Net indirect taxes	6.98	1.80	4.56	2.51	-0.42	2.15
Correlation with 1986/1985[d]		1.000		0.998	-0.939	0.990
R^2 for 1986/1985[e]		1.000		0.853	-0.585	0.950
Private consumption	69.31	0.81	69.00	-1.24	-0.51	-1.78
Private investment	15.04	1.09	21.46	1.81	-0.58	1.32
Government consumption	14.01	-0.02	12.68	-0.06	-0.38	-0.44
Government investment	3.75	-0.06	1.87	-0.06	-0.07	-0.13
Exports	18.40	-3.40	12.50	-0.42	-0.69	-1.07
Imports	20.51	-3.20	17.51	0.03	-2.23	-2.10
Correlation with 1986/1985		1.000		0.397	0.766	0.834
R^2 for 1986/1985		1.000		0.154	0.522	0.670
Indirect taxes and subsidies	4.99	2.38	2.78	3.32	-0.38	2.98
Tariffs	1.99	-0.58	1.78	-0.81	-0.03	-0.83
Social security payments	11.35	0.04	11.63	-0.19	-0.03	-0.22
Net direct taxes/transfers	-9.36	-0.84	-5.77	-0.66	0.92	0.25
Government capital income	1.77	-0.13	1.51	-0.06	0.01	-0.04

Government spending	17.75	-0.08	14.55	-0.12	-0.45	-0.56
Government deficit	7.02	-0.95	2.62	-1.72	-0.94	-2.70
Correlation with 1986/1985		1.000		0.984	-0.184	0.868
R^2 for 1986/1985		1.000		0.788	-0.464	0.348

Notes:

[a] Actual data are derived from *Contabilidad Nacional de España*, Base 1980, Serie 1980–1985, Datos Definitivos, 1986 Provisionales y 1987 Avance. See Kehoe, Polo, and Sancho (1995) for details.

[b] See note (c) for Table 4.7.

[c] All variables except the unemployment rates are expressed as percentages of GDP.

[d] Correlation coefficient with actual changes 1986/1985. When necessary (Imports, Government spending), the change is multiplied by −1 so that all changes sum to zero.

[e] R^2 in predicting actual changes 1986/1985.

exogenous shocks. What is surprising is how well the model does without doing this. Another is to come up with better elasticities in consumer demand functions and production functions. Another possibility is to use the changes that actually take place to calibrate certain parameters. Kehoe and Serra-Puche (1991), for example, use the change in imports that took place in Mexico between 1980 and 1983, in response to a sharp fall in the terms of trade, to calibrate the Armington elasticity of substitution between imports and domestic production in a similar model of the Mexican economy. The results in the previous section suggest many other possible improvements in the model: that the fall in the price of oil was not passed on to purchasers of energy products to the extent our model predicts, for example, might indicate that our assumption of perfect competition in this market should be modified.

Another obvious challenge is to figure out what types of policy change or exogenous shock this model is capable of analysing and what types it is not. It probably comes as a surprise to some readers that the model does so well even though it takes intertemporal factors into account in very simplistic ways, if at all. Certainly, we should not expect the model to perform as well in evaluating the impact of, say, a tax reform that significantly changes the tax rate on capital income. An interesting project would involve using a fully specified dynamic applied general equilibrium model, such as that of Auerbach and Kotlikoff (1987), Goulder and Summers (1989), or Jorgenson and Yun (1990), to analyse a policy change such as that analysed here. The results of the dynamic model would then be compared with the results of the static model and with the actual data.

Another issue that we should mention is that of data availability. This is a constant limitation in this line of research. The reader will have noticed that throughout the analysis we have had to use a model calibrated to the 1980 SAM to analyse changes that took place six years later. Furthermore, it is only in 1990 that there were sufficient data to evaluate the performance of the model. In fact, the version of the model constructed in 1985 did not even use a complete SAM for 1980 (see Kehoe et al., 1985b for the SAM that was used at the time). The later improvement in the SAM accounts for the differences in simulation results between, for example, Kehoe et al., 1985a and Kehoe et al., 1989. The basic predictions concerning consumer prices and major macroeconomic variables were present, however, even in earliest version of the model. Obviously, the model improves with more and better (for example, more recent) data. How much data do we need, and how good do they have to be, to have confidence in our simulation results? This chapter brings us one step further to answering these questions. More work remains to be done.

Notes

This chapter draws heavily on Kehoe and Kehoe (1994) and Kehoe, Polo, and Sancho (1995). The research was sponsored by the Air Force Office of Scientific Research, Air Force Material Command, USAF under grant F49620-94-1-0461. The US Government is authorised to reproduce and distribute reprints for governmental purposes notwithstanding any copyright notation thereon. The views expressed herein are those of the author and not necessarily those of the Air Force Office of Scientific Research, the US Government of the Federal Reserve Bank of Minneapolis, or the Federal Reserve System.

5 The development of econometric methods at the DAE

Ron Smith

5.1 Introduction

The history of econometrics is now a flourishing little sub-discipline: see, for instance, Epstein, 1987; Pesaran, 1987b; Morgan, 1990; de Marchi and Gilbert, 1989; Qin, 1993; and Keuzenkamp and Magnus, 1995. In addition, *Econometric Theory* regularly publishes interviews with the pioneers of econometrics. This interest is as much methodological as historical, since the pioneers of econometrics had to confront very fundamental issues which remain a matter of dispute today. In this history the DAE plays a central role. Epstein (1987, p. 142) says that 'the influence of this English work was comparable to that of the Cowles Commission in establishing directions for econometric research.' The English work was initially done at the DAE, but Epstein, like Gilbert (1986), sees leadership of the English school of econometrics leaving Cambridge for London in the 1950s. Like Cowles, after a period of developing econometric methods the DAE turned its attention to other topics.

There were many achievements in econometric methods during the first decade of the DAE, but two were of particular importance. The establishment of the text-book, single-equation, time-series regression framework with its standard notation and tests as the work-horse of econometrics, and the use of tight economic theory in estimation of consumer demand models, exemplified by Stone (1954b). Of the DAE work, Gilbert (1986) says: 'Demand analysis is widely perceived by the economics profession as being one of the great success stories of postwar applied econometrics. This is to a large extent because of the close relationship between economic theory and econometric practice apparent in work in this area...'.

The quality of the work was recognised at the time. Klein (1952, p. 104), reviewing Stone (1951), says: 'Econometricians will be delighted to see sound publications like this coming out of England where the lack of a large scale movement by scholars towards econometrics has retarded achievements commensurate with the best British traditions in Economics.' Harberger (1955) reviewing Stone (1954a) says: 'This volume and the series which it initiates are sure to take a place on that narrow bookshelf labelled "classics of econometrics".'

In some ways Cambridge was an odd place to lead econometrics. Prominent figures at Cambridge were not only hostile to econometrics, but well informed about its methodological lacunae. Keynes had roundly condemned the whole enterprise in his vituperative but perceptive review of Tinbergen[1] and the prejudice persisted. Stone (1978) makes a persuasive case that Keynes subsequently changed his mind about econometrics, but if Keynes relented, the Cambridge Keynesians did not. Leading figures at Cambridge including Kahn, Kaldor and Joan Robinson were deeply sceptical about the validity of probabilistic inference in economics and the hostility to econometrics remained.

Given this context, the standard questions: Who? When? What? Why? become quite sensitive. *Who* should be counted in the DAE can be a matter of fine judgement because there was constant movement of personnel to and from other institutions, in particular the Faculty,[2] and because there was a constant flow of distinguished visitors who worked for a time in the DAE. This often raises questions of attribution about what really was DAE work, and some may differ with my judgments. The *when* I shall consider is the period 1945–1970. It is the first 25 years of the DAE and covers the tenure of the first two Directors. The story of econometrics in Cambridge after 1970 is rather different. Who and when we should be discussing may be matters of judgement, but *what* we are talking about, the definition of econometrics, is absolutely central and different definitions of econometrics can lead to quite different stories.

There was then, and is now, a variety of definitions of econometrics. Tintner (1953) gives a nice contemporary discussion of the large variety of alternative definitions of econometrics then used, by someone who had worked in the DAE. Samuelson, Koopmans and Stone (1954) say 'econometrics may be defined as the quantitative analysis of actual economic phenomena based on the concurrent development of theory and observation, related by appropriate methods of inference'. Current usage of the term econometrics is much narrower, focusing on the development of appropriate methods of inference and I shall tend to use this narrow definition. To try and review the actual applied econometric work which was, and is, the main product of the DAE would be almost impossible and it will only be mentioned in passing where it directly relates to methods.

Although the DAE work was done in a wider context of discovery, I shall largely ignore the contributions that others made elsewhere. This is partly a question of occasion – I come to praise the DAE, not to bury it in citations to related literature – and partly a question of attribution. The practice in econometrics of attaching people's names to tests and procedures means that most people who have taken an econometrics course recognise Durbin–Watson and Cochrane–Orcutt, DAE work. Only real specialists know the contribution of von Neumann, the Andersons and Champernowne in this area.

5.2 Origins and objectives

The establishment of the DAE was approved by the University in 1939, but it had a purely formal existence until the end of the war as a Committee of Management chaired by Keynes.[3] Stone was appointed Director from July 1945 and real operations began in 1946. It was initially supported by funds from the University, the Rockefeller Foundation, the Nuffield Foundation and the National Institute of Economic and Social Research. Establishing a successful research institute is not easy and the DAE was fortunate in its founder. Keynes did battle with the University to establish it; helped raise money for it;[4] appointed the right Director with an indefinite tenure;[5] provided a research agenda that was to prove a major stimulus for applied econometrics; and then died leaving the Director a free hand.

Richard Stone was in his early 30s when he became Director. He was subsequently knighted in 1978 and awarded the Nobel Prize in 1984 for his work on national accounts (see Stone, 1986; Deaton, 1987, 1993; Pesaran, 1991). In a Faculty where such qualities were quite rare, he was a polite, gentle, tolerant person; but he was quite uncompromising in his academic objectives. The discussions of research policy in the first two *Reports* of the DAE provide a very clear statement of his early objectives.

The *First Report* says:

The Department's programme, though in one sense wide in scope, is intended to form a unity, and the object of this section is to discuss the nature of the programme and the aims which it serves. We see the aims of applied economics to be as follows. Through the processes of observation and testing it should develop economic theories so that they stand established as applicable to the actual world, and on these foundations it should seek to provide the basis for making reliable predictions. The realization of these aims presupposes a certain degree of progress taking place at one time along a number of different lines. In the first place the theories to be tested must be stated with sufficient exactness to be brought into relation with observations. Secondly, the necessary observations must be brought into being if they are not already available. Thirdly, the procedures for testing hypotheses under non-experimental conditions must be developed so that they are suited to the conditions of economic problems. The Department's research programme has been conceived as a group of interrelated investigations which should yield results along each of these main lines of activity. (*First Report*, pp. 3 and 4)

This policy is consistent with Frisch's editorial in the first issue of *Econometrica* (Frisch, 1933), in which it was the unification of statistics, economic theory and mathematics that constitutes econometrics. However, use of the term econometrics is rare in the *First Report*. What would now be called econometric theory is discussed in the *First Report* under the heading '(b) Statistical Methods in Economics'. When the term econometrics is used in the *First Report*, it tends to be in reference to an estimated model of an economy. For instance, it reports Klein giving a seminar on an econometric model of Canada and in the course of the discussion of work on statistical methods, it says: 'These investigations [into serial correlation] are in the nature of preliminary work on problems whose solution is preparatory to the construction of a general econometric model for the British economy' (p. 15). The *Report* also notes that Professor Tintner was invited by the Faculty to give a course of lectures on econometrics during the academic year 1948-9. Tintner (1952) is one of the first generation econometrics texts.

In addition to statistical methods, the other two headings were (a) National Income, Product and Social Accounting Projects and (c) Verification and Estimation of Economic Relationships. In the *Second Report* an additional objective was added. The first three were essentially the same, but given the progress in restating economic theories in a form which allowed them to be tested empirically, in collecting the relevant data and in developing the statistical tools for the testing of economic hypotheses, the DAE could add a fourth objective: actually to make the tests.

5.3 Activities

The activity under the Statistical Methods heading in the two years covered by the *First Report* is quite spectacular. R. C. Geary spent 1946-7 in the DAE working on time-series models, testing for normality, errors-in-variables models and instrumental variables. T. W. Anderson visited the Department for the summer of 1948, contributing a paper on 'The Asymptotic Distributions of the Roots of Certain Determinantal Equations', commenting on aspects of one of Geary's papers. Orcutt was working on properties of time series and with Donald Cochrane, an Australian PhD student, on their eponymous correction for serial correlation. Gerhard Tintner, who was in the DAE in the academic year 1948-49, was working on tests of significance in time series and developing a unified theory of multivariate analysis which would include as special cases: discriminant analysis, factor analysis, canonical correlation and weighted regression. Under heading (c) 'Verification and Estimation of Economic Relationships', Stone and Prest were analysing market demand; Duesenberry, Orcutt and Roy were estimating consumption functions; Tintner was trying to test whether labour demand and supply functions were homogenous of degree zero in wages and prices. Under heading (a) 'National Income, Product and Social Accounting Projects', James Durbin, who had just joined the DAE, was working on the sampling problems involved in the construction of a set of social accounts for Cambridgeshire. Despite the apparently parochial nature of the Cambridgeshire project it was to generate fundamental work in statistical theory, not only on sampling by Durbin (see Phillips, 1988), but also the substantial amount of work on the log-normal distribution, collected together in Aitchison and Brown (1957).

In the *Second Report*, progress under the heading '(c) The development of Statistical and Other Methods of Analysis' continues to be spectacular. Stone is working on prediction from autoregressive schemes and linear stochastic difference systems, Cochrane and Orcutt continue their work on correcting for serial correlation, while Durbin (who left the DAE for the London School of Economics at the end of 1949) and Geoff Watson (another Australian who joined the DAE in October 1949) worked on testing for it. Watson was also working on the distribution of quadratic forms and their ratios. The work of Tintner on multivariate analysis continues, and Tintner and James have published separate papers on Carnap's theory of probability.

Under other headings, Tobin, Prais, Houthakker and Farrell are working on demand; Stone, Utting and Durbin are working on sampling; A. D. Roy is working on the distribution of income, and theoretical issues involved with national accounts and index numbers are being investigated.

5.4 Time series

In terms of econometric theory, the central work is on time series. In retrospect, one could interpret this work in terms of the development of the textbook regression model. Stone and the other workers at the DAE recognised that lack of independence in time-series data was a major methodological obstacle to the application of regression. In confronting this problem, the DAE work shifted the focus from concern with the autocorrelation structure of the data to the autocorrelation structure of the disturbance or equation error; developed the Durbin-Watson test to detect such disturbance serial correlation and the Cochrane–Orcutt procedure to remove it; and showed, in a range of applications, that these procedures 'worked'. So, by Stone (1954a) the text-book regression approach to time-series econometrics was established as a reliable tool and Stone could provide the elegant exposition that text books would copy. While the conclusion of this story seems true, the process was much more complicated and uncertain than it suggests.

Firstly, in 1946 it was still not obvious in Cambridge that regression was the appropriate technique and that econometrics would come to be dominated by regression in all its weird and wonderful forms. The errors-in-variables model had not been fully supplanted by the errors-in-equations model. Empirically, Stone used confluence analysis (see the discussion in Hendry and Morgan, 1989) and principal components. The breadth of statistical methods being investigated is striking. These covered not only the other multivariate methods that Tintner was working on but also pure distribution theory, both for inference and for modelling empirical size distributions. Sorting out fairly technical issues in mathematical statistics, such as the distributions of quadratic forms and roots of determinants, seemed central to developing econometrics. It was Stone who suggested that Geary work on determinants, having noted that the roots of the same determinant played a central role in both Hotelling's principal component and Tintner's errors-in-variables models, though in one case it was the largest and the other the smallest. The roots of a determinant were also the basis of the LIML estimator which Anderson had developed with Rubin (see Phillips, 1986).

Secondly, Cambridge was still concerned about the fundamental legitimacy of time-series regression analysis. The *First Report* (p. 4) says: '[I]t has long been recognized that economic time series, which inevitably form a large part of the data available to the economist, do not in general satisfy the assumptions underlying the classical methods of regression analysis'. Although Mann and Wald (1943) had provided an asymptotic basis for the estimation of stationary linear stochastic difference equations, the practical relevance of these results was not clear. Both small samples and stationarity remained issues. Orcutt (1948) showed the small sample downward bias of the estimated coefficient of the lagged dependent variable. Stationarity was taken more seriously because of the influence of Yule (1926), whose conclusions had been used by Keynes in his attack on Tinbergen. To quote Geary (1948, p. 149): 'It is scarcely an exaggeration to state that statisticians of the writer's generation were so frightened by Udny Yule's famous paper on "Nonsense Correlations" that we came to regard economic time series as so much dynamite, to be handled at all times with extreme caution and not to be handled at all if one could avoid it.' This was the problem Stone and his colleagues had to confront.

It is obvious to a modern reader, reawakened to the dangers of spurious regression and familiar with stochastic trends, cointegration and Johansen (the roots of determinants return), and it was obvious to them, that Stone, Orcutt, Geary and Anderson were working on a fundamental econometric problem. However, it is likely that, for much of the intervening period between then and now, Stone (1947b) and three 1948 *Journal of the Royal Statistical Society* (JRSS) Series B papers – Orcutt (1948), Geary (1948) and Anderson (1948) – would not have seemed 'econometric' at all, quite alien to the spirit of the text-book model the DAE did so much to establish.

The papers were all concerned to characterise economic time series. Stone (1947b) used principal components to show that nearly all the variance of US national accounts data could be accounted for by three factors. Orcutt (1948) used Monte Carlo methods to show that the whole set of 52 economic series used by Tinbergen might have been obtained by drawings from the population of series generated by a first-order autoregression in first differences with a coefficient of 0.3. There was clearly a simple common structure to economic time series, but it was not obvious how this should be interpreted. Geary (1948, p. 51) puts this rather nicely. After removing deterministic polynomial trends from the series and examining the residuals, he says: 'It is the writer's conviction that the figures are trying to tell us something of importance in regard to the inter-relationships of economic time series if only we could discover what it was.'

With hindsight about the dangers of non-stationarity, many of the DAE instincts seem right, e.g. Stone's preference for first differencing and Orcutt's continuing caution about time-series regression, despite his role in establishing the text-book model. Stone was clearly aware of the limitations of first differencing, Stone and Prais (1953) have a very clear discussion of the effect of the unit root on forecast error variance. Of course, despite the emphasis on mathematical statistics, the economics was never forgotten. For instance, the demand studies showed that in many cases most of the explanation was provided by the trend rather than the economic component, prices and income, and Farrell was set to try to provide an economic interpretation of this.

One notable feature of the development of the standard regression model at the DAE is that simultaneity was almost completely ignored. To many, the treatment of simultaneity is the defining characteristic of Cowles Commission econometrics and the simultaneous equations model tends to be what is covered in the econometrics chapter, should they have one, of statistical text books on multivariate analysis. The neglect of simultaneity had been previously criticised, e.g. in the Klein (1952) review of Stone (1951). The DAE were certainly familiar with the issues and Geary had done work on instrumental variables (IV) at the DAE, though the fact that IV was a solution to endogeneity as well as errors in variables was not then apparent. Stone (in Pesaran 1991, p. 103) comments: 'It is perhaps surprising that I did not discuss Haavelmo's simultaneous equation system. In principal I fully agreed with it but I thought that with many other difficulties in time series regression analysis, this one could perhaps be left over for the time being. In my work it got left over for ever, I am sorry to say. I did experiment with instrumental variables but I never had any luck with them and they never appeared in my published works.' Epstein (1987, p. 149) discusses the neglect of simultaneity in more detail.

5.5 Cross-section and distributions

Stone (1954a) was the culmination of almost a decade of work on applied demand analysis at the DAE, by an eminent group of workers, including Prest, Houthakker, Farrell, Prais, and Tobin. This covered a vast amount of work on data construction, economic theory, econometric methods and estimation. The initial objective of the project on the analysis of family budgets was to provide cross-section estimates of income elasticities which could be combined with time-series data to improve the precision of estimation. However, as can be seen from Prais and Houthakker (1955), the project covered a much wider range of theoretical and econometric issues including equivalence scales, rationing, estimating non-linear Engel curves and various technical problems in cross-section analysis such as grouping and the treatment of heteroscedasticity. Like the other DAE work, Prais and Houthakker are remarkably clear in setting out the relevant economic theory, the characteristics of the data that are to be modelled, and the statistical methods to be employed; econometrics as unification of those elements is very obvious. Concern for what we would now call diagnostic or mis-specification testing is also obvious. For instance, they suggest using the Durbin–Watson test on the residuals of a regression where the data were ordered by an explanatory variable as a diagnostic for non-linearity.

In almost everything the DAE was doing – sample surveys, family budgets, income distribution, ownership of durables, aggregation and many other issues – skewed distributions, in particular the log-normal, played a central role. Aitchison and Brown (1957) pulled together this work and established the distribution as a powerful tool. They say (p. 1): 'Some critics will ask if anything can be contained in such a study other than the well known properties of the normal distribution and the logarithmic function. We hope to make it clear as the work proceeds that there is an adequate rejoinder to this criticism.' There was and the book remains a widely used reference. They cover the properties of the distribution, various mechanisms for its genesis, testing for log-normality, parameter estimation, probit analysis, analysis of variance, truncated and censored distributions and a range of applications, many arising from DAE work.

5.6 Links to statistics

The DAE at this time had very close links with mathematical statistics, which was strong in Cambridge. Wishart was on the Management Committee of the DAE for the first decade, Stone supervised graduate students taking the Diploma in Statistics, and many of the staff were trained as statisticians. This orientation is obvious in where they chose to publish: the *Journal of the Royal Statistical Society* (JRSS) was by far the most popular outlet. Whether it was wise to favour the JRSS so much is another question. Fisher (1976) reports Farrell as expressing regret at publishing in the JRSS, because it was not widely read in the US. Papers were also published in other statistical journals, including *Biometrika* and the *Journal of the American Statistical Association* (JASA), and in all almost half the publications were in statistical journals.

Table 5.1 summarises where the papers listed in the Reprint Series in the first three *Reports* were published. The classification is inevitably somewhat arbitrary and it would be anachronistic to impute a modern economist's fascination with core journals to the DAE of the 1940s and 1950s. The list should be taken as an indication of audience rather than content. Many of the papers could have been published in statistical, economic or accounting journals. Papers published in the economic journals dealt with technical statistical questions and not all the JRSS papers were on statistical methods; they also included papers on data construction, applied work and bibliographies of the application of mathematical statistics to economics. Reprint No. 29, Stone, Utting and Durbin's paper on 'The Use of Sampling Methods in National Income Statistics and Social Accounting', seems to have been published in both the *Review of the International Statistical Institute* and *Accounting Research*. The latter journal was a popular outlet. This had been founded by Frank Sewell Bray, the head of a leading London accountancy firm, who had close research links to the DAE.

Table 5.1. *Publication patterns in the first three* Reports

	1	2	3	Total
Statistical				
JRSS	5	7	7	19
Biometrika	1	2	1	4
JASA	0	2	1	3
Others	0	4	2	6
TOTAL				32
Economic				
Economic Journal	5	3	4	12
Econometrica	0	1	2	3
Economica	0	1	0	1
Review of Economics and Statistics	0	1	0	1
Review of Economic Studies	0	0	4	4
London & Cambridge Economic Service Bulletin	1	3	3	7
Other	0	2	10	12
TOTAL				40
Accounting	3	3	2	8
TOTAL	15	29	36	80

5.7 Computing

Considerations of calculation have always shaped the development of statistical and econometric methods and the DAE invested heavily in improving methods of computation, whether by hardware, software or basic research. The first three *Reports* list the computors on the staff and the inventory of calculating machines, which were so constantly in use that at least one was normally out of action for repair. Prais and Houthakker (1955, p. 64) report that calculation of the results presented in the book required about two persons engaged in full-time computation for a period of three years, in addition to the use of punch card equipment and the electronic computer.

Durbin's comments on the constraints imposed by calculation, in Phillips (1988), are illuminating. They bring out the delicate diplomacy involved in negotiating with computors, the articles that were not published because the calculations were never completed, the avenues that were not explored because the computational burden seemed intractable and the worry that published tables were wrong because of numerical errors. For instance, in response to the question: 'Was it very difficult at the time to do these numerical calculations?' [for the Durbin–Watson tables] Durbin says (p. 131):

We thought at the time that they were horrendously difficult calculations, but one of the assets of the DAE was that we had a room there with perhaps eight or ten young ladies operating desk calculators, supervised by an older lady of forbidding demeanour. They did the computing. We were very concerned about the accuracy of these tables, as everybody was, doing computing in those days. What we tried to insist on was for the girls to do all the calculations twice. But of course this was rather boring from their point of view. To some extent you had to play a game when you were organising this type of computing, in getting the right amount of checking and getting it done properly. There was always a doubt in our mind whether the tables really were accurate to the order that we claimed they were.

As Durbin describes, subsequent electronic calculation showed the tables to be accurate.

During its first decade, the human computors at the DAE (not all of whom were women) were starting to be displaced by electronic computers. Berndt (1991, pp. 2–6) provides a short historical perspective on computers and econometrics, in which the DAE features prominently. Orcutt had done his PhD thesis in Economics at Michigan on the use of electronic devices to undertake complex mathematical computations. This led to the 'regression analyser', an analog machine. Orcutt built a prototype at MIT and Stone invited him to Cambridge, with the expressed hope that, as Orcutt reports, 'I would bring the machine and put it to use in developing tests of significance of apparent relationships between autocorrelated economic time series' (Berndt, p. 3). The analyser made Orcutt's Monte Carlo experiments feasible. Digital rather than analog machines were to become the econometrician's tool and again the DAE was in the lead. Berndt says that, apparently, the first article published by an econometrician based on results from a digital electronic calculator having a stored memory program is Houthakker (1951). The DAE were using EDSAC (the Electronic Delay Storage Automatic Calculator) of the University Mathematical Laboratory, one of the first digital computers. Brown, Houthakker and Prais (1953) describe this work. They comment that about 70 hours of labour by a human computor with an electric desk machine were replaced by 7 minutes of machine time. The first program for the inversion of large matrices (using the Choleski method) was developed by Houthakker and Prais. Both Prais and Houthakker (1955) and Aitchison and Brown (1957) contain chapters on computation problems, including a description of the use of EDSAC.

Work on developing software for econometrics, in particular matrix algebra and regression packages, and computational methods for the large-scale modelling required by the Growth Project, continued at the DAE. In this Lucy Slater, who was appointed to the DAE in 1956, played a major role. Outside economics she was known for her work on hypergeometric functions (e.g. Slater, 1966). Whereas in the 1950s Cambridge had been ahead of the world in computing, during the 1960s the DAE was handicapped by the type of computers used at the Mathematical Laboratory. These were unreliable and non-standard research machines not designed for the large-scale data processing of the sort involved in econometrics. The *Fifth Report* (p. 15) mentions the difficulties caused by problems with the TITAN computer and the computing for the Singh-Whittington Company Accounts project had to be done on the IBM 7090 at Imperial College. However, it was not only the computing facilities that were to become less conducive to econometrics at the DAE.

5.8 The move away from econometric methods

The *Fourth Report* for the period July 1954 to December 1957 describes the major changes affecting the DAE over that period. In July 1955 Richard Stone resigned as Director to become P. D. Leake Professor of Finance and Accounting, the rules for this Chair having been written to preclude him holding both posts. Stone (in Pesaran, 1991) commented that he was a little put out, as he had come to think of the Department as his, but that it really worked out for the best. He continued to work in the Department with a research group. There was also a review of the DAE by the General Board of the University. The *Fourth Report* notes (p. 12) that previously the Department was virtually a separate unit within the Faculty, and that 'an important feature of the years 1954–57 has been a closer integration of the department with the Faculty. The new relationship was reflected in the view expressed by the General Board in its report that the Department might be considered the laboratory of the Faculty.'

The new Director was Brian Reddaway, who remained Director till 1970. Harcourt (1987) describes Reddaway: 'He has one of the finest critical minds in the profession; he remorselessly reveals flaws in logic and ignorance of the nature and use of data alike.' His two major reports on the effects of UK Direct Investment Overseas and the Selective Employment Tax are characteristic of his practical policy-oriented style of analysis. Reddaway had a mathematical training (a First in Part I of the Cambridge Mathematics Tripos), but did not regard the elaborating of econometric techniques as in the forefront of his interests or expertise. He shared the general Cambridge doubts about the applicability of econometrics to complex economic processes, where numerous factors, many unmeasurable, interacted and relationships were likely to change through time. Econometrics was left to Stone's group, to become the Growth Project in 1960. In effect, the DAE was split into two largely separate groups, though in finance and formal organisation they were a single entity.

Within the main part of the DAE under Reddaway, work which did not require much probabilistic inference flourished on a wide variety of topics. Links with the Faculty were encouraged, aided by the collocation of the DAE and Faculty in Sidgwick Avenue from 1962. Within the Growth Project applied econometrics flourished, but the development of what would now be seen as econometric methods had ceased to be a central priority for Stone. He had obtained the tools he required; he could now apply them to answer other more fundamental questions. It is possible that had he had the resources he had earlier he might have continued to hire mathematical statisticians and econometric theorists, but the priority was the application of the methods.

In the later 1950s and 1960s, the DAE did a large amount of applied econometric work, much of it very innovative, particularly on consumer demand, corporate behaviour and the modelling of the economy as a whole, particularly in the Growth Project. There was also fundamental technical work on empirical methods in economics, particularly input–output and the measurement of efficiency, but there are few titles in the *Reports* that would be recognised today as work in econometric methods. Unlike the earlier years, it became rare for the practical problems to generate methodological solutions. Exceptions are: G. R. Fisher (1957) on maximum likelihood estimation with heteroscedastic errors, which arose out of the project on the determination of stock market prices, and F. E. A. Briggs (1962) on the influence of measurement errors on the correlations of ratios, which arose out of Salter (1960).

While it is true that using a narrow definition of econometrics, as the development of methods, accentuates the break, a break there certainly was. Most historians of econometrics have noted this transition away from the study of econometric methods. They have tended to attribute it to the shift in Stone's interest, whereas Cambridge people tend to attribute it to the general hostility to econometrics. The abstract of Gilbert (1986) begins: 'In the immediate postwar decade, work in the Department of Applied Economics at Cambridge was instrumental in establishing the now standard regression model as the major statistical tool in applied economics. Subsequently, the focus of British econometrics shifted to the London School of Economics.' Gilbert discusses the various factors which gave the LSE an advantage, including a teaching programme that produced well-trained econometricians, something Cambridge lacked. Epstein (1987, p. 149) says of the DAE over this period: 'Sophisticated econometrics was not seen as offering a great return in devising development strategies and other very ambitious economic policies. The problems of statistical theory uncovered by Stone's demand work were left for others to tackle.'

Epstein gives as an example of the problems left for others to tackle the comparison of the small sample properties of LIML and OLS. A more obvious example is that of a characteristically Cambridge methodological problem, structural stability. In his review of Tinbergen, Keynes had identified this as a central weakness of econometrics, though Tinbergen had made considerable efforts to check the structural stability of his equations. What is more, what have become the standard tests arose out of a characteristically Cambridge application: consumer durables, which was the subject of DAE work by Stone and Rowe, Farrell, Cramer, Pyatt, and Bain. Chow was taught by Houthakker, who had been at the DAE, and saw, from a Chicago perspective, the importance of extending the standard consumer theory to durables (see Pagan, 1995). One problem he faced was determining whether the equations continued to fit. In solving this problem he brought the analysis of covariance test to econometric notice and developed the predictive failure test, introducing the tests that bear his name.

5.9 The development of other methods

It is quite clear that Stone would not have accepted the narrow current definition of econometrics that I am using here. In Pesaran (1991, p. 108), Stone was asked whether he thought the input–output approach complementary to the econometric approach and replied: 'I must confess that I am not up-to-date in terminology as I have always thought that input–output techniques were an integral part of econometrics.'

The first stage of the input–output work had been inevitably to construct a set of accounts for 1948. The forecasting performance of input–output was then assessed and input–output became an integral part of the Growth Project model. A range of technical work on methods was required to develop the input–output core. This included techniques to update the coefficients and modify the strict proportionality requirements. The model also involved substantial applied econometric work to estimate the other demand and supply relationships involved. What distinguished the model from the standard 'Keynesian' macro-models pioneered by Klein was the consistent disaggregation within the context of the complete social accounting matrices that Stone had developed. It was designed to provide a tool for exploring alternative long-term scenarios rather than short-term forecasting. Kenway (1994) discusses the evolution of macro-models in the UK and contrasts Stone's vision with that of James Ball who developed the London Business School model, after working with Klein. Both visions survive as working models. Ironically, Stone's ambitious academic vision is now commercially self-sustaining as Cambridge Econometrics, while the Business School model remains dependent on public funds.

Another example of a very widely used empirical method that originated in Cambridge that would not today be called econometrics is data envelopement analysis. Probably the most cited Cambridge economics paper of the 1950s is Farrell (1957). Farrell had worked in the DAE and then moved to the Faculty. At the DAE he had worked on irreversible demand functions, to explain the trend, and demand for cars. He also did considerable work on the theory of the firm (see Fisher, 1976) and his 1957 paper used the theory of production to operationalise the measurement of efficiency and its decomposition into allocative and technical components. The *Fourth Report* of the DAE proposes applying the technique to coal mines and Farrell and Jolly did investigate the structure of the British coal mining industry. The technique was widely adopted, particularly once large linear programs could be solved quickly. Following Charnes, Cooper and Rhodes (1978) the technique is generally known as data envelopement analysis and although there have been important extensions, e.g. to handle increasing returns to scale, the method is almost universally attributed to Farrell. Fare, Grosskopf and Lovell (1985) discuss some of the extensions. The method is non-parametric, no form is assumed for the production function, and deterministic, the efficient frontier being derived directly from the observations in the sample. It handles multiple outputs without difficulty and corresponds directly to the economic notion of a production function. In this it differs from econometric approaches, e.g. stochastic frontier analysis, where a specific form for the production or cost function and a distribution for the unexplained errors are required.

5.10 Conclusion

Stone in his British Academy Lecture says, 'I am glad that Moggridge has reminded us of a phrase that I often heard Keynes use in the later years of the War. A propos of the White Paper on Employment Policy of 1944, Moggridge quotes Keynes as saying that "theoretical economics has now reached a point where it is fit to be applied" and foreseeing "a new era of Joy through Statistics" as the policy came into operation'.

What might have surprised Keynes is how much of the joy came through mathematical statistics, but joy there certainly was. The comments of Prais and Houthakker in the 1970 Preface to the second impression of their 1955 book capture the spirit of much of the work:

We are conscious, more than ever, that there are passages in the book that follows breathing an air of optimism for which maturer years may have substituted an air of caution! Some passages (such as those dealing with electronic computation) may be somewhat dated though even these, we think, retain their validity. But we have let the words stand as we wrote them if only to serve as a reminder of the ebullient spirit that then permeated applied economics, not least at the Department in Cambridge bearing that name. If progress is to be made in economics as in the natural sciences, we remain convinced that it is essential for economists not only to work in teams, but more especially in teams that include mathematicians and statisticians; that idea was put into practice by Professor Richard Stone at the time we were fortunate enough to be engaged there on this project. In presenting the second impression of this book to the public, we are conscious of our debt to him for his stimulation and interest in our work and for providing such a congenial atmosphere in which to carry it out. (p. xxvii)

Notes

I am very grateful to all the people who discussed the early days of the DAE with me.

1 This review is discussed by Pesaran and Smith (1985), Morgan (1990) and O'Donnell (1995) who argues that Keynes's attitude to mathematics was misinterpreted.
2 Of course the DAE is part of the Faculty, but I shall follow common usage and treat the Faculty as just the teaching part.
3 The other members were David Champernowne, Austin Robinson, Joan Robinson, Gerald Shove, Piero Sraffa and Dennis Robertson.
4 Stone, in Pesaran (1991), says the first grant from Rockefeller was primed by Keynes.
5 Of course, the other members of the Committee of Management also had an input.

Part Two

Combining data and analytic techniques

6 Takeovers, institutional investment and the persistence of profits

Andy Cosh, Alan Hughes, Kevin Lee and Ajit Singh

6.1 Introduction

This chapter is concerned with the inter-relationship between the shareownership characteristics of companies, their takeover activity and the impact upon them of competitive forces affecting the persistence of their profits. It reflects three strands of work carried out in the DAE since its foundation 50 years ago. The first is the pioneering work on estimating the wealth of the nation by Jack Revell which led, *inter alia*, to the first systematic analysis of UK shareownership patterns (Revell and Moyle, 1966; Moyle, 1971). The second is the work on company growth, profitability and takeovers making use of the major company panel dataset constructed at the DAE during Brian Reddaway's period as Director (Singh and Whittington, 1968; Singh, 1971; Meeks, 1977; Kumar, 1984; Cosh, Hughes and Singh, 1980). The third is work using the same database on the prediction of profitability by Whittington (1971).

The paper revisits the question of the impact of merger on corporate profitability using UK data for the 1980s. This is familiar territory and is also one of the few areas of economics where there is more or less unanimity of empirical findings. Mergers research from many different countries over diverse time periods has established that mergers normally have a negative or neutral impact on corporate profitability.[1] The present paper brings three new dimensions to the re-examination of this question. Firstly, it is concerned not just with the average impact of mergers, but also with the dispersion of post-merger outcomes. Although the average outcome may be neutral or negative, some mergers do nevertheless succeed. Can such successful mergers be predicted on the basis of the pre-merger characteristics of merging firms? Secondly, we focus here on the role of institutions as share owners and how their presence may influence the outcome of the merger and takeover process. Thirdly and most importantly, we provide a more rigorous *counterfactual* for analysing the impact of mergers than that used in most previous studies. For the latter purpose, we locate our analysis within a general discussion of the forces affecting company profitability over time. This is important because the counter-factual used in merger studies is central to testing the usual maintained hypothesis that a shareholder-welfare motivated merger should raise share returns and/or profitability. Mueller (1986) and others have argued that there operate general forces of a competitive kind which generate a ten-dency (which may be weak and which may leave some companies with per-sistent above-profit performance) for profits to converge toward competitive norms. If this is so, then high profitability firms will tend to experience some erosion of their relative superiority over time, and *vice versa* for low profitability firms. Moreover, if the most profitable firms acquire the least profitable, as advocates of the market for corporate control would expect, then arithmetically speaking the combined profit-ability of the merged entity will be lower than the profitability of the acquirer alone.

The implications for studies assessing the impact of merger on profit-ability are clear. Firstly, there will be an averaging effect from combining sets of differently performing assets. This can be handled in empirical work by making an appropriate before and after comparison of the post-merger acquiring firm's performance with the weighted average pre-merger per-formance of the two firms. (For a discussion of averaging effects in the US context, see Mueller, 1986 especially pp. 173 ff. UK studies dealing explic-itly with this issue include Singh, 1971; Meeks, 1977; Cosh, Hughes and Singh, 1980; Kumar, 1984; Cosh, Hughes, Lee and Singh, 1989.) The second implication is that competitive forces themselves may have led to profit changes *without merger* and the relative strength and direction of these for the acquiring and acquired firm should be taken into account in setting up a counterfactual test of merger effects. This is a much less straightforward issue since we need to specify a dynamic profit generation model to compare pre- and post-merger profitability. Moreover, we should like to purge pre-merger profits of the effects of previous mergers. Merger is so widespread in the UK that finding samples of firms free from mergers over extended periods is virtually impossible. This has led the authors of a recent overview of work on profits' persistence to argue that the proper modelling of merger/profitability inter-relationships was a long way off (Geroski and Mueller, 1990, p. 201). Our approach here is to focus on periods of time which, whilst too short to model explicitly the time-series movements of profitability of individual firms, are long enough to pick up post-merger effects. In doing so, we consider carefully the econometric implications of evaluating the forces determining post-merger outcomes on such short-period cross-sectional data, in the context of a dynamic competitive process which acts to erode profitability extremes and imparts a dynamic path to profits over time.

We do this by making use of samples of acquired firms and a matched sample of acquiring and non-acquiring companies. We also allow for possible samples selection biases in assessing merger impacts from samples of surviving companies.

The remainder of this chapter is organised in six sections. Section 6.2 briefly reviews existing literature and outlines the hypotheses to be tested here. Section 6.3 considers the econometric issues involved in modelling merger outcomes in the context of a tendency for profits to regress to equilibrium values and proposes a way forward involving matched samples which is used on the data described in section 6.4. Section 6.5 outlines the characteristics of the acquired and acquiring companies and of average merger outcomes and the role of institutions in our sample period. Section 6.6 then provides our analysis of the determinants of post-merger outcomes allowing for sample selection and regression to the norm issues. A final section outlines our main conclusions.

6.2 Post-merger performance, pre-merger characteristics of institutional investors and regression to the norm: conceptual issues and previous results

Studies of the impact of merger within the profit maximisation paradigm assume that to be 'successful' mergers must raise the profitability of participating companies, and that for this improvement to represent a welfare gain it must not be due to the exploitation of customers or suppliers through enhanced monopoly or monopsony powers. A number of arguments have been advanced as to how these gains might arise involving enhanced efficiency through economies of scope or scale, either at the individual plant or overall corporate level. Whatever the pre-merger profit performance of the merging companies relative to their industry norms, the implication here is that merger should enhance it by shifting the production possibility frontiers which they face. Where mergers are for scale reasons we might expect mergers with relatively small pre-merger sizes to have the most scope for post-merger scale-related profit gains, so pre-merger size should help predict post-merger success.

Another view of the impact of mergers on profitability emphasises selection through the capital market. This links pre-merger profit and growth performance to post-merger success. Causation here works through shifts in performance arising from movement towards the production possibility frontier. This argument is based on the view that merger leads to efficiency improvements not through any scale or complementarity factors, but simply through the replacement of inferior by superior management of existing assets in the market for corporate control. The more dynamic and profitable the acquirers, and the more sluggish and unprofitable their targets, the bigger the potential improvements in the profitability of asset use should be by shifting the performance of the latter towards existing best practice. The most dynamic and profitable acquirers pre-merger should have greatest potential for raising post-merger performance in the companies they acquire.

Given that the motivation behind merger in these approaches is essentially profit maximising, it may nonetheless be the case that the intention to improve performance is thwarted by the problems of implementation alluded to in the organisational literature on mergers. This suggests that 'successful' outcomes are more likely the more horizontal the acquisition, and the less likely are 'culture' clashes. Diversifying mergers and the acquisition of smaller companies by large holding companies appear from this and other literature to be most likely to lead to problems of control loss and inferior post-merger performance. (Kitching 1967, 1973; Hunt *et al*. 1987; Ravenscraft and Scherer, 1987; Hughes, 1993). On the other hand, there are some arguments to suggest that where diversification occurs by merger it may be more easily integrated than in horizontal acquisition, given the predominance of divisionalised management structures in the typical large diversified firm and the purchase of human as well as physical capital in the merger process (Williamson, 1975; and for a survey, Hughes, 1993). These approaches suggest that the direction of merger and the absolute size of acquiring companies will influence post-merger success.

The analysis so far has assumed profit maximisation as the motivating force behind merger, with the spread of post-merger profit performance put down to variations in managerial competence to manage the merger process, or to variations in the potential for improvement represented by the pre-merger performance of merging parties. It has been argued, of course, that the objective of merger is not in all cases the pursuit of profit and that those mergers inspired by the pursuit of managerial self-interest are not intended to improve profitability. These then may lead to the appearance of 'unsuccessful' mergers in profit terms and account for the poor average performance so often noted in the literature. Indeed if mergers are more frequently used as a means of growth by 'managerial' than by owner-controlled firms then the problem is compounded.

There are a number of reasons for arguing that this might be the case. First, following Penrose (1959), it may be argued that merger eases the managerial staff constraint on growth by the acquisition of skilled experienced management along with productive assets. In effect, a merger growth strategy pushes the demand growth curve (in a Marris-type model) out to the right, enhancing the growth possibilities for management for any rate of profit. Second, to the extent that merger is particularly appropriate as a method of diversification to stabilise profits, then risk-averse management may adopt a merger-intensive growth strategy (Amihud and Lev, 1981). The link between merger and management control has also been emphasised by Reid (1968) and by Mueller (1969). The latter has argued, in a manner echoed later by Jensen (1986), that large mature managerial companies with access to substantial internal cash flows will have in effect a lower discount rate than the market in general and thus regard all other companies as undervalued takeover targets. Thus corporate age and the freedom from shareholder interference should weaken the drive to pursue profit-motivated takeover.

The burden of these arguments has been to imply that if owners of equity were more active in monitoring the managers of more mature companies, they would be more likely to perform in a manner consistent with shareholder value maximisation. In this context, institutional shareholders may have a critical role to play as a countervailing force either to property-less, inside management, or to entrenched managers with substantial ownership rights (Cosh and Hughes, 1987; Cosh, Hughes, Lee and Singh, 1989; Charkham, 1995).[2] We should therefore include the presence prior to merger of a significant shareholding by financial institutions as a pre-merger characteristic likely to influence post-merger profitability outcomes favourably. The importance of doing so is emphasised by the increased significance attached to the potential disciplinary role of institutions as their shareownership has grown. Whereas in 1969 insurance companies, pension funds, unit trusts and investment trusts held 34.2% of all UK listed market securities by value this had risen to 58.9% by 1985, and to 61.2% by 1993 (Cosh, Hughes, Lee and Singh, 1989; CSO, 1994).

So far we have focused on the individual pre-merger company characteristics which might predispose merger outcomes to be more or less unsuccessful in terms of enhanced profitability. In measuring the success or failure of a particular merger, however, a counterfactual estimate of profits in the post-merger period is required with which to compare the actual post-merger outcomes. One common method is to compare the post-merger profitability with the weighted average pre-merger profitability of the parties to a merger with both sets of data normalised by mean industry or economy-wide profitability to adjust for common average trends in performance. This also deals with the averaging effect discussed earlier. It does not, however, pick up any effects on profitability which would have been expected to occur on the basis of the pre-merger characteristics of individual companies, and in particular of their pre-merger relative profitability. The most important argument here is based on the notion of Galtonian regression to the norm, in which inter-company rivalry leads to a competitive process in which profitability extremes are competed away over time (Downie, 1959; Mueller, 1986; Mueller (ed.), 1990). This suggests that in the absence of merger profit changes might be expected to occur in a predictable fashion based on past profits. It is important therefore to allow for these possible effects in assessing merger-related outcomes.

There have been some attempts to do so in the recent merger literature. Ravenscraft and Scherer consider 67 lines of business acquisitions in the period 1965–74 and analyse the relationship between their post-acquisition profitability averaged over the period 1974–77 ($POSTPI_i$) and their pre-merger profitability in the year before acquisition ($PREPI_i$), and asset growth in the period 1974–77 ($GROW_i$). To allow for variations in overall profit rate movements when aggregating across the various pre-merger event years, they adjust each line of business profit rate by a variable $MACRO_i$ which reflects the ratio of overall manufacturing profit rates in the particular merger year to overall average manufacturing profit rates in the period 1974–77. They report the following result (t-ratios in parentheses):

$$POSTPI_i = -2.84 + 0.10\ PREPI_i + 0.15\ GROW_i$$
$$\qquad\quad (1.31)\quad (0.81)\qquad\quad (0.81)$$
$$R^2 = 0.034,\ n = 67$$

The coefficient on $PREPI_i$ is not significantly different from zero, but is significantly different from $1 (t = 7.18)$ so that there is regression towards the 'normal' rate of profit. They test for the impact of merger on this 'regression' effect by estimating the same equation on a pooled sample of their 67 lines of business and 261 corporations which survived as independent companies on the Compustat data tapes from 1965 to 1980, and which had assets of less than $50 million and profit rates on assets of 15% or higher in 1965. The median size and profit characteristics of this group were close to that of the 67 acquired lines of business in 1965. In the regression the 261 corporations are represented by their 1965 $MACRO_i$ adjusted profit rates for $PREPI_i$ and their average profit rate and growth in the period 1974–77. The 67 acquired lines of business are identified within the sample by a dummy variable taking the value of 1 for an acquired business and zero for the non-merging corporations. They estimate two equations, first for the full 261 plus 67 sample and second for 67 plus a restricted surviving group of 179 corporations with 1966 and 1967 profit rates at least 70% of their level in 1965. The results are as follows:

$$POSTPI_i = -4.55 + 0.32\ PREPI_i - 0.19\ (DUM_i \times PREPI_i) + 0.24\ GROW_i$$
$$(4.68)\quad (5.76)\qquad\quad (2.78)\qquad\qquad\qquad\quad (3.48)$$
$$R^2 = 0.157, n = 328$$
$$POSTPI_i = -3.5 + 0.40\ PREPI_i - 0.29\ (DUM_i \times PREPI_i) + 0.19\ GROW_i$$
$$(3.13)\quad (5.06)\qquad\quad (3.54)\qquad\qquad\qquad\quad (3.36)$$
$$R^2 = 0.160, n = 246$$

Both equations report coefficients on $PREPI_i$ consistent with regression to the norm with a faster 'regression' to the norm for acquired firms (mostly falls). The second equation (which removes those survivors with substantial profit falls after 1965) exhibits less regression to the norm overall and a commensurately bigger relative effect for merged firms. The consistently positive significant coefficient on growth suggests that acquired lines of business were not used as 'cash cows' and starved of investment funds. They conclude that acquisition activity lowers profitability and that part of this is due to Galtonian regression to the norm from unsustainably high pre-merger performance.

Ravenscraft and Scherer's treatment of merger and regression to the norm is based on the approach of Mueller (1986) who examined the cross-section impact of mergers on the persistence of profitability using rates of return on assets for US corporations for seven sub-periods in the years 1947–74. His basic estimating equation involves regressing rates of return (π) on assets in time period $t+1$ on rates of return in time period $t-1$ (i.e. lagged two periods); assets acquired as a percentage of asset size (ACQ) in period t; and the interaction of ACQ and π_{t-1}. The detailed estimates vary by time period but the coefficients on π_{t-1} indicate regression to the norm whilst the coefficient on $ACQ.\pi_{t-1}$ is negative, often significantly so, implying that merger enhances regression to the norm. The coefficient on ACQ itself is usually significantly positive when rates of return are measured gross of interest payments. This is not the case for net of interest profit rates. This reflects the use of heavy debt financing in the US conglomerate merger waves of the 1960s. In the period 1962–67, Mueller interprets his results as showing that for firms earning roughly double the average rate of return (gross of interest) mergers tended to reduce profitability, for all other companies they tended to raise it. When profit rates are measured net of interest, mergers tended to reduce profitability for the majority of companies (i.e. all companies with profitability greater than one third of the sample mean).

Cubbin and Geroski (1990) follow a different route in attempting to measure merger impacts within an analysis of profit persistence. They estimate separate time-series profit equations on annual data for each of 239 UK quoted companies in the period 1951–77 of the form:

$$\pi_{it} = \alpha + \lambda \pi_{it-1}$$

and attempt to explain the estimated parameters for each company in terms of industry and company specific variables, including the number of acquisitions a company makes in the period 1951–73. This latter variable is negatively related to α, λ and $\alpha/(1-\lambda)$ (where the latter is interpreted as an estimate of the long-period equilibrium rate of profit of the firm). Acquisition activity, *ceteris paribus*, reduces profitability and speeds up regression to the norm. They recognise that their sample has potential selection biases because it focuses on surviving firms and also because it may reflect the 'averaging' effect of merger. They therefore construct a separate panel of 217 'pseudo' companies, adding back to each surviving 'real' company over the period 1951–77 the assets and profits of each firm it acquired over each year prior to acquisition. Estimates of their basic profit equation for this adjusted sample suggest that purging merger effects raises the proportion of firms which appear able to sustain long-run profits above the norm. In particular they note that '[t]he higher incidence of significant α's in the current sample may also be due in some way to the reduced scope for a profit rate dilution effect of mergers in our (purged) sample' (p. 164). They also find that attempts to explain cross-firm estimates of α, λ and $\alpha/(1-\lambda)$ suggest a negative merger impact when acquisition intensity is measured by the number of acquisitions.

Thus each of these studies has followed a somewhat different path in assessing the strength of the regression towards the mean effect in its analysis of the impact of mergers on profitability. We outline below a further route to the modelling of the dynamics of corporate profitability. However, we must emphasise that our main objective in this exercise is not the dynamics *per se*, but the assessment of the impact of mergers on profitability given the dynamics. We therefore pay particular attention to the econometric problems involved in carrying out such an analysis on the basis of cross-section data for a limited period – a data choice itself dictated by the exigencies of the merger phenomenon. Had our primary interest been in just the dynamics, the appropriate data set would necessarily have involved long time series of profitability for each firm. It is the focus on mergers which requires a relatively short-period cross-section analysis. The latter in turn obliges us to use suitably matched samples of merging and non-merging firms to draw inferences about the effects of mergers.

6.3 Modelling the effects of merger on company profitability

In this section, we consider some of the difficulties encountered in the empirical investigation of the effects of merger activity on company profitability in the existing literature discussed above. We then suggest an approach which attempts to mitigate some of the associated econometric problems which we identify. These difficulties arise from the fact that the population of companies is constantly changing: some companies disappear from the population through failure or through take-over; and those that remain undergo considerable changes in their nature as they evolve over time, possibly involving a sequence of take-overs or restructuring. This means, as we have already argued, that it is unlikely that an investigator can readily construct samples which can be analysed to isolate the effect of a merger using a long run of data for a merging company prior to and following the merger event. There are in any case obvious difficulties of self-selection, since the companies which appear in the sample as 'acquirers' clearly exist (separating them from those which have been acquired or died), and have chosen to engage in merger (separating them from other survivor firms who have not engaged in merger activity).

There have been, as we have seen, some ingenious attempts to establish suitable counterfactuals and to cope with the problems of data limitations in the context of studying the impact of merger on profit persistence. However, the most straightforward approach remains to apply cross-section methods to analyse the effects of mergers in a sample of companies over a shorter time frame which captures genuinely merger-free years (i.e. the sample is chosen to ensure that the effect of the included mergers is not distorted by further merger activity or death). Unfortunately, where an important purpose of the analysis is to consider the effect of merger on the dynamic time path of profitability (e.g. whether mergers help to speed up, or delay the workings of the 'competitive process') there are, as we elaborate below, econometric problems which arise in estimating these dynamics from a cross-section regression. These problems arise whether we consider a sample of merging firms only, or whether we consider a sample of merging and non-merging firms. However, in this latter case, we can obtain an indication of the *differences* that exist between the two groups, so that inferences about the effects of mergers can be drawn more readily. For this reason, in the analysis of merger activity, we favour here the use of cross-sectional methods on a sample of acquiring companies and a carefully selected matching sample of firms not involved in mergers, and focus attention on the differences between these. Of course, the self-selection problems still remain, but there are standard estimation procedures which can be employed to deal with these. Moreover, as we explain below, the choice of the variable on which the match is based can also be used to mitigate some of the effects of self-selection.

In the remainder of this section, we briefly describe the modelling framework that underlies our analysis of company profitability, before turning to the choice of the appropriate econometric methods for use in the analysis. We then elaborate on the arguments outlined above, and describe in more detail the estimation methods that are employed in the empirical work described in section 6.6.

6.3.1 The modelling framework

In general, and ignoring the possible effects of merger for the time being, we might assume that profits in firm i at time t, expressed relative to industry profits, are given by the following linear model:

$$Y_{it} = \alpha_i + \beta X_{it} + \lambda Y_{it-1} + \varepsilon_{it}. \tag{6.1}$$

The terms '$\alpha_i + \beta X_{it}$' capture the factors which systematically influence (relative) profits while the intercept α_i captures the factors which influence firm i's profits and which are not time-varying. We assume β, λ common to all firms. The ε_{it} represent random shocks which impact on firm i's profits (e.g. a strike in time t, or an unexpected increase in demand). The presence of λY_{it-1} indicates that there is a degree of inertia in profitability. If there is an increase in warranted/equilibrium profits, because X_{it} rises, then profits only gradually rise (assuming $1 > \lambda > 0$); the speed of adjustment depends on λ (large λ corresponds to slow adjustment). Equally, if there is a positive shock (an unexpected increase in demand, say) then the effect dies away only gradually. Equation (6.1) can be considered to be a 'structural relationship', in which case X_{it} is likely to include variables, measured at time t, which are determined simultaneously with profitability (e.g. firm growth). Alternatively, equation (6.1) can be considered as the 'reduced form' equation for profitability (based on a system of equations explaining profitability, growth, and other variables), in which case X_{it} will include all those variables, measured at time $t-1$, which influence the endogenous variables in the system. The λ coefficient can be interpreted as capturing the workings of the 'competitive process' (e.g. Downie, 1959; Clifton, 1977) exerted directly on profitability in the 'structural' interpretation of (6.1), or exerted indirectly on all the endogenous variables of the system in the 'reduced form' interpretation of (6.1). A small λ (close to zero) means firms take advantage of changes in 'warranted' profits quickly, and the effects of random shocks are quickly eliminated.[3]

One main aim for this study is to find the effect of merger activity on profitability. In terms of the above formulation much of the discussion in section 6.2 can be regarded as being concerned with the possible effect merger has on the speed of adjustment. To consider the effects of merger activity, we can use the following generalised version of (6.1):

$$Y_{it} = \alpha_i + \beta X_{it} + \gamma merg_{it} + \lambda Y_{it-1} + \phi(merg_{it} \times Y_{it-1})$$
$$+ \psi(merg_{it} \times X_{it}) + \varepsilon_{it}, \tag{6.2}$$

where $merg_{it} = 1$ if a merger has occurred in firm i at time t or zero if no merger has occurred in firm i at time t. The inclusion of the variable $(merg_{it} \times Y_{it-1})$ allows the speed of adjustment to differ in the two cases. An estimate of $\phi = 0$ means there is no difference in adjustment speeds with or without merger; $\phi < 0$ means adjustment is quicker with mergers; $\phi > 0$ means adjustment is slower with mergers. The inclusion of $(merg_{it} \times X_{it})$ is also important. In the *absence* of this variable, a different speed of adjustment will *force* X_{it} to have different long-run effects on Y_{it} since where

$merg_{it} = 1$, $\left(\dfrac{\partial Y_{it}}{\partial X_{it}}\right)_{LR} = \dfrac{\beta}{1 - (\lambda + \phi)}$ while when $merg_{it} = 0$, $\left(\dfrac{\partial Y_{it}}{\partial X_{it}}\right)_{LR} = \dfrac{\beta}{1 - \lambda}$ in the

long run. Including the variable $(merg_{it} \times X_{it})$ allows

$$\left[\left(\frac{\partial Y_{it}}{\partial X_{it}}\right)_{LR} \text{ when } merg_{it} = 0\right] = \left[\left(\frac{\partial Y_{it}}{\partial X_{it}}\right)_{LR} \text{ when } merg_{it} = 1\right] \text{ if } \psi = \frac{-\beta\phi}{1 - \lambda}.$$

6.3.2 Some econometric considerations

The most straightforward way of looking at these models, *assuming no data constraints*, would be to use a fixed-effect pooled regression. This uses data for many firms over many years, pools all the data, and estimates a single regression with separate 'intercepts' for each firm obtained using firm-specific dummies. In this case, where we have assumed that the parameters in the regression are common to all firms, pooling is acceptable.[4] In general, however, there are considerable data constraints in work of this type, the result of which is that we are typically faced with just two observations for each company: one prior to the merger, and one following the merger.[5] In these circumstances, only cross-sectional regression methods are available. If the model was static (i.e. $\phi = 0$ and $\lambda = 0$), a standard cross-section would give consistent estimates of β, γ and ψ. If the model is dynamic (i.e., $\lambda \neq 0$ and $\phi \neq 0$), and we know $\Psi = (-\beta\phi)/(1-\lambda)$, so that the *long-run* elasticities $(\partial Y_{it}/\partial X_{it})_{LR}$ are the same for $merg_{it} = 0$ and $merg_{it} = 1$, then this same cross-section will give consistent estimates of the long-run elasticities (see Pesaran and Smith 1995b). But if $\Psi \neq (-\beta\phi)/(1-\lambda)$, then these cross-section estimates are not consistent. Moreover, and this is particularly relevant here, standard cross-section analysis can say nothing about the dynamics themselves (i.e. the value of λ).

In this paper, we consider a 'Barro cross-sectional regression' in which we include a lagged Y_{it} on the RHS of a cross-section regression, i.e. across firms we regress Y_{it} on Y_{it-1}, X_{it}, $(merg_{it} \times Y_{it-1})$ and so on.[6] The aim is to obtain an estimate of λ and hence examine the dynamics directly. However, Barro cross-sections suffer from econometric problems of their own.[7] To see this, consider the simple relationship

$$Y_{it} = \mu_i + \lambda Y_{it-1} + \varepsilon_{it}$$
$$= \mu + \lambda Y_{it-1} + (\mu_i - \mu) + \varepsilon_{it}.$$

Denote the inter-firm variance in intercepts, i.e. $v(\mu_i)$ by σ_μ^2 and denote the time-series variability, $v(\epsilon_{it})$, by σ_ε^2, assumed the same for all firms. Then it is straightforward to show that in the cross-section regression of Y_{it} on an intercept and Y_{it-1}, the estimator of λ is given by $\hat{\lambda}$ where:

$$E(\hat{\lambda}) = \lambda + (1-\lambda) \frac{\sigma_\mu^2}{\left[\sigma_\mu^2 + \frac{(1-\lambda)}{(1+\lambda)} \sigma_\varepsilon^2 \right]}.$$

If the cross-section variability (σ_μ^2) is large relative to the time-series variability (σ_ε^2), so that relative profits across firms varies by a great deal compared to the variation in a single firm's profitability over time, then

$$\frac{\sigma_\mu^2}{\sigma_\mu^2 + \frac{(1-\lambda)}{(1+\lambda)} \sigma_\varepsilon^2} \approx 1 \text{ and } E(\hat{\lambda}) \approx \lambda + (1-\lambda) \approx 1,$$

irrespective of the true value of λ.[8] Hence, the estimated coefficient on Y_{it-1} says little about the dynamics and simply reflects the relative size of these variances.[9]

However, some information can be gained by use of *matched samples*. If we have two samples in which σ_μ^2, σ_ε^2 are the same in both samples, then we can run two Barro cross-sections (one on each sample). If we find $\hat{\lambda}$(sample 1)$>\hat{\lambda}$(sample 2), then the true λ(sample 1)$>\lambda$(sample 2). Moreover, in the (pooled) cross-section regression (i.e. using both samples together) where we regress Y_{it} on an intercept, μ_i, Y_{it-1} and $(merg_{it} \times Y_{it-1})$, then the estimated coefficient on $(merg_{it} \times Y_{it-1})$ is given by $\hat{\phi}$ where:

$$E(\hat{\phi}) = \phi - \phi\sigma_\mu^2 \left\{ \frac{(1+\lambda)(1+\lambda+\phi)\sigma_\mu^2 + (1-\lambda)(1-\lambda-\beta)\sigma_\varepsilon^2}{[(1+\lambda)\sigma_\mu^2 + (1-\lambda)\sigma_\mu^2][(1+\lambda+\beta)\sigma_\mu^2 + (1-\lambda-\beta)\sigma_\varepsilon^2]} \right\}$$

$$= \phi \frac{2[1-\lambda(1+\beta)\sigma_\mu^2\sigma_\varepsilon^2]}{2[1-\lambda(1+\beta)]\sigma_\mu^2\sigma_\varepsilon^2 + (1+\lambda)(1+\lambda+\beta)(\sigma_\mu^2)^2 + (1-\lambda)(1-\lambda-\beta)(\sigma_\varepsilon^2)^2}$$

Hence, it appears that, although we are unable to obtain reliable point estimates of the speed of adjustment of company profitability, we are able to obtain some information on the effect of mergers on this dynamic process by comparison of a sample of companies who have engaged in merger with a sample of companies who have not. Biases also render the estimated effect of mergers unreliable, but they do so by underestimating their effect; evidence of significant effects based on these cross-sections would therefore provide strong evidence to support the view that mergers are important.

6.3.3 Self-selection issues

Even if we abstract from the difficulties experienced in estimating the effects of merger on the dynamic processes involved in modelling company profitability, there remain problems in the empirical work because of the problem of self-selection. In the empirical exercise to be carried out here, the self-selection problem arises in two forms. First, the sample of companies to be analysed, whether engaged in merger activity or not, is of 'survivors' in the sense that they exist during the two periods for which data are collected (i.e. at least seven years during the late 1970s/early 1980s in our analysis). It is important that both the merging and non-merging samples of companies survived for the same reasons, since otherwise comparison of the determination of profitability in the two samples could be dominated by the (unequal) influences of the factors affecting survival, and may not provide an adequate reflection of the influence of merger on profitability. Second, even assuming that the merging and non-merging samples differ only in those characteristics which affect profitability (when it is known that both groups are 'survivors'), it is important to recognise that the decision to enter into a merger is unlikely to be independent of the process determining the company's profitability. For example, imagine that we observe that merging companies have higher profits than non-merging companies. But the merging companies might have achieved high profits even if the merger had not taken place, and the observed link between merger and profitability might be obtained because the factors which result in high profits are correlated with those which encourage a company to decide to take over another.

In fact, treatment of these self-selection issues is relatively straightforward. The first problem, relating to the fact that only survivors are considered in the analysis, can be remedied if we choose our sample of non-merging companies so that they match the merging companies according to the variable (or variables) which distinguish 'survivors' from 'non-survivors'. In our own previous work (Cosh *et al.*, 1989), we observed that victims were routinely smaller than average, so that the primary factor distinguishing the victims of takeovers, both from their acquirers and from the companies in the industry as a whole, was their size. If the sample of non-merging companies is chosen so as to match the acquiring sample by size, therefore, then the analysis can proceed on the assumption that both sets of companies provide an equally representative reflection of the properties of 'survivors', and differences between them can be attributed to the effects of mergers alone (see the next section for further discussion of the distinguishing features of acquired companies).

The effect of self-selection in the analysis of 'treatment effects' has been widely discussed (see, for example, Greene, 1993, p. 713), and is also relatively straightforward to take into account using Heckman's (1979) two-stage treatment of sample selection as a specification error. Specifically, we can complement the profitability equation given in (6.2) with the following model of the decision to engage in merger activity:

$$merg_{it} = \begin{cases} 1 \text{ if } merg_{it}^* = \pi Z_{it} + v_{it} > 0 \\ 0 \text{ if } merg_{it}^* = \pi Z_{it} + v_{it} < 0 \end{cases} \tag{6.3}$$

where $merg_{it}^*$ is an unobserved underlying latent variable, influenced by Z_{it}. The self-selection issue arises if ϵ_{it} and v_{it} are correlated, since the effects picked up by the merger dummy in (6.2) will, in these circumstances, confuse the effect on profitability due to the merger and the characteristics of the merging firms as they relate to post-merger profitability (i.e. the typical firm engaging in merger might have achieved high profits anyway, so that it would be wrong to ascribe all the effects of high profitability to the merger itself). Now, abstracting from the dynamic issues, and under the assumption that ε_{it} and v_{it} are from a bivariate normal distribution, with $\varepsilon_{it} \sim N(0,\sigma_\varepsilon^2)$, $v_{it} \sim N(0,1)$ and correlation of ρ, then:

$$E[Y_{it}|merg_{it}=1] = \alpha + (\beta+\psi)X_{it} + \gamma + E[\varepsilon_{it}|merg_{it}=1]$$

and

$$E[Y_{it}|merg_{it}=0] = \alpha + \beta X_{it} + E[\varepsilon_{it}|merg_{it}=0]$$

and hence

$$E[Y_{it}|merg_{it}=1] = \alpha + (\beta+\psi)X_{it} + \gamma + \rho\sigma_\varepsilon^2 mills_{it}$$
$$E[Y_{it}|merg_{it}=0] = \alpha + \beta X_{it} + \rho\sigma_\varepsilon^2 mills_{it}$$

where $mills_{it} = \dfrac{\phi(\pi Z_{it})}{\Phi(\pi Z_{it})}$ if $merg_{it}=1$, and $mills_{it} = \dfrac{-\phi(\pi Z_{it})}{1-\Phi(\pi Z_{it})}$ if $merg_{it}=0$.

Hence, the effect of the merger decision on the profitability equation can be identified by construction of the $mills_{it}$ variable, and by its inclusion in the profitability equation. As usual in the implementation of the Heckman two-stage procedure, the inclusion of this term requires use of an estimate of the variance/covariance matrix for the parameters which is adjusted to take into account the heteroscedasticity induced by the self-selection process when testing hypotheses. Given the biases that arise owing to the use of Barro cross-sectional regression methods, it seems inappropriate to rely too heavily on such hypothesis tests. On the other hand, this adjustment might be important, and a pragmatic approach would be to consider hypothesis tests based on both unadjusted and adjusted variance/covariance matrices to give an indication of the robustness of the results obtained and inferences drawn.

6.4 Merger sample and variable definitions

Our sample consists of 59 companies involved in a merger in the years 1981–83 (i.e. $t = 1981$, 1982 or 1983) for which data were available on the Exstat UK Company Accounts databank for the relevant pre-merger and post-merger periods (i.e. $(t-4)$ to $(t+3)$ for acquirers), and for which we were able to gather shareholding information for the acquirer in the year prior to merger. The Exstat database is intended to be comprehensive in its coverage of the UK quoted company sector. Around 2,400 non-financial records existed on the database for the early 1980s. All companies identified in the database coding system as having lost their independence through merger were listed for analysis. There were 143 in the three years 1981–83. We were able to obtain the necessary seven years of accounting data and information on pre-merger shareholdings for 59 of these. The major reason for exclusion from the sample was an insufficient run of years of data, either because the acquirer was relatively new to the population or was acquired or lost quotation soon after merger, or because the acquired was also a newcomer. An inspection of other lists of major mergers in these years in the financial press and elsewhere suggested that the Exstat records were reasonably comprehensive at the top end of the size distribution of acquisitions. We estimated that the total consideration paid for our sample of 59 mergers was around £1.7bn, with 16 costing less than £5m to effect and 11 costing over £25m. The largest of the latter amounted to £250m. This may be roughly compared with the official estimate of £4.2bn paid to effect a total of 931 acquisitions of UK independent industrial and commercial companies (quoted and unquoted) in the period 1981–83. Of these, 27 cost over £25m, and 821 less than £5m (*Business Monitor*, various issues). Our sample therefore emphasises the larger end of the size spectrum of acquisitions in the UK in this period, which is to be expected since it is where the majority of quoted companies are located. Even so, a substantial proportion of our sample cost less than £5m to effect.[10] In addition to our 59 merging companies, a matched sample of 59 non-merging companies was drawn from the Exstat database which most closely matched our acquirers by size and industry group. It was also possible to obtain institutional investment holdings data for 47 of these. The following variables have been used in the analysis:[11]

(a) $LSIZE_i$ log(size), pre-merger, measured by the logarithm of net assets in year $(t-1)$, where t is the year of the merger

(b) $PREPROF_i$ pre-merger profitability, measured by the % pre-tax return on net assets averaged over the three pre-merger years $(t-3)$ to $(t-1)$

(c) $PERFIMP_i$ short-run improvements in performance, measured by the change in pre-tax return within the three pre-merger years (i.e. $(t-1)$ less $(t-3)$)

(d) $PREGRO_i$ pre-merger growth, % change p.a. in net assets in the three pre-merger years (i.e. $(t-4)$ to $(t-1)$)

(e) $POSTPROF_i$ post-merger profitability, measured by the % pre-tax return on net assets averaged over the three post-merger years $(t+1)$ to $(t+3)$

(f) $HORZ_i$ dummy variable taking the value 1 when acquirer and acquired are drawn from the same industry group, and 0 otherwise

(g) $INST_i$ dummy variable taking the value 1 when acquirer has a significant institutional shareholding of 5% or more in the year prior to merger, and 0 otherwise

(h) $MERG_i$ dummy variable taking value 1, when company engages in merger, and 0 otherwise

(i) AGE_i number of years since company registration.

To control for industry differences and changes in the economic environment, the variables (a) to (e) were all measured as differences from the mean values for other companies in their industry groups.[12]

6.5 Takeovers in the sample: an overview[13]

Before turning to an analysis of the links between pre-merger characteristics and post-merger profitability, it is helpful to summarise the principal characteristics of the take-over process as a whole in our sample, since this reveals the likely nature of potential selection biases in our later analysis. We also pay particular attention here to the role of institutional investment in the merger process. The evidence presented below also bears *inter alia* on two main hypotheses:[14] (a) the strong hypothesis, that the increasing domination of the stock market by institutional investors has led to a change in the behaviour of all companies in the market whether or not they have an institutional presence; (b) a weaker hypothesis, that only the behaviour of companies in which the institutions have a sizeable shareholding will be affected. Table 6.1 shows the pre-merger characteristics of the acquired and acquiring companies compared with their industry averages. It shows that the acquired companies were significantly smaller and performing worse than their industry averages. However, this under-performance in terms of profitability, growth and share return was significant only for companies acquired by acquirers with a significant institutional holding (F acquirers). Indeed, the companies which were acquired by companies without a significant financial holding (N acquirers) showed better pre-merger performance in both share return and short-run change in profitability than their industry averages. On the other hand, it can be seen that acquiring companies were performing better than their industry averages in the period immediately prior to merger announcement in terms of profitability and share return. This above-average performance was more marked for N acquirers which were also larger than their industry averages. But the average size of F acquirers was less than their industry averages and their pre-merger performance was not so superior – short-term profitability and change in profitability were significantly better, but pre-merger growth was lower than industry averages and the other variables were not significant. These findings suggest that we should find significant differences between acquirers and acquired in both the F group and the N group, but for slightly different reasons. In the case of the F group the acquired were significant under-performers and the acquirers were marginal over-performers; whilst in the N group, it was the acquirers which were the significant over-performers with the acquired as marginal under-performers. These expectations were confirmed by Table 6.2 which provides a univariate pre-merger performance comparison of acquirers with that of those they acquired. In both F and N groups the pre-merger performance of the acquired companies was noticeably worse and they were found to be significantly smaller than their acquirers.

Multivariate discriminant analysis was used to assess the collective discrimination between acquiring and acquired companies achieved by our variables and to discover which variables are most important in a multivariate context.[15] The impact of financial institutions' shareholdings on the merger process is examined in two ways. First, in Table 6.3 we present the results of an analysis of the characteristics of acquirers as a whole *versus* the acquired as a whole. Then, the discrimination between acquirers and acquired on the basis of their pre-merger characteristics is contrasted

Table 6.1. *Pre-merger characteristics – the sign test – comparison of acquirers and acquired with their industry averages*

Variable	Sample	Whole sample			Sample of acquirers with financial holding (F)			Sample of acquirers without financial holding (N)		
		Sample size	Comparison with industry average	Significance level (two-tail) (%)	Sample size	Comparison with industry average	Significance level (two-tail) (%)	Sample size	Comparison with industry average	Significance level (two-tail) (%)
Size	Acquired	59	Smaller	0.1	25	Smaller	0.1	34	Smaller	0.1
Size	Acquirer	59	Smaller	—	25	Smaller	5	34	Larger	—
1-yr profitability	Acquired	59	Lower	5	25	Lower	5	34	Lower	—
1-yr profitability	Acquirer	59	Higher	0.1	25	Higher	5	34	Higher	0.1
3-yr profitability	Acquired	59	Lower	5	25	Lower	5	34	Lower	—
3-yr profitability	Acquirer	59	Higher	0.1	25	Higher	—	34	Higher	0.1
Growth	Acquired	59	Slower	1	25	Slower	0.1	34	Slower	—
Growth	Acquirer	59	Slower	—	25	Slower	5	34	Faster	—
Change in profitability	Acquired	59	Better	—	25	Worse	—	34	Better	—
Change in profitability	Acquirer	59	Better	1	25	Better	5	34	Better	—
Share return	Acquired	47	Lower	—	19	Lower	5	28	Higher	—
Share return	Acquirer	47	Higher	—	19	Higher	—	28	Higher	10

Table 6.2. *Pre-merger characteristics – the sign test – comparison of acquired and with their acquirers*

Variable	Whole sample			Sample of acquirers with financial holding (F)			Sample of acquirers without financial holding (N)		
	Sample size	Comparison of acquired with acquirer	Significance level (two-tail) (%)	Sample size	Comparison of acquired with acquirer	Significance level (two-tail) (%)	Sample size	Comparison of acquired with acquirer	Significance level (two-tail) (%)
Size	59	Smaller	0.1	25	Smaller	0.1	34	Smaller	0.1
1-yr profitability	59	Lower	0.1	25	Lower	0.1	34	Lower	—
3-yr profitability	59	Lower	0.1	25	Lower	0.1	34	Lower	1
Growth	59	Slower	1	25	Slower	—	34	Slower	5
Change in profitability	59	Worse	1	25	Worse	1	34	Worse	—
Share return	47	Lower	0.1	19	Lower	0.1	28	Lower	5

Table 6.3. *Multivariate analysis – pre-merger characteristics – discrimination between acquirers and acquired*[a]

Variables	Whole sample	Acquirers with financial holding	Acquirers without financial holding
Standardised discriminant function coefficients			
Size	0.69	0.76	0.86
1-yr profitability	—	1.82	—
3-yr profitability	—	-1.00	—
Growth	0.28	—	0.41
Change in profitability	—	-1.22	-0.39
Share return	0.63	0.88	0.49
Tests of significance			
Significance level (%)	0.1	0.1	1.0
Canonical correlation	0.54	0.76	0.59
% correctly classified	77.7	84.2	78.6
Number of companies	118	50	68

Note:
[a] The variables used in each sample are differences from their industry averages.

Table 6.4. *Multivariate analysis – pre-merger characteristics – discrimination between those with and those without a significant financial holding[a]*

Variables	Acquired companies	Acquirers
Standardised discrimination function coefficients		
Size	0.63	0.99
1-yr profitability	0.64	—
3-yr profitability	—	—
Growth	—	0.49
Change in profitability	—	−0.57
Share return	—	0.67
Tests of significance		
Significance level	1	0.1
Canonical correlation	0.49	0.63
% correctly classified	61.0	80.9
Number of companies	59	59

[a] The variables used in each sample are differences from their industry averages.

for the sample of acquirers with financial holdings to those acquirers which have none. Second, in Table 6.4, these variables are used to discriminate F acquirers from N acquirers and F acquired from N acquired. In general, the results are supportive of the univariate findings. The significant differences found between acquirers and acquired are reflected in the strong statistical significance and the success of the discriminant function in correctly classifying companies as acquirers or acquired. The importance of size and the unimportance of profitability as a characteristic distinguishing acquirers as a whole from the acquired as a whole, is shown in the discriminant function.

As might have been expected from the univariate results, the good pre-merger share return of acquirers means that this variable too, along with growth, is a significant discriminator. It could, of course, be argued that the importance of the share return variable suggests that the stock market disciplinary mechanism is working in the interests of stockholders. However this interpretation is not straightforward since, as we have seen, the acquired companies were not significantly underperforming relative to the market prior to acquisition. Moreover, a key question from the acquiring company's shareholders point of view is not so much how their company is performing pre-merger, but what impact the merger has on subsequent returns.

Comparing the results of our analysis here with those of previous merger studies suggests that the characteristics of the selection process as a whole have not been significantly modified by the increased importance of financial institutions. The influence of the latter might nonetheless be manifested in the acquisition behaviour of companies in whose shares they held significant stakes. We tested this in a multivariate context by recomputing discriminant functions for F acquirers and their acquired and N acquirers and their acquired.

The analysis, also presented in Table 6.3, shows that in both F and N groups size remains a significant discriminator. It is, however, less important in discriminating between F acquirers and their acquired. Moreover in the F group the profitability and share return variables are the most important discriminators. In the N group on the other hand, size and growth remain the most important. Although the share return enters as a significant discriminatory variable for both groups, it is less important in the N group. The change in profitability in the pre-merger period appears in both the discriminant functions, but the interpretation of its appearance is made difficult by its strong positive correlation with 1-year profitability. These results are entirely consistent with our univariate findings, and reinforce our tentative conclusion that any beneficial impact of financial institutions is to be felt at the level of the firms in which they hold significant equity stakes, rather than in terms of the takeover process as a whole.

So far, we have concentrated on discriminating between acquirers and their acquired. Now we can turn in Table 6.4 to the related but separate question of the extent to which it is possible to discriminate between companies acquired by F and N acquirers respectively, and between F and N acquirers themselves. The analysis of acquired companies suggests, as did the univariate tests for that period, that acquiring companies with a strong institutional presence were more likely than other acquirers to seek out small and unprofitable companies. No doubt this in part reflects their own relatively small size, which along with their relatively low growth, improving profits and high share return, distinguishes them from other acquirers. Whether this acquisition strategy led to further profit or improved share return is taken up next.

The impact of merger was assessed by comparing the post-merger performance of the acquirer relative to its industry with its pre-merger performance relative to its industry. The pre-merger performance of the acquirer is measured simply for the acquirer itself, and as a weighted average of the pre-merger performance of the acquirer together with the company it acquired. The latter measure corrects for the averaging effect discussed earlier.

The implications of the findings presented in Tables 6.5 and 6.6 are clear

Table 6.5. *Merger effect – the sign test – the change in performance of the acquirer relative to its industry*

Variable	Whole sample			Sample of acquirers with financial holding (F)			Sample of acquirers without financial holding (N)		
	Sample size	Comparison of after with before	Significance level (two-tail) (%)	Sample size	Comparison of after with before	Significance level (two-tail) (%)	Sample size	Comparison of after with before	Significance level (two-tail) (%)
Size	59	Smaller	—	25	Same	—	34	Smaller	—
1-yr profitability	59	Lower	10	25	Lower	—	34	Lower	—
3-yr profitability	59	Lower	—	25	Same	—	34	Lower	—
Growth	59	Faster	—	25	Faster	—	34	Slower	—
Change in profitability	59	Worsens	—	25	Improves	—	34	Worsens	5
Share return	47	Lower	—	19	Higher	—	28	Lower	5

Table 6.6. *Merger effect – the sign test – the post-merger performance of the acquirer relative to its industry compared with the weighted average pre-merger performance of the acquirer and the acquired relative to its industry*

Variable	Whole sample			Sample of acquirers with financial holding (*F*)			Sample of acquirers without financial holding (*N*)		
	Sample size	Comparison of after with before	Significance level (two-tail) (%)	Sample size	Comparison of after with before	Significance level (two-tail) (%)	Sample size	Comparison of after with before	Significance level (two-tail) (%)
Size	59	Larger	5	25	Larger	1	34	Same	—
1-yr profitability	59	Lower	—	25	Same	—	34	Lower	10
3-yr profitability	59	Lower	—	25	Same	—	34	Lower	—
Growth	59	Lower	—	25	Faster	—	34	Slower	—
Change in profitability	59	Worsens	10	25	Same	—	34	Worsens	5
Share return	47	Lower	–	19	Higher	—	28	Lower	10

despite there being few statistically significant results. For the sample as a whole there is significant deterioration in the short-term profitability of acquirers relative to industry averages. This is, *ceteris paribus*, to be expected given the lower profit performance of the acquired relative to their acquirers in this period. It is therefore not surprising to find that this change switches from weakly significant to statistically insignificant when the pre-merger weighted performance of the acquirer and acquired are compared with the acquirer's post-merger data. This confirms the usefulness of allowing for averaging effects in this context. The picture is however worse for N acquirers than for F acquirers on either basis so that averaging is less important here. Thus we find that merger appears to have worsened the profitability, growth, profit change and share performance of the N acquirers. On the other hand, the acquirers with financial holdings appear to have fared better than the N acquirers. Growth and share returns appear higher for the F acquirers although insignificantly so, and profitability is unchanged relative to the industry average. Further analysis reveals that the decline in profitability of the N acquirers represents a move from being significantly above their industry averages to being insignificantly above and the same is true for share return. On the other hand, in the case of growth and change in profitability they have moved from above to below average. Our univariate analysis revealed that F acquirers were less successful pre-merger in terms of growth and 3-year profitability than N acquirers. It could therefore be argued that there was more scope for them to improve relative to the N acquirers in these areas.

The differences in the impact of merger on performance between acquirers with, and those without, institutional holdings can be tested more directly using the Mann–Whitney test. This test confirms that the merger effect is better for the F acquirers and their superior relative performance is statistically significant at the 5% level or better in terms of the effect of merger on both 1-year and 3-year profitability and the post-merger change in profitability, and at the 12% level for share returns. These significant differences arise only when comparing the post-merger performance of the acquirer with the weighted average pre-merger performance of the acquirer and its acquired combined (i.e. relating to the results presented in Table 6.6 and not Table 6.5).

The Mann–Whitney test revealed no significant differences between the changes in performance of F and N acquirers relative to their industries. On the other hand, the post-merger performance of the acquirers and the acquired was found to be significantly better in the F group relative to the N group. These findings are reflected in the multivariate analysis, presented in Table 6.7, since the discrimination between F and N acquirers in terms of their change in performance is much higher when the change in per-

Table 6.7. *Multivariate analysis – merger effect – the change in performance of the acquirer relative to its industry – discrimination between those acquirers with and those without a significant financial holding*[a]

Change variables	Acquirer after compared with acquirer before		Acquirer after compared with weighted average of acquirer and acquired before	
	Stepwise	Direct	Stepwise	Direct
Standardised discriminant function coefficients				
Size (not included)	—	—	—	—
1-yr profitability	—	0.88	—	0.25
3-yr profitability	1.00	0.24	1.00	0.79
Growth	—	0.08	—	−0.20
Change in profitability	—	−1.02	—	−0.63
Share return	—	0.52	—	0.52
Test of significance				
Significance level (%)	17	75	2	19
Canonical correlation	0.21	0.25	0.35	0.40
% correctly classified	66.1	61.7	67.8	66.0
Number of companies	59	59		

Note:
[a] The variables used are post-merger differences from industry averages compared with pre-merger differences.

formance is measured relative to the weighted average of the acquirer and its acquired. In this case a reasonable degree of discrimination is achieved, with the change in 3-year profitability from before to after the merger emerging as the dominant variable. Indeed, it can be seen that, owing to the strong positive correlation between this variable and all the others, the inclusion of other variables adds little to the discrimination achieved. This reinforces the conclusion of our univariate analysis.

In summary, for the sample of acquirers as a whole we find a generally insignificant worsening of relative performance. This appeared to be due to the relatively inferior post-merger performance of acquiring firms in which there was no significant institutional presence. These acquirers suffered a relative deterioration in performance much as the majority of previous studies of UK mergers have led us to expect. On the other hand the F acquirers show a positive (albeit insignificant) port-merger performance. This finding raises the question of whether the superior merger effect for F acquirers is due to the presence of institutional investors themselves (through motivational or expertise effects), or to the other pre-merger characteristics of these acquirers, in particular their tendency to be somewhat below the average pre-merger profitability of N acquirers. This is explored further in the analysis which follows.

6.6 Regression results

The central purpose of this section of the paper is to consider whether the long-run level of company profitability (relative to its industry average) can be explained by company characteristics; whether the determination of this long-run level differs in companies engaging in merger compared to those who do not; whether the 'competitive process' (associated with the speed of adjustment to the long-run equilibrium) is enhanced by merger activity; and how the influence of institutional investors identified in the preceding section can be interpreted in this framework. In particular, we question whether the acquirer's decline in profitability relative to its industry average is simply a reflection of its superior relative profitability pre-merger. If this were found to be the case, it would both provide an alternative explanation for the superior merger effect of F acquirers discussed above and would call into question the typical counterfactual assumption used in many merger studies.

To do this we draw upon the modelling framework presented in section 6.3. This required the creation of a matched sample of 59 companies for the same time period as our merger sample. Each company in this sample matched one of our acquirers by size and industry group, and none had engaged in merger activity in this period. Our matching was designed to control for differences in profitability due to different competitive circumstances which might arise between a randomly selected sample of firms and a sample in which firms which might become victims have been omitted (as is the case here). As discussed in the previous section of the paper, company size is the primary determinant of the likelihood of the company being taken over, and matching by size therefore ensures that the merging and non-merging firms can be considered to have the same 'survivor' characteristics, and differences between them can therefore be ascribed to the merger effect.

However, it is also important that the two samples have similar characteristics in terms of the time-series and cross-section variability of the firms' profitability series. As discussed in the earlier sections, biases in the estimators of the coefficients on the dynamic terms in the profitability regression are influenced by the relative size of these variance terms, and it is important that the biases in the two samples are comparable if inferences are to be drawn through comparison of the two samples. As it turns out, matching by size and industry provides samples which have very similar cross-section variation in firm profitability.[16] Since there is no *a priori* reason to believe that the time-series variation would differ significantly between the samples, we proceed on the assumption that the biases affecting the two samples are also comparable across firms and industries. The comparison of the findings for these two groups allows us to draw inferences about the effect of merger itself.

Our first approach estimates the profitability equation using OLS and the results are presented in Table 6.8. In this table, column (1) examines directly the difference in adjustment speeds between the acquirers and the matched sample and provides a point of reference with the previous literature in this area. It shows that the adjustment coefficient on $PREPROF_i$ (λ in our earlier discussion) is between zero and unity and that merger appears to accelerate this adjustment. Both of these results are statistically significant. The full set of explanatory variables is introduced in the equation reported in column (2). The inclusion of further variables supports the conclusions derived from column (1). Company size has a weak, positive effect on profitability within the matched sample, but this effect is not found amongst the acquirers. The results suggest that rapid growth in the earlier period reduces subsequent profitability, but this effect is not present for the acquirers. The result for the sample as a whole echoes the findings of Whittington (1971) for the UK quoted sector in the period 1948–60. The result for the acquiring sample is consistent with a Penrose effect in which merger allows the pursuit of fast growth without diseconomies of growth adversely affecting profitability. For the matched sample there is a significant, positive relationship between current profitability and the previous period's performance improvement. However, it appears that merger largely eliminates this effect on profits. Company age is unrelated to profitability in these samples, but there is some evidence for a negative impact in the case of horizontal mergers (which is in accordance with previous studies for the UK). Overall, the impact of merger appears to eliminate, or reduce the impact of a company's history on its current profitability. This accounts for the higher intercept term for the sample of acquirers.

In order to examine the impact of institutional investor presence on this process we introduced the institutional dummy variable. Lack of information for some of our matched companies restricted the sample to 47 acquirers and their matched companies. Column (3) of Table 6.8 presents the findings for this sample and a comparison with the full sample shown in column (2) shows that our previous findings apply equally to this restricted sample. Columns (4) and (5) then present the results when the institutional dummy is introduced. Its inclusion reinforces our earlier conclusions about the impact of the other variables and about the adjustment process. Furthermore, a significant institutional presence appears to be associated with higher profitability and this effect is greater amongst the acquirers. On the other hand the statistical significance of these findings is poor.

Finally, column (6) provides comparable results in which the acquirer's prior period profitability is replaced by the average profitability of the acquirer and acquired together (weighted by their assets in that period). It can be seen that this has very little impact on the estimated coefficients for the sample of acquirers and requires no qualification of our earlier conclusions.

The OLS results suffer potentially from sample selection bias. We therefore also employ Heckman's two-stage procedure to check for this. The first stage involves the estimation of a probit model of the decision to merge and these results are presented in Table 6.9. The first two columns relate to the full sample of acquirers and matched companies and the last two columns are for the restricted sample with institutional investor data. A reasonable degree of discrimination is achieved in each case, with profitability in the pre-merger period having the greatest degree of explanatory power, although pre-merger growth also shows in these equations. This corroborates our finding in the previous section of this paper that acquirers were significantly more profitable than their industry averages. The insignificant coefficient on size reflects the success of our matching procedure.

The second stage of the Heckman approach involves calculation of the inverse Mills ratio from equations (2) and (4) of Table 6.9. This variable is then included as an additional explanatory variable in an attempt to

Table 6.8. OLS regression analysis of company profitability

Dependent variable: $POSTPROF_i$ = company i's profitability relative to industry average

	(1)	(2)	(3)	(4)	(5)	(6)
$CONST$	-2.1864	-4.7762	-2.4599	-3.4588	-4.3585	-4.3315
	(1.67)	(1.98)	(0.75)	(0.99)	(2.64)	(1.65)
$MERG_i$	3.4232	8.9504	7.1171	5.8616	5.9756	6.3712
	(1.79)	(2.33)	(1.58)	(1.20)	(2.54)	(2.82)
$PREPROF_i$	0.7390	0.6429	0.7153	0.7477	0.7578	0.7570
	(3.81)	(3.49)	(3.29)	(3.40)	(3.56)	(3.56)
$LSIZE_i$	—	1.4071	1.4101	1.6656	1.7337	1.7274
		(1.82)	(1.62)	(1.82)	(2.12)	(2.11)
$PERFIMP_i$	—	0.4560	0.5724	0.5702	0.5722	0.5722
		(4.23)	(4.74)	(4.75)	(4.90)	(4.91)
$PREGRO_i$	—	-0.2947	-0.4546	-0.4902	-0.4995	-0.4986
		(1.75)	(2.14)	(2.27)	(2.43)	(2.43)
$INST_i$	—	—	—	2.5103	3.6688	3.6061
				(0.84)	(1.65)	(1.62)
AGE_i	—	0.0332	-0.0073	-0.0080	—	—
		(0.70)	(0.13)	(0.14)		
$(MERG_i \times PREPROF_i)$	-0.4838	-0.4142	-0.4789	-0.4548	-0.4935	-0.4975
	(1.94)	(1.67)	(1.59)	(1.49)	(1.68)	(1.67)
$(MERG_i \times LSIZE_i)$	—	-1.5109	-1.8982	-1.5307	-1.7773	-1.9132
		(1.40)	(1.56)	(1.17)	(1.55)	(1.64)
$(MERG_i \times PERFIMP_i)$	—	-0.3347	-0.4660	-0.4934	-0.4848	-0.5055
		(2.04)	(2.59)	(2.74)	(2.76)	(2.91)
$(MERG_i \times PREGRO_i)$	—	0.1761	0.3390	0.4077	0.4141	0.4047
		(1.00)	(1.54)	(1.82)	(1.93)	(1.89)
$(MERG_i \times INST_i)$	—	—	—	2.6132	—	—
				(0.57)		

	(9)	(9)	(2)	(3)	(3)	(3)
$(MERG_i \times AGE_i)$	—	-0.0670	-0.0296	-0.0249	—	—
		(0.96)	(0.37)	(0.31)		
$HORZ_i$	—	-3.1600	-5.0485	-4.7081	-5.4746	-5.3311
		(1.18)	(1.53)	(1.43)	(1.79)	(1.74)
N	118	118	94	94	94	94
$\overline{R}^2$	0.1372	0.2844	0.3387	0.3462	0.3643	0.3632
σ_e	10.0603	9.1616	9.3771	9.3244	9.1939	9.2019
LLF	-437.8142	-421.920	-336.7823	-335.0766	-335.5044	-335.5860
$\chi_{FF}^2(1)$	0.3668	1.4301	1.9434	2.1565	2.4923	2.4354
$\chi_R^2(r)$	27.8650	—	3.3502	—	0.8516	0.9114
	(9)	(9)	(2)	(3)	(3)	(3)

Notes:

Results refer to regressions of the form

$$POSTPROF_i = \alpha + \alpha_0\, MERG_i + \alpha_1\, PREPROF_i$$
$$+ \alpha_2\, LSIZE_i + \alpha_3\, PERFIMP_i + \alpha_4\, PREGRO_i$$
$$+ \alpha_5\, INST_i + \alpha_6\, AGE_i$$
$$+ \beta_1\, (MERG_i \times PREPROF_i) + \beta_2\, (MERG_i \times LSIZE_i)$$
$$+ \beta_3\, (MERG_i \times PERFIMP_i) + \beta_4\, (MERG_i \times PREGRO_i)$$
$$+ \beta_5\, (MERG_i \times INST_i) + \beta_6\, (MERG_i \times AGE_i)$$
$$+ \beta\, HORZ_i + \varepsilon_i$$

estimated using OLS on a sample of 118 or 94 companies ($N=118$ or $N=94$). Owing to missing observations, $INST_3$ and $MERG_i INST_i$ are omitted when $N=118$.

Figures in parentheses are (absolute) t-values. $\overline{R}^2$ is the square of the adjusted correlation coefficient. σ_e is the standard error of the equation. LLF is the log-likelihood of the regression, $\chi_{FF}^2(1)$ is Ramsey's RESET test of functional form, and $\chi_R^2(r)$ is the LM test of r linear restrictions (col. (4) is unrestricted where $N=118$, and col. (5) is unrestricted when $N=94$).

$PREPROF_i$ Columns (1)–(5) = the pre-tax return is measured for the acquirer alone

Column (6) = the acquirer's pre-tax return is measured as the weighted average of the acquirer and the acquired.

Table 6.9. *Probit analysis of companies' merger decision*

Dependent variable: $MERG_i=0$ if company does not engage in merger, 1 if company does engage in merger

	(1)	(2)	(3)	(4)
CONST	−0.18312	−0.07587	−0.00133	−0.09510
	(0.693)	(0.626)	(0.004)	(0.691)
$PREPROF_i$	0.03378	0.03116	0.04062	0.03960
	(2.105)	(2.004)	(2.091)	(2.117)
$LSIZE_i$	−0.05294	—	−0.03059	—
	(0.738)		(0.375)	
$PERFIMP_i$	0.01189	—	0.01651	—
	(1.006)		(1.361)	
$PREGRO_i$	0.01466	0.01441	0.01293	0.01476
	(1.650)	(1.806)	(1.447)	(1.830)
$INST_i$	—	—	−0.01467	—
			(0.00288)	
AGE_i	−0.00088	—	−0.00288	—
	(0.193)		(0.563)	
N	118	118	94	94
LLF	−77.0945	−77.9520	−60.0869	−61.3416
LLF_0	−81.7914	−81.7914	−65.1558	−65.1558
P	70/118	75/118	57/94	61/94

Notes:
Results refer to probit regression of the form
$$MERG_i=1 \text{ if } \gamma_0+\gamma_1 PREPROF_i+\gamma_2 LSIZE_i+\gamma_3 PERFIMP_i+\gamma_4 PREGRO_i$$
$$+\gamma_5 INST_i+\gamma_6 AGE_i+v_i>0$$
0 otherwise
where the idiosyncratic component of the underlying latent variable is assumed to be normally distributed. Owing to missing observations, $INST_i$ is omitted when $N=118$.

Figures in parentheses are the (absolute) values of the ratio of the estimated coefficient and the asymptotic standard error. LLF refers to the value of the log-likelihood of the estimated model. LLF_0 is the value of the model under the assumption that the slope coefficients in the probit model are all zero. P is the proportion of companies correctly assigned to the merger/non-merger groups.

distinguish between the merger sample selection effect and the effect of merger itself. There was found to be a high correlation between the calculated inverse Mills ratio and the merger dummy and so the latter was excluded from the second-stage OLS runs. The Heckman regression results are presented in Table 6.10 along with the unadjusted and adjusted t ratios.

The main conclusion is that the estimated coefficients are very similar to those obtained by OLS analysis. The t-ratios are generally higher and give us greater confidence in our earlier conclusions. The importance of the effect of merger on the path of profitability is confirmed and is shown by the statistical significance of the coefficients for the interaction terms including the merger dummy variable in the Heckman equations.

6.7 Conclusion

Our overall conclusions may be summarised briefly. We did not find that size in our acquiring sample was significantly related to profitability in our profit equations, and conclude that, in our sample, scale effects were not a significant factor in determining post-merger profit outcomes. We did, however, find that rapid growth-by-acquisition avoided the future falling off in profitability performance that was experienced by rapidly growing non-acquirers. We conjecture that this is consistent with acquisition growth avoiding management and related diseconomies of expansion in the manner hypothesised by Penrose. We also found that expansion by horizontal merger was likely to reduce future profitability. This is also inconsistent with most scale-based arguments for horizontal acquisitions. It is more consistent with control loss arguments in which horizontal expansion is less likely to benefit from divisionalised management structures than diversified expansion by merger. We found no evidence of life cycle effects in our sample.

Our overall findings on the pre- and post-merger characteristics of firms involved in take-over were much the same as the studies covering previous periods when institutional investors were a less significant component of stockownership patterns in the UK. In that sense, their increased presence appears not to have greatly affected the selection process as a whole. We did find, however, that acquiring companies with significant institutional investment holdings (F acquirers) were associated with mergers which had relatively positive post-merger outcomes compared with mergers where the acquirers did not have such holdings present (N acquirers). We also found that the F acquirers were somewhat less profitable pre-merger than the N acquirers and sought out significantly less profitable targets.

These results on merger outcomes were derived using the standard counterfactual basis for estimating merger effects. This assumes that the best estimate of post-merger profitability in the absence of merger is the pre-merger level of the merging companies profitability relative to their industry mean. This counterfactual neglects the insight into the dynamic

Table 6.10. *Heckman two-stage regression analysis of company profitability*

Dependent variable: y_i = company i's profitability relative to industry average

	(1)	(2)	(3)	(4)	(5)	(6)
CONST	−0.5215	−0.5656	−0.8773	−0.7087	−1.5896	−1.3022
	(0.55,0.61)	(0.29,0.43)	(0.39,0.51)	(0.29,0.35)	(1.08,1.33)	(0.91,1.15)
$MILLS_i$	2.6403	5.4705	4.3665	3.5884	3.6845	3.9719
	(2.19,2.48)	(2.31,3.39)	(1.58,2.08)	(1.20,1.47)	(2.54,3.15)	(2.78,3.54)
$PREPROF_i$	0.7998	0.7522	0.8270	0.8394	0.8515	0.8571
	(4.09,4.55)	(3.99,5.97)	(3.70,4.95)	(3.63,4.51)	(3.91,4.89)	(3.93,5.07)
$LSIZE_i$	—	1.4139	1.4186	1.6725	1.7348	1.7255
		(1.83,2.67)	(1.63,2.15)	(1.82,2.24)	(2.12,2.63)	(2.11,2.68)
$PERFIMP_i$	—	0.4542	0.5709	0.5689	0.5712	0.5709
		(4.21,6.00)	(4.73,6.09)	(4.74,5.74)	(4.89,5.94)	(4.88,6.08)
$PREGRO_i$	—	−0.2474	−0.4172	−0.4594	−0.4669	−0.4621
		(1.44,2.10)	(1.93,2.54)	(2.10,2.58)	(2.28,2.83)	(2.26,2.88)
$INST_i$	—	—	—	2.5048	3.6662	3.5699
				(0.84,1.02)	(1.65,2.03)	(1.61,2.04)
AGE_i	—	0.0321	−0.0085	−0.0090	—	—
		(0.68,0.99)	(0.15,0.20)	(0.16,0.20)		
$(MERG_i×PREPRO_i)$	−0.5221	−0.4124	−0.4838	−0.4587	−0.4968	−0.5034
	(2.10,2.32)	(1.67,2.48)	(1.60,2.12)	(1.50,1.85)	(1.69,2.09)	(1.68,2.14)
$(MERG_i×LSIZE_i)$	—	−1.5042	−1.8983	−1.5306	−1.7719	−1.9547
		(1.39,2.04)	(1.56,2.07)	(1.17,1.44)	(1.55,1.92)	(1.67,2.14)
$(MERG_i×PERFIMP_i)$	—	0.3344	0.4664	0.4937	0.4853	0.51269
		(2.04,2.91)	(2.59,3.34)	(2.74,3.32)	(2.77,3.36)	(2.94,3.66)
$(MERG_i×PREGRO_i)$	—	0.1718	0.3372	0.4082	0.4117	0.3977
		(0.98,1.41)	(1.53,2.01)	(1.81,2.22)	(1.92,2.37)	(1.86,2.36)
$(MERG_i×INST_i)$	—	—	—	2.6205	—	—
				(0.58,0.71)		
$(MERG_i×AGE_i)$	—	−0.0653	−0.0288	−0.0241	—	—
		(0.94,1.36)	(0.36,0.47)	(0.30,0.37)		

$(HORZ_i)$	—	-3.1217	-5.0175	-4.6827	-5.4508	-5.218
		(1.17,1.69)	(1.52,1.97)	(1.42,1.73)	(1.78,2.18)	(1.70,2.15)
N	118	118	94	94	94	94
$\bar{R}^2$	0.1487	0.2838	0.3387	0.3461	0.3641	o.3616
σ_ϵ	9.9928	9.1658	9.3777	9.3251	9.1954	9.2136
σ_u	4.8556	5.8851	5.2649	4.8456	4.927	5.0634
ρ	0.5438	0.9295	0.8293	0.7405	0.7479	0.7844
LLF	-437.0200	-421.9741	-336.7880	-335.0840	-335.5192	-335.7054
$\chi_{FF}^2(1)$	0.6658	1.4429	2.0220	2.2279	2.5626	2.4076
$\chi_R^2(r)$	26.7689(10)	0.2880(1)	3.3629(8)	0.0166(1)	0.8829(4)	1.2800(4)

Notes:

Results refer to restricted versions of the following regression

$$POSTPROF_i = \alpha + \alpha_0 \ MILLS_i + \alpha_1 \ PREPROF_i$$
$$+ \alpha_2 \ LSIZE_i + \alpha_3 \ PERFIMP_i + \alpha_4 \ PREGRO_i$$
$$+ \alpha_5 \ INST_i + \alpha_6 AGE_i$$
$$+ \beta_1 \ (MILLS_i \times PREPROF_i) + \beta_2 \ (MILLS_i \times LSIZE_i)$$
$$+ \beta_3 \ (MILLS_i \times PERFIMP_i) + \beta_4 \ (MILLS_i \times PREGRO_i)$$
$$+ \beta_5 \ (MILLS_i \times INST_i) + \beta_6 \ (MILLS_i \times AGE_i)$$
$$+ \beta \ HORZ_i + \gamma \ MERG_i - e_i$$

estimated using OLS on a sample of 118 or 94 companies ($N=118$ or $N=94$). Owing to missing observations, $INST_i$ and $merg_i INST_i$ are omitted when $N=118$. Here $MILLS_i$ is the inverse of the Mill's ratio, calculated using the Probit regression results of Table 6.9 column (2) for columns (1)–(2), and using the probit regression results of Table 6.9 column (4) for columns (3)–(6).

Figures in parentheses are the (absolute) values of the ratio of the estimated coefficient and the unadjusted (OLS) and adjusted standard errors respectively (see text for discussion). R^2 is the square of the adjusted correlation coefficient. σ_ϵ and σ_u are, respectively, the unadjusted and adjusted standard errors of the equation, ρ is the estimated correlation coefficient between the error term of the profitability regression equation and the idiosyncratic element of the latent variable underlying the decision to enter into merger. LLF is the log-likelihood of the regression, and $\chi_{FF}^2(1)$ is Ramsey's RESET test of functional form. χ_r^2 is the LM test of r linear restrictions (based on the unadjusted var/cov. matrix).

$PREPROF_i$ Columns (1)–(5) = the pre-tax return is measured for the acquirer alone

Column (6) = the acquirer's pre-tax return is measured as the weighted average of the acquirer and the acquired.

path of profits provided by the literature of regression to the norm. When we carried out an analysis of the persistence of profits using appropriately constructed matching samples of acquiring and non-acquiring firms, and allowed for potential sample selection biases, we found that regression to the norm exists in the absence of mergers, and is reinforced by their presence. The existence of regression to the norm implies that the standard counterfactual is biased against finding positive normalised post-merger impacts where acquirers exhibit better than the norm pre-merger profitability. This is of course typically the case, and has important implications for existing merger results which do not correct for this effect. In the context of testing for differences in merger outcomes between F and N acquirers in our sample, ignoring regression to the norm will lead us to bias our results towards finding more favourable outcomes for F acquirers. This is because they were typically less profitable pre-merger than were the N acquirers. The fact that F acquisitions produced a positive difference between post-merger and pre-merger normalised profitability suggests, however, that as a group they were able to offset to a greater degree the regression effect experienced by N acquirers. In that sense the presence of institutional investors has a beneficial impact on merger outcomes.

Notes

Partial financial support from the ESRC's Initiative on the Analysis of Large and Complex Datasets (grant no. H519255003) is gratefully acknowledged by the first three authors, as is ESRC support under the Survey and Database programme of the ESRC Centre for Business Research.

1 For recent surveys of the international evidence on the effects of mergers on profitability, see Hughes (1993), Singh (1992, 1993). It is important to note that these studies, which have generally been carried out by industrial organisation economists, are based on accounting data. There is however another set of studies which use a different method – the so called 'event' studies methodology – and arrive at a very positive assessment of the impact of mergers. This research, which is normally the province of finance specialists, is based on stock market data. The dependent variables in these investigations are the share prices of the merging companies. Such studies have also been reviewed in the survey articles mentioned above. The latter point out that the differences in the results of the two types of study are more apparent than real and go on to show how these can be reconciled.

2 See, however, Demsetz who has argued that ownership structure is endogenous and has no independent effect on performance (Demsetz, 1983).

3 In all discussions, we ignore the possibility that $\lambda = 1$. If $\lambda = 1$, then: (i) the model explains profit *growth* in terms of X_{it}, and says nothing about levels; and (ii) random shocks have an effect on profit levels which persist indefinitely, and in principle π is unbounded.

4 Heterogeneity in parameters in a *dynamic* model of this sort (i.e. with $\lambda \neq 0$) would mean that pooling gives inconsistent estimates. See Pesaran and Smith (1995b) for further discussion.

5 Hopefully, these observations relate to time periods which are sufficiently long for the effects of short-term volatility to be eliminated. In our own work, the pre- and post-merger periods are the 3-year time intervals before and after the year in which the merger takes place.

6 This is termed a Barro cross-section as it has been popularised by Robert Barro in work on cross-country growth and convergence (regressing the change in output over a length of time on output in the initial period across countries, $i = 1, \ldots, n$). See Barro and Sala-i-Martin (1995).

7 These are elaborated in detail in Lee *et al.* (1997).

8 Note that,

$$E(\hat{\lambda}) = 1 - \frac{\sigma_\mu^2}{\left[\sigma_\mu^2 + \frac{(1-\lambda)}{(1+\lambda)}\sigma_\varepsilon^2\right]} + \lambda \left(1 - \frac{\sigma_\mu^2}{\left[\sigma_\mu^2 + \frac{(1-\lambda)}{(1+\lambda)}\sigma_\varepsilon^2\right]}\right),$$

i.e. $\hat{\lambda}$ is a weighted average of the true λ and unity, with weights dependent on σ_μ^2, and σ_ε^2, and λ itself.

9 The intuition behind the bias is as follows: when running the cross section, one assumes a common intercept (α), placing the deviations ($\alpha_i - \alpha$) into the error. Usually this is reasonable, as this term is not correlated with the other regressions in the x-sectional regression. But when one of the regressors is the lagged value of y_{it}, it is clear that ($\alpha_i - \alpha$) is correlated with the regressor. This results in bias, and the bias is larger the greater this correlation (based on σ_μ^2) relative to time-series movement (based on σ_ε^2).

10 For an analysis of smaller non-quoted acquisitions in this period, see Cosh and Hughes (1994a, 1995).

11 Apart from the institutional holding variable, all the data are drawn from the Exstat UK Company Accounts database.

12 The definition of industry group used throughout is that which appears in the UK Stock Exchange official list and includes about 100 industry groups.

13 This section draws upon some of the results of Cosh *et al.* (1989).

14 For a fuller discussion, see Cosh *et al.* (1989).

15 In contrast to the preceding non-parametric univariate analysis, the multivariate discriminant analysis makes the strong assumption of multivariate normality in the exogenously determined RHS variables. The extent to which results are robust to the violation of this assumption depends on the extent of the presence of multivariate skewness and kurtosis, and on the precise nature of the interdependencies between the RHS variables; this latter point is particularly relevant when the RHS variables include discrete variables. There are no uncontroversial procedures for dealing with, or indeed testing for, the presence of multivariate non-normality, although it has been suggested that, if possible, data should be transformed to achieve approximate univariate normality. In fact, all the variables involving profits and the share returns variable pass

Kolmgorov–Smirnov tests of univariate normality and can therefore be used with some degree of confidence. The variable which least approximates normality is, as usual, the size variable and it is for this reason that the log transformation is used in the discriminant analysis. Obviously, univariate normality is a necessary but not sufficient condition for multivariate normality, and in the absence of further evidence on the validity of the multivariate normality assumption, the results obtained are to be treated with appropriate reservations (see, for example, Singh, 1971).

16 A test of the equality of cross-firm variance in profitability in the two samples provided a test statistic valued at 1.53 which compared to the $F(58,58)$ distribution is insignificant.

7 Semi-parametric estimation of the company size–growth relation

Andy Cosh, Alan Hughes, Hyehoon Lee and Stephen Pudney

7.1 Introduction

In the applied literature, a common finding of studies covering the last 15 years or so has been that firm growth and failure rates decline with firm size and age (Schmalensee, 1989; Hall, 1987; Evans, 1987a,b; Storey *et al.* 1987; Dunne and Hughes, 1994). This is in contrast to studies covering earlier periods for the United Kingdom which showed that firm growth was positively related to size (Singh and Whittington, 1968, 1975; Samuels, 1965; Prais, 1976; Hart, 1965; Kumar, 1984; Samuels and Chesher, 1972). Both sets of studies contradict a celebrated hypothesis attributed to Gibrat which holds that growth is independent of firm size. It has been argued that the result for earlier periods may reflect higher rates of growth by merger amongst larger companies (Hannah and Kay, 1977; Hughes, 1993), whilst the result for more recent years may be attributable to selection bias.

When we estimate size–growth relationships with company panels, an unavoidable problem is sample attrition. Some companies may cease to exist during the period covered by the panel. Whereas slow-growing large firms may simply slip slowly downwards through the size distribution for a considerable length of time before ceasing to trade, a smaller company is likely to hit the boundary of extinction much sooner. Small firms which have slow or negative growth may be more likely to disappear from the sample in any given time interval than are large firms. If slow-growing small firms have a greater likelihood of failure than slow-growing large firms, then estimates of growth by size, based on surviving firms only, will be biased towards finding a negative size–growth relationship. However, as we discuss below, there are some conceptual difficulties with this line of reasoning, and also serious identification problems. Recent applied studies have in any case found that a negative size–growth relationship remains even after correcting for possible sample selection bias (Dunne and Hughes, 1994).

145

The main focus of this chapter is methodological: to examine the robustness of these results to decisions that are typically made about econometric specifications (usually linear regressions and probits) to be used in the analysis. We do this by implementing some recent semi-parametric estimators which are based on the Nadaraya–Watson kernel approach, and which generalise the standard regression and probit estimators. We focus on the relationship between two aspects of firms' development – their growth and failure rates – and firm size, allowing also for the influence of age and broad industrial sector. We do this for a large stratified sample of UK quoted and unquoted companies covering the whole corporate sector size range in the period 1976–1982. We find results which give grounds for concern about the use of standard linear parametric techniques.

The chapter proceeds as follows. Section 7.2 discusses alternative econometric approaches and introduces a decomposition of the joint mortality/growth distribution which simplifies the application of semi-parametric estimators. Section 7.3 surveys semi-parametric estimation techniques available for estimation of each component of the joint distribution. Section 7.4 describes our dataset. Sections 7.5 and 7.6 report and analyse estimation results produced by the parametric and semi-parametric approaches respectively. Section 7.7 compares the joint distribution of firm growth and mortality based on the alternative approaches and section 7.8 concludes.

7.2 Alternative approaches

Define the following notation: y_0 and y_1 are measures of the size of the firm in periods 0 and 1. If the firm dies between these two dates, y_1 is undefined, and a dummy variable ζ takes the value 1 if death occurs and 0 otherwise. A vector z contains a number of other variables to be used to explain or describe firm growth. Our objective is to study the distribution of $\{y_1, \zeta\}$ conditional on $\{y_0, z\}$, which underlies the evolution of the company population through time. Note that we are dealing here only with the processes of firm growth and death, not with the births of new firms.

Our first objective is to estimate the conditional probability density/mass function of $\{y_1, \zeta\}$ conditional on $\{y_0, z\}$. Since we are seeking to analyse the relation between growth and size (and death and size), we focus particular attention on the role of y_0. We are particularly anxious to avoid imposing *a priori* assumptions about the way in which y_0 enters the distribution. To estimate the distribution of $\{y_1, \zeta | y_0, z\}$ directly would be possible using classical parametric methods, notably maximum likelihood. These methods are widely available in standard software packages, and are consequently very widely used (see Dunne and Hughes (1994) for a typical example in the context of company growth). However, the parametric approach brings with it additional incidental assumptions (typically normality and linearity), which may have a critical influence on the results. Under the parametric approach, the joint distribution of $\{y_1, \zeta\}$ would be specified as a partially-observed bivariate normal distribution with mean vector specified to be linear in y_0 and z. These assumptions could be relaxed within the parametric framework, for example by specifying flexible distributional forms (see, for example, Gallant and Nychka, 1987; Gabler *et al.*, 1993), and with more general specifications used for the conditional mean vector. However, these generalised specifications are not often used in practice.

An alternative approach is to use techniques that are non-parametric as far as possible. To introduce the idea of non-parametric regression, consider the following regression model, which ignores firm death and any other explanatory variables besides y_0:

$$E(y_1|y_0)=g(y_0) \tag{7.1}$$

The non-parametric approach consists in estimating the entire function $g(.)$ without restricting it to some parametric family such as the set of linear functions. The best-known of these methods use variants of the Nadaraya–Watson kernel smoothing technique (see Silverman (1986) and Härdle (1990) for surveys, and Deaton (1989) and Pudney (1993) for examples of their application in economics). The Nadaraya–Watson estimator of the value of the mean function $g(y_0)$ at an arbitrary point y_0 is as follows:

$$\tilde{g}(y_0)=\frac{\sum_{j=1}^{n} k\left(\frac{(y_0-y_{0j})}{\lambda_j}\right)y_{0j}}{\sum_{j=1}^{n} k\left(\frac{(y_0-y_{0j})}{\lambda_j}\right)} \tag{7.2}$$

where $k(.)$ is a suitable kernel function (usually symmetric and non-negative), which integrates to unity. The estimator (7.2) can be interpreted as a sample analogue of the population regression $E(y_1|y_0)=\int y_1 dF(y_0,y_1)/\int dF(y_0)$, where F is used as generic notation for a cumulative distribution function (cdf). It can also be viewed as a (rather sophisticated) smoothed form of a simple bar chart plotting group means of y_1 against ranges of values for y_0. The degree of smoothing in (7.2) is controlled by a set of bandwidth parameters λ_j which may vary (for instance, to give a higher degree of smoothing in regions where observations are sparse). Wherever we apply expressions like (7.2) in this study, we use the two-stage adaptive method of Breiman *et al.* (1977) to generate bandwidths. It is convenient for our purposes to use a globally differentiable kernel such as the Gaussian pdf,[1] to avoid difficulties with gradient-based optimisation techniques.

Estimators of this type have the enormous theoretical advantage of robustness against functional mis-specification. However, there are circumstances in which kernel-type estimation performs poorly. One such case involves discrete explanatory variables. Although kernel regression has good asymptotic properties in such cases (see Bierens, 1994), it will nevertheless tend to work very badly in finite samples when the explanatory variables contain dummies which define a very fine partition of the sample into cells. For example, consider the following model where y_0 is continuous and (for simplicity) assume z is a vector of 0/1 dummies:

$$E(y_1|y_0,z)=g(y_0,z) \qquad (7.3)$$

In this case, for a sufficiently small bandwidth, kernel estimation of $g(.)$ is equivalent to computing separate non-parametric regressions of y_1 on y_0 in each of the cells of the sample cross-classification defined by the dummies z. When there is a very large number of cells defined by the partition z, within-cell sample sizes will be small and thus the separate cell-specific regressions subject to high degrees of sampling error. This type of model is the rule rather than the exception in micro-econometrics, so this is an important drawback. A second limitation of kernel techniques is that their performance deteriorates very rapidly as we increase the number of explanatory variables. Again, high dimensionality tends to be a feature of micro-econometrics.

An intermediate approach is semi-parametric: we specify the statistical problem in such a way that it involves both non-parametric and parametric elements. In the previous regression example, this might amount to the following specification:

$$E(y_1|y_0,z)=g(y_0,z'\gamma) \qquad (7.4)$$

leading to the problem of estimating the unknown bivariate function $g(.)$ and unknown vector γ. This has two obvious advantages over (2): the dimension of $g(.)$ is reduced and the linear form $z'\gamma$ is continuously-variable if z contains a continuous variable, and usually moves us much closer to continuous variability even if z is entirely discrete.

In practice there is no clear dividing line between the semi-parametric approach and a suitably general parametric approach. In the former, we treat the degree of flexibility of the functional forms essentially as something to be estimated automatically from the data, while in the latter we treat it formally as fixed *a priori*, but in practice usually determine it by means of *ad hoc* model selection criteria (such as a score test for mis-specification, or a likelihood-based criterion like that of Akaike). It is interesting to note that Gallant and Nychka (1987) proposed a technique based on a particular series-expansion as a semi-parametric method, with the order of the expansion treated as a quantity increasing with the sample size according to a pre-defined rule, whereas Gabler *et al.* (1993) implemented it as a fully parametric technique with the order of the expansion fixed at a level suggested by model selection criteria. One could regard the latter approach as a formal adaptive version of the former, in which case its statistical properties could in principle be derived. In the hands of an intelligent applied statistician, there may in any case be little to choose between the two interpretations.

The presence of firm death in the process complicates matters significantly, since it divides the sample into two separate regimes. Rather than estimate the distribution of $\{y_1,\zeta|y_0,z\}$ directly, we break it down into separate components which can be more easily estimated in a robust way using simple semi-parametric estimators. Consider the joint probability density/mass function $f(y_0,y_1,\zeta|z)$, which has two components. Each component can be decomposed as follows:

Dying firms

$$f(\zeta=1|y_0,z)=\frac{f(y_0|\zeta=1,z)\,f(\zeta=1|z)}{f(y_0|z)} \tag{7.5}$$

Surviving firms

$$f(y_1,\zeta=0|y_0,z)=f(y_1|y_0,\zeta=0,z)(1-f(\zeta=1|y_0,z))$$
$$=f(y_1|y_0,\zeta=0,z)\left[\frac{f(y_0|\zeta=0,z)\,(1-f(\zeta=1|z))}{f(y_0|z)}\right] \tag{7.6}$$

where we use the symbol f as generic notation for any pdf. The expressions (7.5) and (7.6) are particularly convenient for applied work, since the components on the right-hand sides appear in forms that are relatively easy to estimate using semi-parametric methods.

Note that our objective here is only to estimate as flexibly as possible a conditional distribution. There is a further question, not addressed in this study, concerning the structural significance that can be attributed to such a distribution. It is well known, for example, that a dynamic model containing firm-specific random or fixed effects will be inconsistently estimated by simple regressions, either on a full panel or a simple cross-section (see Nickell, 1981; Arellano and Bond, 1991; Pesaran and Smith, 1992). This is an issue concerning the estimation of distributions conditional not only on y_0,z, but also the unobservable effects. It does not affect our ability to estimate the purely observable distribution (5)–(6), which may be attributed a descriptive rather than structural role. Our aim here is not to construct a model that is structural in any sense, but to focus on other possible biases that might stem from the use of conventional linear regression and probit models, rather than more flexible forms.

7.3 Estimation techniques

There are four separate components of the distribution (7.5)–(7.6). The probability $f(\zeta=1|z)$ is a binary response function of the sort which is conventionally estimated using maximum likelihood probit or logit analysis. The pdfs $f(y_0|z)$ and $f(y_0|\zeta=1,z)$ can be thought of as (not necessarily normal or linear) regressions of y_0 on z in the full population and the subpopulation of dying firms respectively. The conditional distribution $f(y_1|y_0,\zeta=0,z)$ is again a regression relationship, this time defined on the population of surviving firms, but involving both y_0 and z as conditioning variables. We consider three separate estimation approaches for these three classes of relationship.

7.3.1 Binary response models

There is now a long list of available semi-parametric estimators for the simple binary response model, although relatively few applications of them as yet. Table 7.1 lists some of the semi-parametric estimators that have been proposed in the econometrics literature. There is a standard interpretation of the binary response model involving the specification of a latent indicator which generates a positive response by crossing a (zero) threshold. Thus:

$$\zeta=\mathbb{I}(z'\beta+\upsilon>0) \tag{7.7}$$

where β is a fixed parameter vector (subject to an arbitrary normalisation); $\mathbb{I}(A)$ is the indicator function, equal to 1 if the event A is true and 0 otherwise; and υ is an unobservable satisfying $E(\upsilon|z)=0$ (or some analogous location restriction). Note that the distributional form of υ and the scedasticity function $\text{var}(\upsilon|z)$ are left unspecified.

An alternative model is the following direct specification for the response probability:

$$f(\zeta=1|z)=G(z'\beta) \tag{7.8}$$

where $G(.)$ is an arbitrary non-negative function. This model is equivalent to the latent variable model only under special assumptions. For instance, when υ and z are independent and heteroscedasticity is ruled out, then $G(.)$ is the common cdf of $-\upsilon$ whatever value of z we choose to condition on. If

Table 7.1. *Estimation methods for the binary response model*

Technique	Reference	Comments
Maximum score estimator (MSCORE)	Manski (1975)	Estimator of scaled coefficients of latent regression only; no homoscedasticity; unknown limiting distribution; convergence at rate slower than $\sqrt{n}$
Smoothed MSCORE	Horowitz (1992)	Estimator of scaled coefficients of latent regression only; no assumption of homoscedasticity; convergence at rate $\sqrt{n}$ to normal limiting distribution; asymptotically efficient in the absence of further assumptions
Semi-parametric maximum likelihood	Cosslett (1983)	Estimator of β and $G(.)$; assumes homoscedasticity ($\sigma(z)=\sigma$); convergence at rate $\sqrt{n}$ to normal limiting distribution; asymptotically efficient under homoscedasticity
Empirical likelihood	Klein and Spady (1993)	Estimator of β and $G(.)$; assumes homoscedasticity; convergence at rate $\sqrt{n}$ to normal limiting distribution; asymptotically efficient under homoscedasticity
Maximum rank	Han (1987)	Estimator of β only; no assumption of homoscedasticity; convergence at rate $\sqrt{n}$ to normal limiting distribution

there is heteroscedasticity in the latent variable model then the scedasticity function is $\mathrm{var}(\upsilon|z)=\sigma^2(z)$ and:

$$f(\zeta=1|z)=G\left(\frac{z'\beta}{\sigma(z)}\right) \tag{7.9}$$

where $G(.)$ is now the cdf of $-\upsilon/\sigma(z)$. Thus (7.8) is not generally valid as a representation of (7.7) unless σ happens to be a function of the same linear form $z'\beta$ as appears in the latent indicator. Even in that case, the resulting function of $z'\beta$ that gives the response probability will not necessarily have the properties of a cdf, as is assumed in probit or logit analysis. Note that it is not always possible to express the model (7.8) in the form of a hetero-scedastic latent indicator model (7.9), since the implied function $\sigma(z)$ may not exist or may be negative.

The estimators detailed in Table 7.1 are all based on the optimisation of some objective function. Specifically:

MSCORE

$$\hat{\beta}=\arg\max_{\beta}\sum_{i=1}^{n}(2\mathbb{I}(\zeta_i=1)-1)\mathbb{I}(z_i'\beta\geq0) \qquad (7.10)$$

Smoothed MSCORE

$$\hat{\beta}=\arg\max_{\beta}\sum_{i=1}^{n}(2\mathbb{I}(\zeta_i=1)-1)\Phi\!\left(\frac{z_i'\beta}{\mu_n}\right) \qquad (7.11)$$

Semi-parametric ML

$$\hat{\beta}=\arg\max_{\beta}\left(\max_{G(.)}\sum_{i=1}^{n}\Big(\zeta_i\ln G(z_i'\beta)+(1-\zeta_i)\ln\big(1-G(z_i'\beta)\big)\Big)\right) \qquad (7.12)$$

Klein–Spady

$$\hat{\beta}=\arg\max_{\beta}\left(\max_{G(.)}\sum_{i=1}^{n}\Big(\zeta_i\ln\hat{G}(z_i'\beta)+(1-\zeta_i)\ln\big(1-\hat{G}(z_i'\beta)\big)\Big)\right) \qquad (7.13)$$

Maximum rank correlation

$$\hat{\beta}=\arg\max_{\beta}\sum_{i=1}^{n}\sum_{j<i}\Big(\mathbb{I}(\zeta_i>\zeta_j)\mathbb{I}(z_i'\beta>z_j'\beta)+\mathbb{I}(\zeta_i<\zeta_j)\mathbb{I}(z_i'\beta<z_j'\beta)\Big) \qquad (7.14)$$

In these expressions, μ_n is a bandwidth sequence, $\Phi(.)$ is the normal cdf, and $\hat{G}(.)$ is a non-parametric kernel regression of ζ on $z'\beta$.

7.3.2 Regressions on z

The most general form of semi-parametric regression would involve the following conditional expectation function:

$$E(y_0|z)=g(z'\beta) \qquad (7.15)$$

where $g(.)$ is some unknown function and β is again a normalised parameter vector.[2] Models of this kind are not easy to estimate. If there is a continuously-distributed variable in the z vector, then an appealing approach is to use the following kernel least-squares estimator. For any given value β, we compute the non-parametric kernel regression of y_0 on the constructed index variable $z'\beta$ and evaluate the residual sum of squares. An optimisation algorithm is then used to minimise the residual sum of squares with respect to β. Thus:

$$\hat{\beta}=\arg\max_{\beta} \sum_{i=1}^{n}\left(y_{0i}-\hat{g}(z_i'\beta)\right)^2 \tag{7.16}$$

where $\hat{g}(.)$ is the non-parametric regression of y_0 on $z'\beta$.

7.3.3 Regressions on y_0 and z

Ideally, one would like to estimate the distribution $f(y_1|y_0,\zeta=0,z)$ by fitting a very flexible model of the following form:

$$E(y_1|y_0,\zeta=0,z)=g(y_0,z'\beta) \tag{7.17}$$

where $g(.,.)$ is an unknown function and β is a (normalised) parameter vector. This specification suggests a least-squares estimator that minimises the following criterion:

$$\hat{\beta}=\arg\max_{\beta} \sum_{i=1}^{n}\left(y_{1i}-\hat{g}(y_0,z_i'\beta)\right)^2 \tag{7.18}$$

In the application discussed below, we simplify this procedure still further by introducing an additivity assumption so that the model becomes:

$$E(y_1|y_0,z)=g(y_0)+z'\beta \tag{7.19}$$

The reason for this is that trivariate kernel regression produces estimates that converge at a slower rate than bivariate kernel regression ($O_p(n^{-1/3})$ rather than $O_p(n^{-2/5})$), so that if the additivity assumption is valid the properties of the estimator should be considerably improved.

Least-squares estimation of this type of model is equivalent to the estimator discussed by Robinson (1988) (see also Härdle, 1990, section 9.1). The additive semi-parametric regression estimator can be motivated by an analogue of the formulae for partitioned linear regression, where:

$$\hat{\beta}=(\hat{Z}'\hat{Z})^{-1}\hat{Z}'\hat{y}_1 \tag{7.20}$$

$$\hat{g}=P(y_1-Z\hat{\beta}) \tag{7.21}$$

where Z, X and y are data matrices, $\hat{Z}=Z-PZ$ and $\hat{y}=y-Py$ are the residuals from regressions of Z and y_1 on y_0 and P is the projection matrix

$y_0(y_0'y_0)^{-1}y_0'$. In the semi-parametric case, the transformation P is replaced by a kernel smoother, P^*, with i,j th element:

$$p_{ij}^* = \frac{k\left(\frac{(z_i - z_j)'\beta}{\lambda_j}\right)}{\sum\limits_{r=1}^{n} k\left(\frac{(z_i - z_r)'\beta}{\lambda_j}\right)} \qquad (7.22)$$

Experimentation has revealed little need in this case for the use of a trimming function, as suggested by Robinson (1988), to eliminate the influence of observations with small estimated x-densities.

7.4 Data

Our estimates make use of a dataset prepared at the ESRC Centre for Business Research, Cambridge. The dataset is based on a size-stratified sample of UK companies whose computerised accounts for the years 1976–1982, prepared by the Business Statistics Office, Newport, were available *via* the ESRC Data Archive at the University of Essex. We describe the salient features of this sample and the way in which we have checked and augmented it for the analysis reported here (and for the analysis in companion papers dealing with the economics of company failure and acquisition activity (Cosh and Hughes, 1994a, 1995; Cosh, Hughes and Kambhampati, 1993)). This has involved, *inter alia*, the analysis of the microfiche records of several hundreds of individual company records obtained from Companies House, London and Cardiff to trace the fate of companies leaving the sample in the course of the sample period; to augment the accounting records of sample companies with details of company age; to obtain information on the characteristics of directors; and to extract accounting data for acquired companies in the aftermath of acquisition. The first two of these data augmentation exercises are directly relevant to this paper.

7.4.1 The Business Statistics Office sample

The sample of companies whose accounts form the basis of our analysis is one of a number of samples which have been constructed by the Board of Trade and successor government departments in the aftermath of the 1948 Companies Act to assist in the National Accounts analysis of company profitability and finance. Summary statistics relating to these samples have appeared regularly in *Business Monitor MA3 – Company Finance* and its predecessor publications. Until the late 1970s the analysis was based on a panel of the largest (primarily quoted) companies which was periodically rebased to exclude companies falling below certain size criteria and to include companies newly rising above them (Lewis, 1979). This exclusion of smaller companies was then rectified by the construction of a size-stratified sample of around 3000 independent industrial and commercial companies drawn from the official list of all companies registered in Great Britain in 1975. This sample, which we have used as the basis for our work, consisted of the largest 500 companies, a sample of 1 in 2 of the next 1000 largest, a sample of 1 in 70 of 'medium'-sized companies, and a 1 in 360 sample of the remainder. This sample was in turn replaced, in the mid 1980s, by a further sample of around 3000 companies, again based on the Companies House Register, but including the top 2000 companies in 1981 and a 1 in 300 sample of the remainder. After minor adjustment to the larger companies component of this sample in 1985 there was a major rebasing in 1990 to ensure the inclusion of the largest 2000 companies of 1987.

Of these three potential sources of company data, the first contains very few small and medium-sized companies and covers a relatively distant historical time period. Of the other two, the third and most recent sample appears, at first, to offer a number of potential advantages. First, compared to both the other samples, it is the most comprehensive in its treatment of births and deaths. This is partly because of improvements in the management of the underlying records system at Companies House. It has been estimated that, in the face of chronic failure to submit accounts on time and pressures arising from keeping pace with the high rates of business registration of the late 1970s and early 1980s, the Companies Registers contained accounts for less than half of all companies which should have been filing by 1984/85 (Knight, 1987). On the other hand the increasing use by small and medium-sized companies of dispensation to submit modified accounts has greatly reduced the range of data available for small and medium-sized companies. The analysis in this paper focuses therefore on the stratified sample drawn in 1975.

For each of these sampled companies, our accounting data are available in principle from 1976 to 1982 or until their exclusion from the panel before 1982. In addition to accounting data, each company in the panel has a number of indicators, including indicators of 'death' either by acquisition, liquidation or other cause. For the purpose of this paper we excluded 168 property companies because of accounting inconsistencies with other industrial and commercial companies in terms of asset valuation. Companies with total assets of less than £50,000 were also excluded from our analysis of growth because of the high incidence of missing data and inconsistent asset records in this size class. The final sample for growth

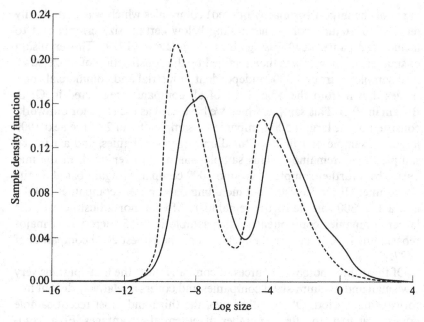

Figure 7.1 Distributions of 1976 and 1982 firm size
In £billion asset value
--- = 1976
— = 1982

analysis consists of 2142 companies of which 527 'died' between 1976 and 1982, and 1615 were 'alive' in both these years.

In the analysis which follows we use total assets as our measure of size (S); this is because sales figures are not universally available and the relatively high ratio of current liabilities to total assets amongst small companies made net assets an inappropriate measure of size for a small but significant portion of our sample.

Figure 7.1 shows a non-parametric kernel estimate of the initial size distribution (in log form). This reveals a very strongly bimodal distribution, reflecting the non-uniform sampling scheme used originally by the Board of Trade. The strong rightwards shift in the distribution between 1976 and 1982 is the result of both company growth in real terms and inflation, since assets are valued in nominal historic cost terms. Figure 7.2 shows a similar non-parametric estimate of the distribution of log age in 1976. Possibly as a result of the non-uniform sampling, there are multiple modes at 6, 16 and 43 years.

Table 7.2 provides a summary of the dynamics of growth and company 'death' in our sample, in the form of a matrix cross-classifying companies

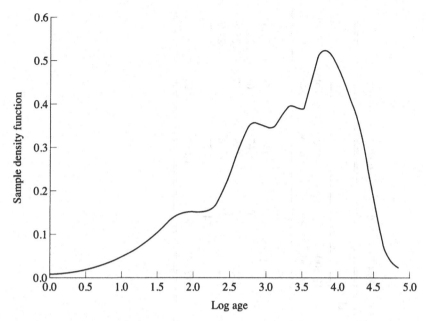

Figure 7.2 Distribution of firm age

by opening and closing total asset size class. Inflation creates a tendency for cell frequencies to be higher to the right of the main diagonal. The matrix nevertheless reveals a clear clustering of firms along the diagonal. Most firms therefore remain in their opening size class (in the case of largest size class only demotions are of course possible). There is a handful of cases of extremely rapid growth, with five companies, for instance, whose 1976 total assets fell in the £100,000–£500,000 range, increasing in size to over £2.5m by 1982. The matrix also reveals a tendency for death rates to fall once the £2.5m size boundary is crossed. For the largest size class the failure rate is approximately one half of that in the three smallest size classes. A separate analysis (Cosh and Hughes, 1994a, 1995) shows that the higher death rate of the smallest size classes is primarily due to liquidation and bankruptcy, since merger deaths are relatively less significant for them than for the middle-sized companies.

The pattern of variations in growth rates of the surviving companies by total asset size class in 1976 is shown in Table 7.3. In addition to the mean and median of growth rates for all survivors and for each of our 6 size classes, this table also reports measures of dispersion, skewness and kurtosis. Table 7.4 reports a matrix summarising tests of significance of differences in mean and median survivor growth rates across all pairs of size

Table 7.2. The distribution of sample companies cross-classified by opening and closing size, survival and death

1976 size class	Total	1982 size class							Total survivors	Total deaths	Death rate %
		<50	50–100	100–500	500–2,500	2,500–12,500	12,500–62,500	>62,500			
50–100	305	21	58	132	7	0	0	0	218	87	28.5
100–500	616	3	10	249	182	4	0	0	448	168	27.3
500–2,500	235	0	0	5	124	36	2	0	167	68	28.9
2,500–12,500	256	0	0	0	4	59	124	2	189	67	26.2
12,500–62,500	431	0	0	0	2	6	214	114	336	95	22.0
62,500–	299	0	0	0	1	0	9	247	257	42	14.1
TOTAL	2,142	24	68	386	320	105	349	363	1,615	527	24.6

Note:
* Size is measured in £000s.

Table 7.3. *Mean growth rates by size of company: survivors only*

	Whole	50–100	100–500	500–2,500	2,500–12,500	12,500–62,500	>62,500
No. of survivors	1,615	218	448	167	189	336	257
percentage points over 1976–1982							
Mean	121	139	142	130	114	99	100
Median	286	76	96	84	91	80	81
St. dev.	170	233	189	231	131	103	107
Kurtosis	4,715	1,722	2,688	7,081	1,014	402	535

Note:
* Size groups measured by total assets in 1976 (size £000).

Table 7.4. *Significance tests of differences in mean and median growth rates*

Size (£000s)	100–500	500–2,500	2,500–12,500	12,500–62,500	>62,500
50–100	−	+	+	+++	+++
	− −	−	−	−	−
100–500		+	+++	+++	+++
		+	+	+	−
500–2,500			+	++	+
			−	+	+
2,500–12,500				+	+
				+	+
12,500–62,500					−
					−

Notes:
+ row av. > column av.; ++ sig. at the 10% level; +++ sig. at the 5% level;
− row av. < column av.; − −sig. at the 10% level.
Upper entry in each cell is the test of means and the lower entry is the test of medians.

classes. This analysis reveals that the smallest three size classes have much greater variance of growth rates than the three largest. It also shows that the distribution of growth rates is positively skewed especially in the smaller size classes, and that the median is therefore a more appropriate measure of central density than the mean. The analysis of differences in means across size classes suggests that the smallest two size classes have significantly higher growth rates than the two largest size classes. In addition, it shows that size class 2 has a higher mean growth rate than size class 4, and that a similar though less significant result applies in a comparison of size class 4 against size class 5. However, none of these results is significant when we compare median growth rates. In fact, only one significant difference emerges, and that is the superior median growth rate at the lower end of size distribution where size 2 compares favourably with size class 1.

7.5 Parametric estimation results

7.5.1 Linear regression and probit

Conventional estimation of relationships like those embodied in the distribution defined by equations (7.5) and (7.6) above is based on linear regression and probit analysis. The first four columns of Table 7.5 give the results of applying these methods. The first column gives the regression of y_1 on y_0 and z, using the sample of surviving firms. The coefficient of y_0 is not significantly different from unity, implying that, in this conditional sense, Gibrat's Law cannot be rejected. Growth is negatively related to the age of the firm, and there are significant industry effects, with industries 2 and 4 (miscellaneous manufacturing and services) tending to grow faster over the period. The degree of fit is extremely high for a cross-section relation, with an R^2 of 0.95.

A conventional approach to testing the validity of a cross-section regression model like this is to use Ramsey's RESET test (Ramsey, 1969), which involves using the square of the fitted value as an additional regressor and testing its relevance using a t-test (in this case used in its asymptotic χ^2 form). The low value of the RESET test statistic indicates no evidence of mis-specification of functional form. Heteroscedasticity is part of the maintained hypothesis underlying the RESET test, and we investigate this using a score test of the null hypothesis of homoscedasticity, which involves essentially a regression of the squared residual on the square of the fitted value with an intercept. The score test then amounts to a t-test on the slope coefficient (again presented in asymptotic χ^2 form here). Once more there is no significant evidence of heteroscedasticity, so this conditional growth regression appears to conform to the assumptions of classical linear regression in these two important respects.

Columns 2 and 3 of Table 7.5 give the regressions of initial size, y_0, on log age and the industry dummies, for the full sample and the sub-set of dying firms respectively. Age has a strong positive effect, with an elasticity of 1.0 or greater. Relative to the norm, industries 1 and 2 (engineering and manufacturing) tend significantly towards large firm sizes and industry 3

Table 7.5. *Parametric estimation results (standard errors in parentheses)*

Covariate	Linear regression/probit				Selectivity model	
	y_1^a	y_0^b	y_0^c	Pr(death)^b	y_1^a	Pr(death)^b
Constant	0.772	3.139	3.810	−0.365	0.766	−0.216
	(0.067)	(0.210)	(0.366)	(0.115)	(2.154)	(0.122)
y_0	0.991	—	—	—	0.991	−0.045
	(0.007)				(0.067)	(0.012)
Log(age)	−0.052	1.310	1.040	−0.122	−0.052	−0.067
	(0.020)	(0.063)	(0.112)	(0.032)	(0.111)	(0.0036)
Industry 1	0.035	0.873	0.658	0.069	0.035	0.107
	(0.051)	(0.173)	(0.325)	(0.095)	(0.170)	(0.096)
Industry 2	0.113	1.043	0.737	0.089	0.112	0.136
	(0.048)	(0.161)	(0.313)	(0.089)	(0.206)	(0.091)
Industry 3	0.054	−0.306	−0.232	0.110	0.055	0.097
	(0.051)	(0.168)	(0.317)	(0.095)	(0.159)	(0.095)
Industry 4	0.185	−0.079	−0.545	0.007	0.184	0.0006
	(0.059)	(0.199)	(0.350)	(0.115)	(0.061)	(0.111)
Number of observations	1,615	2,142	527	2,142	2,142	2,142
σ	0.642	2.428	2.292	—	0.641	—
					(0.023)	
RESET test $\chi^2(1)$	0.067	115.88	22.468	2.792	—	3.580
LM heteroscedasticity $\chi^2(1)$	0.227	0.696	0.645	—	—	—
Selectivity correlation	—	—	—	—	0.014	—
					(5.224)	—
R^2	0.95	0.260	0.214	—	—	—

Notes:
^{a} Based on the sample of surviving firms only.
^{b} Based on the full sample.
^{c} Based on the sample of non-surviving firms.

(retailing etc.) tends towards small firms. The degree of fit is low, with R^2 below 0.3 in both cases: a result that simply confirms the heterogeneity of the stock of firms in existence at a given time. For these two regressions, conventional specification tests give a more negative verdict. The RESET test is highly significant, indicating that the distribution of initial firm size (whether conditioned on subsequent survival or not) has a nonlinear conditional mean function. There is no indication of heteroscedasticity, but the result of the test may be distorted by mis-specification of the mean.

The fourth column of Table 7.5 gives the results of fitting a probit model for the probability that the firm dies between 1976 and 1982. This probit has log age and the industry dummies as explanatory variables; firm size is excluded, so that the result is directly comparable with the semi-parametric estimates of the distribution $f(\zeta=1|z)$ appearing in equation (7.5). We find that the probability of death declines with the age of the firm, but that there are no significant industry effects. Again, we apply the RESET specification test, in the form of a score test for the irrelevance of an additional explanatory variable defined as $(z_i'\beta)^2$, and find a rather marginal result that causes some concern. The null hypothesis is rejected at the 10% significance level, but not at the more conventional 5% level.

Assuming homoscedasticity, we use these four parametric estimates in Section 2.7 below to construct an estimate of the distribution (7.5)–(7.6), as an alternative to the semi-parametric estimates presented in Section 7.6. Before turning to these, we consider the possible use of estimates 'corrected' for sample attrition.

7.5.2 Adjustments for attrition

The regression of y_1 on y_0 and z presented in the first column of Table 7.5 is conditioned on the event that the firm survives through the period 1976–82. There is a large literature in econometrics dealing with the problems of estimating a relationship (such as the size–growth relation) when there exists another correlated process (in this case company death) which randomly excludes individuals from the sampling procedure. Following the work of Heckman (1974) and Hausman and Wise (1979), maximum likelihood (ML) and 2-step parametric estimators are widely available for the following model:

$$y_1 = \beta_1 y_0 + z'\beta_2 + u \tag{7.23}$$

$$y_1 \text{ observed iff } \gamma_0 y_0 + z'\gamma + v > 0 \tag{7.24}$$

where u and v have a correlated bivariate normal distribution. Note that equation (7.24) specifies a linear probit model that is a direct specification of the conditional probability defined by equation (7.5) above. Thus the final column of Table 7.5 can be regarded as a conventional estimate of (7.5).

This selectivity model is widely used, and selectivity-corrected estimates of the firm size–growth relation have been published by Dunne and Hughes (1994). Although firm death can indeed be interpreted as a selection process, it is not obvious that the model (7.23)–(7.24) makes sense in this context. In plain language, (7.23) says that there is a simple relationship that governs the tendency of firms to grow through time, while the probit (7.24) states that there is another separate relationship determining whether or not a firm dies. An estimate of (7.23) thus amounts to a prediction of the rate of growth that a firm either actually achieves or (if it in fact dies) would have achieved. One might argue that this kind of prediction is very hard to interpret in any useful way. In some (but not all) cases,[3] the processes of growth and death are inseparable. Unsuccessful businesses may die because they encounter difficult periods when demand (and thus size) contracts. On this view, negative growth and death are simply two aspects of the same event, and it makes little sense to ask what would have happened to firm growth if the possibility of death had somehow been artificially removed.

Whether or not these reservations are accepted, the ML selectivity estimates appearing in the last two columns of Table 7.5 add little to the simple regression in the first column (see Dunne and Hughes (1994) for a similar result). The estimated correlation between u and v turns out to be very small, with a huge standard error, and consequently the selectivity-corrected firm size regression is virtually identical to the uncorrected regression. Essentially, the selectivity correlation is unidentifiable in this case (as in many other practical applications), and we pursue the approach no further.

7.6 Semi-parametric estimation results

As discussed in Section 7.3, we estimate four separate components of the distribution (7.5)–(7.6); the binary response function for ζ; regressions of y_0 on z for the whole sample and for dying firms; and a regression of y_1 on y_0 and z.

7.6.1 The model for probability of death

There are still very few published applications of semi-parametric estimators for the binary response model. In modelling the probability of a firm's death during the sample period, we initially considered three approaches: Horowitz's (1992) smoothed maximum score estimator; Ichimura's (1993) semi-parametric least-squares estimator applied to a regression of ζ on z; and Klein and Spady's (1993) empirical maximum likelihood estimator. We encountered serious problems in optimising the objective function for Horowitz's estimator, because of the existence of numerous local optima. Even the use of very good starting values in Monte Carlo experiments failed to achieve reliable convergence, and there is a clear need for robust global optimisation algorithms (such as the method of simulated anneal-

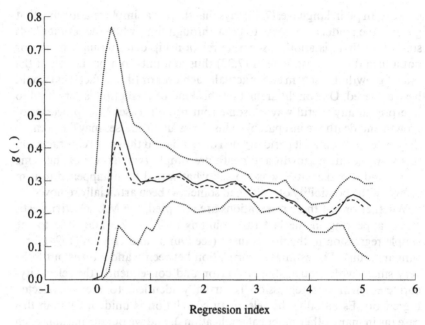

Figure 7.3 Klein–Spady estimation results
——=result from full sample
······=90% empirical confidence interval
---=mean of bootstrap

ing used by Horowitz, 1993) in computing this estimator. We finally opted
for the Klein–Spady estimator, which is asymptotically efficient under
fairly restrictive assumptions. However, Monte Carlo experiments suggest
that Ichimura's (inefficient) least-squares estimator performs nearly as well
in finite samples.

Figure 7.3 and Table 7.6 report the results of applying Klein and Spady's
estimator. When we normalise the coefficient of log age to be unity, the
estimate of the unknown function $G(.)$ in (7.8) turns out to be a decreasing
function of regression index $z'\beta$ for most of the range. Thus, as in parametric estimation, the probability of firm death is predicted to decline with
age. For comparison, we also include in Table 7.6 the coefficients from an
analogous probit model, rescaled so that the coefficient of log age is unity.
In the semi-parametric case, the second of the industry dummies produces
a significant effect, implying a lower inherent survival rate for firms in the
non-engineering sectors of manufacturing industry. In contrast, the corresponding linear probit estimate is not statistically significant.

Table 7.6. *Klein–Spady estimation results (standard errors from 40 bootstrap replications)*

Covariate	Coefficient	Standard error	Normalised linear probit*
Log(age)	1.000	—	1.000
Industry 1	−0.005	0.230	−0.566
Industry 2	0.566	0.219	−0.730
Industry 3	0.074	0.156	−0.092
Industry 4	−0.004	0.154	−0.057

Note:
* Coefficients from Table 5; each coefficient divided by that of log(age).

7.6.2 Regressions of y_0 on z

We estimate the regression of y_0 on z, $g(z'\beta)$, using Ichimura's (1993) semi-parametric least-squares estimator first for the whole sample. The results are presented in Figure 7.4(a) and Table 7.7. The estimates of the unknown function $g(.)$ turn out to be nearly convex and increasing over most of the range of $z'\beta$. The 90% bootstrap confidence interval suggests that $g(.)$ is estimated with good precision and is significantly non-linear. The implied age–initial size relation (after controlling for industry effects) appears predominantly positive, as in the linear regression of Table 7.5. There are three significant industry effects, with industries 1 (metal/engineering) and 2 (miscellaneous manufacturing) characterised by larger firm sizes and industry 3 (retailing etc.) by smaller firm sizes. Again, this conclusion is qualitatively similar to that of the linear regression, but the relative effects of age and industry are quite different. In Table 7.5, the ratios of the coefficients of industry dummies to that of log age are more than double the comparable semi-parametric coefficients in Table 7.7. The fit as measured by R^2 is also considerably improved. Thus semi-parametric estimation does appear to offer a real improvement in flexibility over linear regression here.

In addition to the regression function itself, we have also estimated a scedasticity function by computing a similar semi-parametric regression, using the squared residual as a dependent variable. This procedure estimates the following function:

$$var(y_0|z) = \psi(z'\gamma) \qquad (7.25)$$

The estimate of $\psi(.)$ is plotted in Figure 7.4(b) and the bootstrap confidence intervals suggest that there is no significant variation in the residual

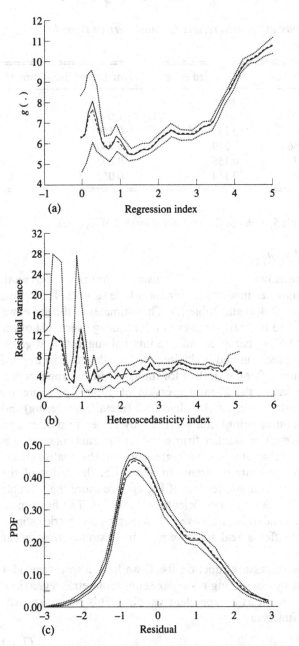

Figure 7.4 Full-sample semi-parametric regression for initial firm size
——— = regression with full sample
········· = 90% confidence interval
--- = bootstrap mean

Table 7.7. *Semi-parametric regression results for full sample (standard errors computed from 40 bootstrap replications)*

Covariate	Regression (dependent variable=log initial size)		Scedasticity (dependent variable=squared residual)	
	Coefficient	Standard error	Coefficient	Standard error
Log(age)	1.000	—	1.000	—
Industry 1	0.239	0.084	0.338	0.206
Industry 2	0.359	0.064	0.194	0.144
Industry 3	−0.114	0.061	0.635	0.374
Industry 4	−0.060	0.079	0.661	0.374
R^2	0.318		0.021	

variance. The low R^2 and insignificant coefficients in the estimate of γ also confirm this. Finally, Figure 7.4(c) plots a kernel estimate of the density function of the regression residual. There is rather strong evidence of positive skewness in the distribution.

Figure 7.5 and Table 7.8 show the results of an analogous semi-parametric regression for initial size in the sub-sample of firms which are observed to die before the end of the observation period. The results are similar, with strong evidence for an increasing and mildly convex relationship. Industry effects are less clear, with only industry 2 (miscellaneous manufacturing) implying a strongly significant increase in size relative to other industries. Again, the semi-parametric regression yields a much better fit than the linear regression in Table 7.5, and also estimated industry effects that are much smaller relative to the age effect.

The evidence on heteroscedasticity is quite mixed in this case. There is some evidence for a lower residual variance for firms near the bottom of the estimated range of values of $z'\gamma$, and the coefficient estimates suggest that this is linked to age and industries 2 (miscellaneous manufacturing) and 3 (retailing, etc). However, the R^2 is low, and heteroscedasticity is not a striking feature of the model.

7.6.3 Regression of y_1 on y_0 and z

The final element required for construction of the joint distribution (7.5)–(7.6) is the density of y_1 conditional on y_0 and z. We estimate this first by using the additive semi-parametric regression estimator described in sub-section 7.3.3 above. The results are reported in Figure 7.6 and Table 7.9. They turn out to be very similar to the ordinary linear regression estimates of Table 7.5. The estimate of the function $g(.)$ is shown in Figure 7.6(a); it is close to linear, with a gradient slightly less than one. To illustrate the implications more clearly, we plot in Figure 7.6(c) the function $g(y_0)-y_0$. Using the pointwise bootstrap confidence intervals as a guide to statistical significance, there is some evidence of a tendency for relatively rapid growth among small firms (with asset values of £0.05m–£0.15m) and also among medium-large firms (asset values in the range £3m–£13m). This is a form of non-linearity that would be difficult to capture using conventional parametric specifications, although the departure from linearity is admittedly not large. This finding is reflected in the fact that R^2 is almost identical for the parametric and semi-parametric regressions.

Turning to the coefficient estimates in Table 7.9, we find very similar estimates to the regression coefficients in Table 7.5, although with slightly larger standard errors, as one would expect. Growth is found to slow with the age of the firm and to be significantly faster than the norm in indus-

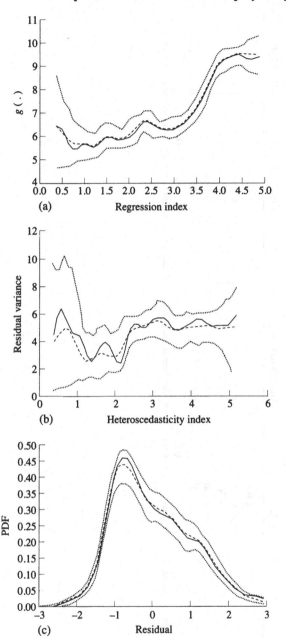

Figure 7.5 Dying firms: semi-parametric regression for initial size
    ——=sample regression
    ······=90% confidence interval
    ---=bootstrap mean

Table 7.8. Semi-parametric regression results for sub-sample of dying firms (standard errors computed from 40 bootstrap replications)

Covariate	Regression (dependent variable=log initial size)		Scedasticity (dependent variable=squared residual)	
	Coefficient	Standard error	Coefficient	Standard error
Log(age)	1.000	—	1.000	—
Industry 1	0.105	0.103	−0.303	0.199
Industry 2	0.365	0.132	0.700	0.263
Industry 3	−0.140	0.116	0.485	0.231
Industry 4	−0.327	0.182	−0.286	0.177
R^2	0.276		0.034	

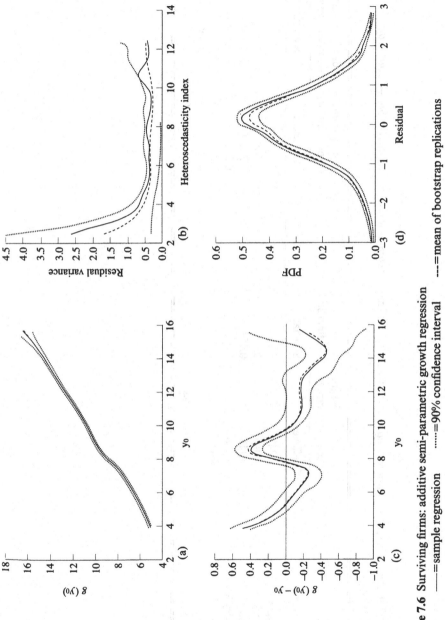

Figure 7.6 Surviving firms: additive semi-parametric growth regression
— = sample regression   ····· = 90% confidence interval   --- = mean of bootstrap replications

Table 7.9. *Additive semi-parametric least squares estimation results (standard errors computed from 40 bootstrap replications)*

Covariate	Regression (dependent variable = log final size)		Semi-parametric scedasticity function (dependent variable = squared residual)	
	Coefficient	Standard error	Coefficient	Standard error
Log(age)	−0.047	0.021	1	–
Industry 1	0.046	0.052	0.265	0.237
Industry 2	0.118	0.053	0.285	0.457
Industry 3	0.056	0.056	0.270	0.444
Industry 4	0.188	0.070	0.380	0.326
Log(y_0)	–	–	0.900	2.000
R^2	0.949		0.014	

tries 1, 2 and 4 (engineering, etc., miscellaneous manufacturing, and services).

We have chosen to investigate the role of heteroscedasticity through the following model:

$$var(y_1|y_0,z)=\psi(z'\gamma+\gamma_0 y_0)$$ (7.26)

with the first element of the vector γ normalised to unity. The function ψ and the parameters γ and γ_0 are then estimated by Ichimura's semi-parametric least-squares regression technique. There is in fact no significant evidence of heteroscedasticity. The estimated function $\psi(.)$, plotted in Figure 7.6(b) together with the pointwise bootstrap confidence interval, shows no significant departure from a constant value. The estimated coefficients presented in Table 7.9 have very large standard errors, and, indeed, are unidentifiable if the true function $\psi(.)$ is invariant. The distribution of the standardised residuals plotted in Figure 7.6(d) is close to the normal.

7.7 The implied distribution of firm growth

The estimates presented above provide three alternative ways of constructing the joint distribution of firm size and death. This mixed discrete/continuous distribution is as follows:

$$f(\zeta=1|y_0,z)=\frac{f(y_0|\zeta=1,z)\,f(\zeta=1|z)}{f(y_0|z)}$$ (7.27)

$$f(y_1,\zeta=0|y_0,z)=f(y_1|y_0,\zeta=0,z)(1-f(\zeta=1|y_0,z))$$ (7.28)

The three possibilities are:

  (i) Estimate the three components of the right-hand side of (7.27) using the static normal-linear regressions and probit in columns 2–4 of Table 7.5 and the first component of the right-hand side of (7.28) using the regression in column 1 of Table 7.5.
 (ii) As (i), except that the left-hand side of (7.27) is estimated directly, using the probit model in column 6 of Table 7.5.
(iii) All components of the right-hand side of (7.27) and the first component of (7.28) are estimated semi-parametrically.

The three approaches entail an increasing degree of flexibility. Approach (i) constructs the distribution from a linear probit and a linear regression. Thus the estimated distribution depends on only two parameter vectors, estimated within the linear-homoscedastic-normal framework. Approach (ii) maintains the assumptions of linearity, homoscedasticity and normality, but introduces further flexibility through the decomposition of (7.27) into three components. Thus the estimated distribution involves four separately-estimated parameter vectors. Approach (iii) takes this a step further by relaxing the linearity, normality and homoscedasticity assumptions by means of semi-parametric techniques. The three resulting estimates are plotted in Figures 7.7–7.9 below. The two parts of the distribution (7.27)–(7.28) are plotted separately. Expression (7.27) is plotted for each of the five industrial sectors, holding log age constant at the sample mean. Expression (7.28) is plotted as a three-dimensional surface, with the four industry dummies set to zero and log age set to its sample mean.

The main drawback of the conventional linear regression-probit approach is clearly in the modelling of firm death. Probit estimation imposes a smooth monotonic relationship between the probability of death and initial size, with variations in the other explanatory variables producing moderate near-parallel shifts in the relationship. In Figure 7.8, some flexibility is introduced through the decomposition (7.27), and this allows non-parallel shifts in response to the explanatory variables. Thus, industry 4 is estimated to have a quite different schedule of size-specific mortality rates to industry 5. Taking this flexibility still further using the semi-parametric approach, Figure 7.9(a) suggests the existence of both heterogeneity across industries and non-monotonicity with respect to size. Indeed, using these more flexible methods, there appears to be little evidence of any simple relationship between firm mortality and size.

In contrast, conventional linear regression seems to describe the growth component of the distribution (expression (7.28)) pretty well. There is remarkably little difference between the plots in Figures 7.7(b) and 7.9(b), and the evidence of non-linearity in the conditional distribution of growth on size is confined to the level of fine detail apparent in the semi-parametric regression results presented in Figure 7.6(c) discussed above. Of course, this result may be partly an artefact of the remaining assumptions that have not been relaxed here. For example, the additivity assumption imposed on the semi-parametric size–growth regression (7.19) greatly reduces the formidable computing burden of these methods and improves statistical precision, but it also rules out possibly important interactions between size and age or industry.

7.8 Conclusions

Conventional assumptions of linearity, homoscedasticity and normality play important roles in applied econometric analyses of the process of firm evolution and mortality. In this study, we have attempted to investigate the validity of these assumptions in a simple exercise aimed at the estimation

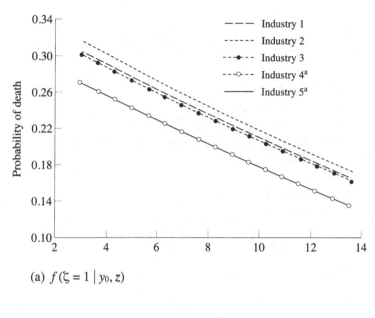

(a) $f(\zeta = 1 \mid y_0, z)$

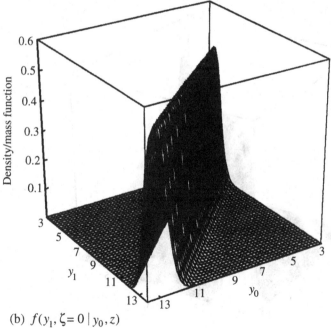

(b) $f(y_1, \zeta = 0 \mid y_0, z)$

Figure 7.7 Linear-homoscedastic-normal model: $f(\zeta = 1 \mid y_0, z)$ estimated directly
Note: [a]The lines representing Industries 4 and 5 are indistinguishable.

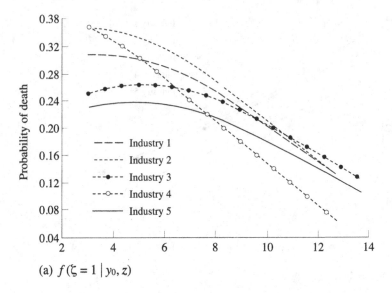

(a) $f(\zeta = 1 \mid y_0, z)$

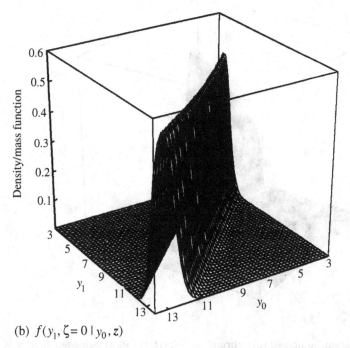

(b) $f(y_1, \zeta = 0 \mid y_0, z)$

Figure 7.8 Linear-homoscedastic-normal model: $f(\zeta=1 \mid y_0, z)$ estimated indirectly

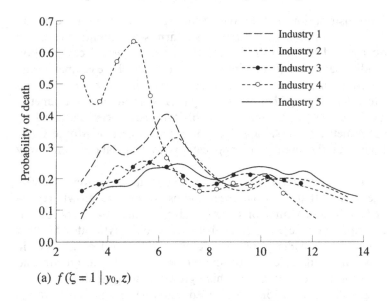

(a) $f(\zeta = 1 \mid y_0, z)$

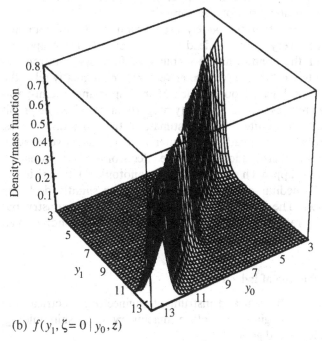

(b) $f(y_1, \zeta = 0 \mid y_0, z)$

Figure 7.9 Semi-parametric model: $f(\zeta = 1 \mid y_0, z)$ estimated indirectly

of the joint distribution of a discrete event (firm death within the period 1976–82) and a continuous outcome (1982 firm size) conditional on the 1976 size, age and sector of the firm. Our approach uses a decomposition of the conditional mortality rate into components which we estimate using kernel-based semi-parametric generalisations of linear regression and probit techniques, together with a partially-linear semi-parametric size–growth regression. Estimators of this type have been discussed by many econometric theorists and have been the subject of Monte Carlo simulations, but the number of applications to real data remains very small.

Applying this approach to a cross-section of companies covering a wide size range, we find that the usual linear homoscedastic size–growth regression fitted to the sub-sample of survivors gives a reasonably good broad-brush description of the conditional distribution of growth rates, but that there is significant evidence of nonlinearity at the level of fine detail. Overall, we find little evidence of any relationship between growth and size, except for a tendency towards high growth among small firms (with asset values £0.05m–£0.15m) and medium-large firms (asset values (£3m–£13m). However, these non-linearities, although apparently statistically significant, are far too fine to be detected by conventional specifications involving quadratic terms or size dummies.

In contrast, we find that the widely used probit model of company mortality performs very poorly indeed. The use of a three-component decomposition of the conditional probability of firm death introduces additional separately-estimated parameter vectors, which greatly relax the restrictiveness of the linear probit model. More importantly, semi-parametric estimation relaxes the monotonicity property imposed by the probit model, and results in a quite different estimate of the mortality process. Whereas the probit model leads us to infer a strong negative relation between mortality and size (allowing for the effects of age and industry), the semi-parametric approach suggests a non-monotonic relation rising to a peak for small–medium-sized firms, then a flat or slightly declining schedule thereafter. The shape of this relation varies across industry, but the peak mortality rate is estimated to occur at a size corresponding to an asset value of around £0.5m in 1976.

Appendix 7A: Definition of industries

Industry 1 metal, mechanical and instrument engineering; electrical and electronic engineering; office machinery etc.; shipbuilding, vehicles, metal goods

Industry 2 food, drink, tobacco, chemicals and man-made fibres, textiles, leather and leather goods, footwear; clothing, non-metallic mineral products, timber; furniture, paper; printing; publishing, other manufacturing, mixed activities in manufacturing: companies with over 50% of activity in manufacturing and which are engaged in 3 or more activities none of which accounts for 40% or more of activity

Industry 3 wholesaling (other than petroleum products), retailing; hotels and catering; repair of consumer goods and vehicles

Industry 4 business services; leasing, other services, mixed activities in non-manufacturing: companies with over 50% activity in non-manufacturing and which are engaged in 3 or more activities none of which accounts for 40% or more of activity

Industry 5 agriculture; fishing and forestry, mineral and ore extraction, oil, construction, transport and communication.

Notes

We are grateful to the Economic and Social Research Council (grant H519255003) for financial support under its *Analysis of Large and Complex Datasets* initiative, and under the *Surveys and Database Programme* of the ESRC Centre for Business Research.
1 The term probability density/mass function is henceforth abbreviated as pdf.
2 Alternatively, one could specify a function of this type for one or more of the quantiles of the conditional distribution. For example see Koenker and Bassett (1978) for a discussion of linear regression quantiles. Henceforth, we restrict attention to traditional regressions specified in terms of the expectation function.
3 This argument remains valid even if other causes are responsible for some deaths. Indeed, the existence of multiple possible causes of death makes the conventional selectivity model still less plausible, since the probit (24) is then attempting to approximate a probability that would involve the parameters of all the separate cause-of-death processes.

8 Wage-earnings in Great Britain during the Industrial Revolution

Charles H. Feinstein

8.1 Introduction

British Economic Growth (1962) by Phyllis Deane and W. A. Cole is widely recognised as one of the most influential of all the books to have emerged from research undertaken in Cambridge at the Department of Applied Economics. It represented the first sustained attempt to estimate historical national income accounts for the United Kingdom, and to make these the basis for the analysis of Britain's economic growth. This work, together with the associated compilation of historical statistics by Brian Mitchell (1962), transformed our knowledge and understanding of the nature and pattern of the developments in Britain in the eighteenth and nineteenth centuries. The application of these quantitative and analytical techniques for the study of the Industrial Revolution and the subsequent phases of economic growth has been enormously influential and stimulating, both here and abroad. Many others have sought to emulate their methodology; some have even borrowed their title; none can claim their originality or their scholarly achievement.

It is thus a great pleasure to be able to contribute to this volume to mark the 50th Anniversary of the DAE, and to pay this tribute to the authors of *British Economic Growth*. More than thirty years later their research is still the essential starting point for any quantitative study of the economic growth of the British economy. Inevitably, however, their demonstration of the data which could be found and of the procedures which could be applied has made it possible for those who followed after them to improve on certain aspects of their work. As they anticipated, some of their findings have been revised and their interpretations challenged.

The aim of this paper is to indicate briefly some of the constructive criticisms which have been made and the issues which have been raised in later work, and then to outline some preliminary results of my own attempts to contribute to the measurement of British economic growth initiated by

Deane and Cole, by compiling a new series of weekly earnings for the period 1770–1880.

8.2 Deane and Cole's estimates and Crafts's revisions

Deane and Cole's estimates of British economic growth were derived by two distinct procedures. For the eighteenth century, indices of aggregate real national product were compiled from the output side, using a variety of quantity indicators for each of the main sectors of the economy. For the nineteenth century, estimates were made of the different categories of nominal income, and these were deflated to obtain series for the real national product. The two GDP series were then spliced in 1800.

These pioneering estimates were quickly challenged by a number of writers, of whom the most persistent and effective was Nick Crafts. He published a succession of critical articles, probing various weaknesses in the Deane and Cole indices for both the eighteenth and the nineteenth centuries. On the income side, he demonstrated that they had chosen an inappropriate price index for the deflation of the nominal series, and that this had seriously distorted their findings for the early part of the nineteenth century (Crafts, 1980). On the output side, he pointed to weaknesses in their procedure for estimating both agricultural and industrial output (Crafts, 1976, 1983). His contribution culminated in an alternative set of estimates of real GDP, based on revised indices for agriculture, industry and services. These covered the whole period from 1700 to 1830 on a consistent output-side basis (Crafts, 1985).

The result of these new estimates by Crafts was a substantial downward revision of the rate of growth of total and per capita real GDP. Independent work by Knick Harley (1982) criticising an earlier index of industrial production constructed by Hoffmann (1955) yielded a similar conclusion. The Deane and Cole estimates had essentially confirmed traditional views of a sharp acceleration in the growth of the economy in the closing decades of the eighteenth century, an interpretation easily consistent with the notion of an economy transformed by an industrial revolution, or – to use Rostow's modern metaphor – of a take-off. By contrast, Crafts and Harley argued that there was no dramatic change, only a gradual rise to a relatively modest rate of growth.

This revisionist attack on a cherished institution inevitably provoked fierce and prolonged controversy.[1] Some critics suggested that the whole attempt at quantification was misguided and that no worthwhile measurement was possible for this early period. Others accepted the value and legitimacy of the attempts to measure economic change over the period of the Industrial Revolution, but were bitterly critical of specific estimates

Table 8.1. *Growth of the British economy, 1700–1831 (annual percentage growth rate)*

A. Real GDP per head

	1700–1760	1760–1780	1781–1801	1801–1831
Deane and Cole	0.45	−0.04	1.08	1.61
Crafts	0.31	−0.05	0.41	0.45

B. Industrial production

	1700–1760	1760–1770	1770–1801	1801–1831
Deane and Cole	0.97	1.06	2.22	3.44
Hoffmann	0.75	1.48	2.66	2.74
Crafts and Harley	0.75	1.12	1.27	2.72
Cuenca Esteban	0.74	1.36	2.61	3.18

Sources: Crafts (1985, p. 45); Crafts and Harley (1992, p. 715); Cuenca Esteban (1994, p. 88).

and methods. In the latter camp, Cuenca Esteban has been an especially polemical participant, arguing for the possibility that 'British economic growth was faster and more sustained than revisionist writers would have us believe' (Cuenca Esteban, 1994, pp. 66–7).

The growth rates implied by his proposed revisions to the index of industrial production are compared with these other estimates in the lower panel of Table 8.1. Although he does not claim that his own estimates have any definitive status, he believes that they do 'serve to reinforce ample qualitative evidence pointing to a major discontinuity in British social and economic development during the last three decades of the eighteenth century'. His recommendation is that 'the dwindling growth rates' obtained 'through ten years of guesswork' by Crafts and Harley 'should in turn be revised in the direction of Hoffmann's and of Deane and Cole's classic, much higher estimates' (Cuenca Esteban, 1994, pp. 68 and 89).

Throughout this dispute, income-based estimates have largely been neglected, and the recent discussion of economic change has focused almost exclusively on the output-based series. However, the incomplete and fragile nature of the available data creates a strong case for the construction, on a consistent basis, of independent estimates of national product from the income side. The present paper on nominal earnings is intended as one step in a larger project designed to do this for the whole period from about 1770 to the late nineteenth century. If the work can be carried through to a satisfactory completion, it will provide a valuable check on the output data, and will also add to our understanding of changes in the structure of incomes during the initial phase of industrialisation.

8.3 New estimates of nominal full-employment earnings

It is now almost a hundred years since a serious attempt has been made to measure the changes in nominal wages over the course of the Industrial Revolution (Wood, 1899). This long interval might be taken to indicate either that it is a foolhardy venture which wise scholars should avoid, or that it is high time there was a new effort.

Any attempt to construct a new index of average nominal earnings during and after the Industrial Revolution has to confront numerous complex problems in the context of a period when the necessary data were seldom collected and even more rarely preserved. Some of the major issues include the changes in the structure of agriculture and in the work of male and female farm labourers and servants; the rise of new manufacturing industries and occupations, and the decline of others, a process illustrated most vividly by the fate of the hand-loom weavers; the impact of successive technological changes such as the spinning jenny, the water-frame, and the mule; the changing role of women and children as the domestic system slowly gave way to workshops and factories; and the shifts in the location of activity, exemplified by the decline of the woollen and worsted textile industry in Norwich and the South-West, and the rise of thrusting new centres in the West Riding of Yorkshire.

Some of the series used for the present index rely for all or most of the period on the well-known indices compiled by previous writers, notably A. L. Bowley and G. H. Wood, and these rest on relatively secure foundations. Over a period of some two decades at the turn of the nineteenth century, these two distinguished scholars energetically extracted and exploited all the then available sources of information on wage rates and earnings, and their main estimates are based on a vast quantity of material, carefully analysed and expertly synthesised.

In 1906, when Bowley reviewed the work that he and Wood had done since his first paper in 1895, he thought that it would in the end be possible to have:

trustworthy accounts of the course of wages in the nineteenth century in industries which include about half our occupied population. We are not likely to be able to construct index-numbers for boot-makers, tailors, unskilled labourers not attached to the industries named, dock labourers, domestic servants, railway men and many others.[2]

Little has changed in this respect since this was written, and it remains the case that it is only possible to cover these additional workers, or to extend the series further back into the past, if we are willing to tolerate lower standards of evidence and of reliability than Bowley and Wood thought acceptable. The case for quantification in the face of the multitude of gaps and uncertainties in the available data is not that it provides definitive estimates (however sharp and secure the results might look when finally set out in neat arrays of printed tables). It is, rather, that it helps to establish orders of magnitude, and to test how robust or vulnerable the estimates are to the different assumptions and judgements the statistician is forced to make in the face of a lack of satisfactory evidence.

Moreover, it is only by attempting to cover these sectors that we can form any judgement of how much difference their inclusion is likely to make to an overall index. It seems especially desirable that this question should be examined, given that conditions in the markets in which these workers offered their labour differed very greatly from those in the major industries. In particular, many of the wage-earners omitted by Bowley and Wood were largely unaffected by any form of technological change. Furthermore, it was usually in these same sectors that there was an excess supply of labour. Trade unions were either non-existent or extremely weak, and the workers' ability to organise in support of claims for higher earnings was correspondingly limited. These factors would tend to depress the level of earnings in these sectors, but it is less clear what their effect would be on rates of change, and this needs to be explored.

The first step in the overall project was the construction of separate estimates of the male and female occupied population of Great Britain at decennial intervals from 1771 to 1881. Each of these totals was classified by sector or occupation, and the estimates for each sector were then further sub-divided to distinguish three categories of income-earners: employers and the self-employed, salaried (white-collar) workers, and manual (blue-collar) wage-earners. The distinction between the latter two groups is inevitably slightly blurred at the margins (for example, the treatment of shop assistants as manual workers is somewhat arbitrary), but in general the basis for the division is clear. Annual estimates of the number of wage-earners in each sector were obtained by interpolation between these benchmarks and provide the weights for the component wage series.[3]

Annual estimates of the movements in earnings were then assembled; so far, these cover 24 separate occupations or industries, accounting for some 80% of the total number of wage-earners in Great Britain in 1851. There are still a number of other sectors for which indices can be compiled, and these additional series will make it possible to deal more adequately with some of the problems of transition noted above, but it is unlikely that they will change the overall picture to any significant degree. The main workers omitted or inadequately covered in this preliminary version are shop assistants; milliners and dress-makers; male and female farm servants in England and Wales; and all wage-earners employed in the manufacture of iron and steel, of metal-using items such as tools, guns, cutlery, chains, needles and nails, of lace, silk, linen and jute textiles, and of food, drink, glass, and timber products. The economic circumstances and labour-market conditions in the industries in which they worked are very varied, and the common factor is simply the difficulty of compiling a continuous series of their earnings. There is thus no reason to assume that the present results are biased by the omission of these sectors.

A few important aspects of the definition of the present indices should be noted. All the series are intended to measure weekly earnings (not wage-rates), assuming full employment. In principle, they should thus capture relevant changes in the composition of the labour force by age, gender, skill or region, and should allow for the effect on earnings of over-time payments and of piece rates or other systems of payment by results. They include an addition for the value of board and lodging where it is a substantial element of the total remuneration, but minor perquisites and allowances are not included. A few of the indices for manufacturing and building cover the whole of the United Kingdom, but the Irish wages in these sectors are too small to have any appreciable effect, and the indices can therefore be treated as relating essentially to Great Britain.[4]

The absolute value of earnings in each industry was generally taken from the estimates of average annual earnings in 1881 obtained in an earlier study (Feinstein, 1990). These in turn were derived by working back from estimates based on the official *Enquiry into Earnings and Hours in 1906* (PP, 1909), checked wherever possible against the information col-lected in the first Board of Trade investigation, *Rates of Wages in 1886* (PP, 1893–94, Pt II). A crucial implicit assumption is thus that all dimensions of the composition of the wage-earners in 1881 are reflected accurately in the level of average earnings at that date, and that the effects of any changes in skill, gender, age or other dimensions as we move back to 1771 are fully incorporated in the earnings indices. This is undoubtedly a rather heroic assumption, given the sweeping changes which occurred during this period. However, it seemed best to proceed in this way so that it would be possible both to specify clearly the basis on which the indices were con-structed, and to test the resulting level of average earnings at various dates against independent benchmarks for those years.

For the aggregate index, each separate earnings series is weighted annu-ally by the corresponding wage-bill, i.e. for each sector or occupation the numbers employed multiplied by the average wage in each year. The movements in the overall index thus measure both the changes in full-employment nominal wages within each sector and the effect of movements between sectors.

In order to illustrate the procedures used to extend the range of sectors contained in the earnings index, I shall describe here four of the new series. These cover agriculture, the cotton industry, the wool and worsted industry, and domestic service. The sources and methods for all the remaining series are set out in Appendix 8A.

8.3.1 Agriculture

This index combines two separate series covering the weekly cash earnings of ordinary adult male and female hired labourers in England and Wales, and a third for male labourers (including farm servants) in Scotland. For England and Wales, total earnings (including allowances in kind, payments for piecework and overtime, and extra money paid at harvest) maintained a roughly constant ratio to weekly cash wages (Bowley, 1899, p. 556; Fox, 1903, pp. 282–90). For Scotland, Bowley incorporates benchmark estimates of the payments in kind to married ploughmen.

From 1770 to 1850, and for Scotland throughout, the index for males is based on Bowley (1899, pp. 562–4, three-year averages); from 1850 to 1881 his estimates for England and Wales were replaced by an index constructed from the wages paid on a sample of farms (Fox, 1903, pp. 331–2; Department of Employment, 1971, p. 38). There are some differences between the Fox and Bowley series where they overlap for the post-1850 period, and the former has been preferred on the grounds that data collected on a consistent annual basis from a sample of farms (even though the number covered is very small) are likely to provide a more accurate indicator of change than the successive independent surveys which are the basis for Bowley's index.[5]

The most worrying feature of this series is the absence of a reliable benchmark between 1795 and 1824. During these years the index first climbs by some 56% to a peak in the period 1807–12, and then falls sharply in a contraction which eliminates most of the preceding rise in nominal earnings. These large movements are entirely dependent on Bowley's interpolation on the basis of very limited information for individual farms, and any statements based on comparisons *within* this period must be heavily qualified.

For female outdoor farm labourers in England and Wales it was possible to obtain benchmark estimates for four years. Interpolation between these points was based on the index for male earnings, assuming a smooth trend in the ratio of female to male earnings between the benchmark years. The resulting series is clearly very imperfect, but allows for the relative decline in women's pay in the late eighteenth and early nineteenth century, and does broadly indicate the trends in the earnings of a previously neglected group of wage-earners.

For 1770, estimates were assembled for some 72 villages from the information on average weekly pay for male and female labourers at different seasons of the year collected by Young on his various tours (Young, 1770, pp. 447–9; John, 1989, pp. 1075–9). Following Young's procedure, annual averages were obtained on the basis that the harvest rate was paid for five weeks, the haytime for six, and the winter for 41; where winter rates were not given the average for the summer weeks was calculated. Because the villages for which Young provides data were predominantly in the North, the figures were grouped by county, and a national estimate was derived as an unweighted average of the 27 counties represented in the dataset. The result for average weekly female earnings is 3s 6d for the full year and 4s 9d for the summer weeks, in each case about 50% of the equivalent male pay in the same set of villages.[6]

For 1833, similar data on male and female wages were extracted from the parish replies to the Rural Queries distributed in 1832 by the Royal Commission on the Poor Law (PP, 1834). In total, over 300 parishes provided usable information on summer or annual wages, and this was again averaged by county to obtain an overall estimate of average annual weekly female wages of 4s 2d, 39% of the corresponding figure for men. This level is consistent with the estimates of 8d to 9d per day by Hasbach (1908, p. 227) and Pinchbeck (1930, p. 88) based on information gleaned from the *Report on the Employment of Women and Children in Agriculture* (PP, 1843).

Data for the two final benchmarks are more readily available in the results of parliamentary enquiries summarised in the *Returns of Wages* (PP, 1887, pp. 411–19) for three quarters in 1860–61 and four in 1869–70. The annual average for the earlier date is 4s 6d per week, equal to 40% of the figure for men, and for the later date 5s 2d, equal to 41%.

8.3.2   The cotton industry

For the period from 1806, Wood has worked exhaustively through the mass of information available for the multitude of different occupations in the cotton industry, and his index (Wood, 1910, pp. 598–9) is carefully weighted to allow for the changes in the composition of the labour force by occupation, sex and age, and for the changing importance of the different components.

Completion of the index for the period before 1806 is very much more difficult. In an attempt to obtain at least a coarse picture of the rapidly changing and poorly recorded developments in these early years, two new indices were constructed – for spinners and for handloom weavers. They were combined in a weighted average, with the latter given twice the weight of the former. The series are intended to cover both domestic and factory workers.

The spinning series, shown in Table 8.2, is itself a very crudely weighted average of estimates of the weekly earnings of women, men and children engaged in five different types of spinning undertaken at home or in the newly-built mills. The estimates are given for eight dates from 1770 to 1806, designed to take account of the changes in earnings and in the composition of the labour force arising from the technological innovations and associated economic changes in spinning, as these are described in the literature on the early cotton industry. It should be possible to improve on both the estimates of wages and the very approximate weights applied in this table, but it makes use of much of the available information and, whatever its imperfections, does at least attempt to deal explicitly with changes which were of crucial importance in the early phase of the Industrial Revolution.

For the hand-loom weavers it is again possible to rely mainly on Wood (1910, pp. 425–33 and 593–6). He gives annual estimates of their weekly earnings from 1797 onwards, showing a figure of 18s 9d at that date, and also quotes estimates from Arthur Young and others for the 1770s and the later decades of the eighteenth century.[7] A starting point of 6s 3d in 1770 and 6s 6d in 1778 was adopted on the basis of the figures Wood quotes, and his comments on these. I have then assumed that handloom weavers' earnings rose rapidly to 18 shillings a decade later, and were steady at that level during the famous 'golden age' when rapidly increasing supplies of cheap yarn created a surge in demand for the services of the weavers. The series then moves up a fraction from 1795 to meet the series given by Wood from 1806 onwards.

8.3.3 The woollen and worsted industry

Both Bowley and Wood tackled the problem of measuring earnings in this industry and provide valuable information, but Wood criticised his colleague's original estimates without himself producing a final index on the lines of his masterly study of the cotton trade.[8] It is not difficult to understand this, given the complexity of the industry, the changes in the composition of the labour force, and the lack of hard information until well into the nineteenth century. Nevertheless, it seemed better to include

Table 8.2. Earnings of men, women and children in cotton spinning, selected dates, 1770–1806 (shillings and pence per week, with rough percentage weights in brackets)

	(1) Hand spindle (women)	(2) Jenny (women)	(3) Throstle (Women and children)	(4) Mule spindle Spinners (men)	(5) Mule spindle Piecers (children)	(6) All spinners (weighted average)
	s d	s d	s d	s d	s d	s d
1770	6 0 (70)	8 0 (30)				6 7
1775	4 0 (60)	6 0 (40)				4 10
1780	3 0 (50)	9 0 (50)				6 0
1790	3 0 (20)	9 0 (45)	4 0 (20)	10 0 (15)		6 11
1795	2 6 (10)	9 0 (40)	4 0 (30)	22 0 (7)	4 0 (13)	7 0
1797	2 6 (5)	8 0 (25)	4 6 (20)	10 0 (50)		8 0
1804	—	—	7 3 (20)	11 6 (80)		10 8
1806	—	—	9 1 (15)	24 0 (28)	5 9 (57)	11 4

Sources: Bowley (1900, p. 119); Collier, (1964, pp. 17, 32, 41 and 91); Hammond and Hammond (1919, p. 56); Mantoux (1928, p. 433–6); Pinchbeck (1930, pp. 139–51 and 191); Unwin (1942, pp. 130–3, 168, 191 and 195–203); Wadsworth and Mann (1931, pp. 401–5).

even a rough estimate rather than to omit the changes in earnings in an industry which was of such importance in the eighteenth century and which was subsequently the subject of revolutionary technical changes, albeit at a slower pace than in the manufacture of cotton.

The present index was compiled separately for 1770–1830 and 1830–1881. For the earlier period I have proceeded on the same lines as for cotton. For spinning, the index is based on a roughly weighted average of estimates aimed at reflecting the changes as hand spinning by women working at home was superseded by the introduction of the jenny, operated by both men and women, and the jenny was in turn replaced in the late 1820s by male-operated mule spindles. The main sources were Bischoff (1842, II, p. 416), Bowley (1902, pp. 112–6), Lipson (1921, pp. 258–60), Palgrave (1926, p. 634) and Pinchbeck (1930, p. 141).

For the handloom weavers a very rough index was pieced together from the few wages quoted, combining series for woollen cloth (weight 4) and for worsted stuff (weight 1) derived from Bowley (1902, pp. 106–8 for Bradford; 1902, pp. 112–4 for Leeds; 1900, pp. 113–4 for Somerset and Gloucester), Palgrave (1926, pp. 634–5), Bischoff (1842, II, pp. 416–9), Lipson (1921, pp. 256–60) and Mantoux (1928, p. 435). The overall index for the woollen and worsted industry was then obtained by combining these two indices for spinning (weight 2) and hand loom weaving (weight 1), and linking this to the corresponding index for the period from 1830.

For 1830 onwards the movements in earnings in all branches of the woollen and worsted industry are represented by estimates for Leeds, Huddersfield and Bradford for selected years by Wood (1909a, p. 93; 1909b, p. 75) and Bowley (1902, p. 117). To obtain an annual series it is necessary to interpolate between their selected years. Since these are simply the years for which information was available in one or other of their sources, I have generally assumed smooth growth between the benchmarks. In so far as the changes in average levels were the outcome of changes in the composition of the workforce – for example, the gradual displacement of men by women in the weaving of woollen cloth – this smoothness may be justified, but the detailed figures could probably be improved by closer study of the trade fluctuations in the industry.

The resulting series for Leeds (weight 1) and Huddersfield (weight 2) were combined to give an index for wool; and the index for Bradford was taken to represent the worsted sector. The values for the woollen and worsted sectors were then combined in a weighted average, with the share of the former declining from about 80% in 1835 to 55% in 1861. The weights were based on employment in the two sectors as shown by the *Factory Returns*, but with an adjustment based on the Census of Population data on occupations to allow for the fact that the proportion of the trade which was still conducted at home in the first half of the nineteenth century was greater for woollens than for worsteds (Baines, 1970, pp. 88–92).

8.3.4 Domestic service

The information available for the earnings of this very large group of wage-earners working in thousands of separate households is severely limited. It is impossible to allow accurately for the many categories from senior cook or butler to lowly scullery maid or stable boy, for the multitude of different wages paid by independent employers in various parts of the country, or for the precise effects on the average of changes in individual earnings with age and length of service. The numbers engaged in this sector are so large, however, that it is worthwhile attempting to form a rough indication of the changes in cash wages and in the value of board and lodging. Many of the sources refer to large establishments and are useful in indicating both changes over time and the dispersion of earnings across the different types of servant, but the level of these payments is well above the average for all households. Separate indices were compiled for female and male domestic servants.

For female cash wages the basic procedure for 1825–1881 was to derive estimates for three benchmark years and then to interpolate between these years. For 1881 a figure of £14 2s was taken from previous work (Feinstein, 1990, pp. 626–8). For a mid-century benchmark a classification of female domestic servants by occupation and age was made using data from the 1851 Census of Occupations (PP, 1851). Cooks, housekeepers, nurses and housemaids, accounting for 22% of the total, were each sub-divided into three age-groups (under 25, 25–40 and over 40), and the larger number of general servants, 78% of the total, was split into seven age-groups. An estimated cash wage was then assigned to each of these 19 age–occupation categories, using information on domestic service from the *Edinburgh Review* (1862, p. 426), Layton (1908, pp. 518–22), Clapham (1934, p. 33), Banks (1954, pp. 71–6), Horn (1986), and Peel (1926, pp. 164–87; 1934, pp. 104–7 and 143–51), and on wages paid to nurses in hospitals and asylums in Abel-Smith (1960, pp. 5–7 and 279) and the *Select Committee on Lunatics* (PP, 1859). This yielded a weighted average of £9 2s for 1850. Interpolation between 1850 and 1881 was based largely on the indices in Layton (1908).

For 1825 a figure of £7 was adopted, partly on the basis of extrapolation by means of Layton from 1850, partly on the sources listed above, together with Adams (1825, pp. 234–97), *A New System* (1825, pp. 424–49) and Pinchbeck (1930, pp. 36). This estimate was then extrapolated to 1770 (£4 12s) by reference to the extensive collection of earnings given in Hecht

(1956, pp. 146–9) and the series for female wages in St Clement Danes given by Snell (1985, p. 416).[9]

For board and lodging there is consistent evidence of a figure of around 10 shillings per week in the late nineteenth century (Feinstein, 1990, p. 628), and it appears to have been much the same as this in the middle of the century (*Edinburgh Review*, 1862, p. 423; Banks, 1954, p. 73). In 1825 this was also quoted as the figure for a large establishment 'when the family is absent' (Adams, 1825, p. 8). However, the writer in the *Review* mentions that 'in the dear days of war and corn-laws the board wages in London were 6 shillings per week for the women', while Pinchbeck (1930, p. 313) quotes a witness before the Factory Commission in 1833 who said that a girl who left home would have to pay 5 shillings a week for board, lodging and washing. Hecht (1956) quotes weekly board wages for a few maids in the late eighteenth century, for which the average is also about 6 shillings. There is also some evidence on the maintenance of apprentices at Quarry Bank Mill (Rose, 1986, p. 107) and at Oldknows (Unwin, 1924, p. 173), and of the inmates of poor law institutions and asylums. The value of farm servants' board was reckoned by Young (1770, p. 509) to be about 4 shillings in 1770, and Marshall put it as rising to about 6 shillings in 1794–6 (quoted in Armstrong and Huzel, 1989, p. 729).

In the light of these figures and the changes in the cost of living, the average weekly cost at twenty-year intervals for all households was taken to be 3s 6d in 1761 and 4s 6d in 1781, increasing with the wartime inflation to 8 shillings in 1801, then falling back to 7 shillings in 1821 and 1841, and finally rising again to 9 shillings in 1861 and 10 shillings in 1881. In real terms this represents a roughly stable allowance from 1761 to 1801, a small improvement between that date and 1841, and then a more substantial rise of some 50% in the last four decades. The intervening years were obtained by interpolating between these estimates by means of the cost of living index.

The corresponding index for the smaller number of male domestic servants was derived in similar fashion from the same sources, but with the advantage that the majority of males were employed in the large households to which much of the surviving evidence relates.[10] The main sources can thus be accepted with less adaptation than was required for their female counterparts.

For the cash wage the principal benchmark was an estimate of £50 for 1886 derived from the data in Giffen's *General Report* on the 1886 wage census (PP, 1893–94, p. 457). In calculating the average, the small number of house stewards and other servants paid more than £140 per annum were excluded as being more appropriately treated as salaried employees. For earlier years, the corresponding estimates were £40 for 1860, £35 for 1830, £25 for 1800 and £18 for 1770.

The value of board and lodging was taken as 12 shillings per week in 1881, 20% above the allowance for women. This was then extrapolated by means of the cost of living index on the assumption that the real value was unchanged over the period back to 1770. The figures for earlier years are thus progressively higher than those for the female servants. At the beginning of the period vails (gratuities) from house guests and visitors were also an important part of the income of servants, but these are regarded as transfer payments, not as part of their earnings.

8.4 The new series and comparison with other estimates

We turn now to the initial results. The provisional indices of nominal earnings are summarised in Table 8.3 in the form of five-year averages with 1770–72 as 100; as already noted these are not the base years. Indices are given for six sectors – agriculture, building (including railway construction), mining and manufacturing, transport, domestic services, and the armed forces – and for the economy as a whole. For the overall average the equivalent in shillings per week is also shown in the final column.

On these estimates we find that average earnings rose slowly from about 7 shillings at the beginning of the 1770s to about 8s 6d in the early 1790s, and then climbed more rapidly during the war-time inflation to peak at about 14s 6d at the close of the Napoleonic Wars. They then dropped back to approximately 12 shillings in the early 1830s before rising very gently to just over 13 shillings per week in mid-century, still below the war-time peak in money terms. Subsequent growth was more rapid, and earnings reached a new peak of almost 19s 6d per week in the mid-1870s. There was thus an overall rise in nominal incomes of approximately 170% over a hundred years.

It is appropriate at this point to enquire how these results compare with previous estimates. We begin with the index compiled by Wood (1899) for selected years from 1790 to 1860. It is an unweighted average of series for 22 towns and two coal fields, covering an unspecified number of urban workers in a variety of industries and occupations. It is thus more limited in scope than the present index, but the latter can be adjusted to a roughly comparable coverage by taking only the series for building, mining, manufacturing and transport in columns 2, 3 and 4 of Table 8.3.[11] As can be seen in Table 8.4, Wood's series initially rises some 7% above the present estimate at the war-time peak, but in the 1830s the present estimate shows a recovery not reflected in Wood's data. The indices then move in harmony through the 1840s and 1850s, with the present series remaining roughly 10% higher. The net result is that the present index shows money earnings improving by almost 20% between 1816 and 1860, while Wood's index indicates no change.

Table 8.3. Average full-time money earnings, Great Britain, 1770–1882 (five-year averages, 1770–72 = 100)

	(1) Agri-culture	(2) Building	(3) Mining and manufacturing	(4) Transport and storage	(5) Domestic service	(6) Armed forces	(7) All sectors 1770–72 =100	(8) All sectors Shillings and pence per week
								s d
1770–72	100	100	100	100	100	100	100	7 2
1773–77	101	105	103	108	101	101	103	7 5
1778–82	103	110	111	138	104	105	109	7 10
1783–87	104	112	118	114	105	99	109	7 10
1788–92	110	118	130	123	110	103	117	8 4
1793–97	137	133	145	172	125	130	140	10 0
1798–1802	167	149	165	197	150	152	166	11 10
1803–07	200	178	186	215	158	145	187	13 4
1808–12	214	205	191	255	188	158	204	14 7
1813–17	206	209	195	233	185	149	200	14 4
1818–22	184	209	174	204	166	142	180	12 11
1823–27	154	208	175	209	163	140	171	12 3
1828–32	157	197	170	204	162	139	169	12 1
1833–37	159	197	176	205	156	139	171	12 3
1838–42	170	210	183	211	168	146	181	12 0
1843–47	164	220	190	212	172	145	185	13 3
1848–52	158	217	191	215	170	141	183	13 2
1853–57	186	230	212	247	198	161	208	14 11
1858–62	189	245	218	235	199	163	213	15 3
1863–67	197	260	234	243	214	168	228	16 4
1868–72	213	277	245	251	230	180	242	17 4
1873–77	244	310	275	271	248	195	271	19 5
1878–82	240	313	257	262	253	201	265	18 10

Table 8.4. *Comparison with Wood's index of average wages in towns, 1790–1860 (1790=100)*

	(1) Wood's index	(2) Present index
1790	100	100
1795	114	116
1800	129	132
1805	144	150
1810	169	161
1816	160	149
1820	151	144
1824	156	146
1831	143	139
1840	139	150
1845	138	156
1850	142	156
1855	161	175
1860	161	177

Sources: (1) Wood, 1899, p. 591.
(2) Centred three-year averages of present estimates for mining, building, manufacturing and transport.

More recently, Williamson (1982) has constructed an index of nominal wages for nine selected years between 1781 and 1851, and for every tenth year thereafter. His series was compiled for a special purpose and differs from the present index in definition and scope. In particular, it covers only adult males and makes no allowance for changes in the composition of the labour force within individual industries. It also has a much narrower coverage, omitting some sectors of particular importance in the transition to the factory economy, for instance the woollen and worsted industries. Nevertheless, both indices incorporate the major Bowley and Wood series (including those for agriculture, building and engineering), and the weight of these common sectors is sufficient to ensure that the general trends indicated by the two indices are very similar (see Figure 8.1).

There are, however, small differences which lead to some divergence in the pattern of movement over the period as the direction of the difference changes. For example, in the late eighteenth century the present series rises by 34% compared to Williamson's 25%. The new index then falls more sharply in the depression following the end of the wars against France, giving a modest net gain between 1797 and 1827 of only 13%, whereas

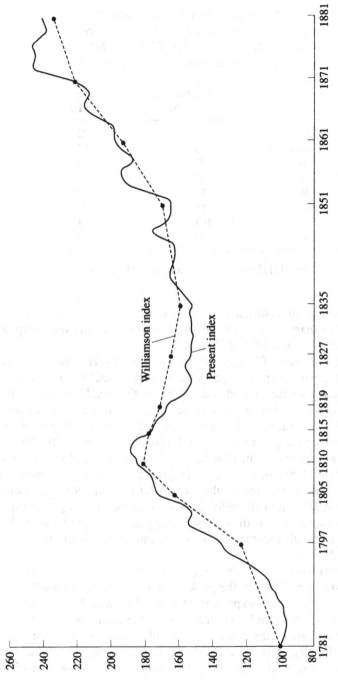

Figure 8.1 Comparison of indices of money wages, Great Britain, 1781–1881 (1781=100)

Table 8.5. *Comparison with Horrell and Humphries's estimates of family income, Great Britain, 1791–95—1860–65 (1836–45=100)*

	(1) Horrell and Humphries	(2) Present index
1791–95	66	72
1796–1800	79	88
1816–20	87	105
1831–35	89	94
1836–40	111	99
1841–45	89	101
1846–50	101	104
1860–65	103	122

Source: (1) Horrell and Humphries, 1992, p. 868.

Williamson suggested a rise of 32%. From then on the new estimates present a marginally more optimistic picture, with an overall improvement between 1827 and 1881 of 57%, rather than 41%.

The estimates of family income collected by Horrell and Humphries (1992) come closer in scope to the present series, and provide a valuable alternative source of evidence regarding the trends in average earnings. Their objective was to measure actual family incomes as measured by a selection of household budgets. These include the earnings of women and children, and in general also include transfer payments in the form of poor relief and grants from charities, and allow for the loss of earnings in periods of depression and unemployment.[12] However, the sample is relatively small, so that the results for non-farm occupations may not be fully representative; and the reliability of many of the budgets must also be rather uncertain. It is thus not surprising that the movements in these estimates of family income do not correspond closely with the present series (see Table 8.5).

The Horrell and Humphries series indicates much less improvement from the early 1790s to the peak in 1816–20, but then rises from there to the late 1830s when the present estimates show a slight fall. There is then a 20% drop in the family incomes series in the early 1840s and a recovery in the latter part of the decade, neither of which is reflected in the present series. Finally, their estimates show almost no improvement in the 1850s and early 1860s, while the present estimates rise by almost one-fifth.

Table 8.6. *Comparison with contemporary estimates of average annual earnings, Great Britain, all sectors, 1760–1884 (£ per annum)*

Date	Source	Contemporary estimate	Present estimate
1884	Levi	46	48
1867	Baxter	40	43
1866	Levi	40	42
1846	Smee	22	34
1803	Colquhoun	28	31
1802	Bell	30–40	30
1800	Beeke	30	30
1760	Massie	17	18[a]

Note:
[a] The present estimate is for 1770.
Sources: Levi (1885), pp. 4–6. Baxter (1868), pp. 51 and 56, adjusted to a full-time basis. Smee (1846), pp. 4–8. Colquhoun (1806), p. 23 for England and Wales; the estimate is given as an average wage per family of £42 and I have assumed – following Beeke (1800), pp. 121–3 – that there were 1.5 wage-earners per family. Bell (1802), p. 137; Bell says that annual average earnings were probably £40, but used £30 for his calculation. Beeke (1800), pp. 121–3. Massie (1760); see also Mathias (1957), p. 43.

To conclude these comparisons, we can check the estimates against the figures for average earnings given by contemporary statisticians such as Massie, Colquhoun, and Baxter. In compiling the present series, I deliberately refrained from using their information on earnings, so that it is appropriate to make such a comparison. There are minor qualifications which might be made at various points, and the reliability and interpretation of some of the contemporary estimates can be questioned.[13] Nevertheless, the general closeness of the agreement in Table 8.6 is very encouraging, and these independent benchmarks suggest that the present index has successfully tracked the main changes in average incomes over the long period from 1881 back to the 1770s.[14]

Overall, therefore, it appears that the new series have helped to refine and extend, but not greatly to change, the basic picture established by earlier scholars. The more comprehensive coverage should increase

Table 8.7. *Growth of real wages and real GDP
per head, Great Britain, 1780–1831 (annual
percentage growth rate)*

	1780–1801	1801–1831
Real GDP per head		
Deane and Cole	1.08	1.61
Crafts	0.41	0.45
Real wages		
Present estimate	−0.09	0.41

Source: See Table 8.1 and text.

confidence in the reliability of the overall movements shown by the index, and the larger number of component series will permit closer analysis of the interesting diversity in movements within and between sectors.

8.5 Real wages and per capita GDP, Great Britain, 1780–1830

Finally, we can return to the issue with which we began and ask what light the new estimates of average real wages can throw on the rate of growth of the British economy during the industrial revolution.[15] The estimates for Great Britain are compared in Table 8.7 with the series for real GDP per head by Deane and Cole and by Crafts. The rate of growth in real wages shown by the new series over the fifty-year period 1780–1830 is marginally slower than the growth of real GDP estimated by Crafts, and is thus even further below the original Deane and Cole estimates. At this aggregate level the new estimates thus offer no support for the attempt by Cuenca Esteban to reinstate the traditional pattern of sharp acceleration in the economy as a whole to a rapid rate of growth during this period.

One probable reason for the differences in Table 8.7 is, of course, the presence of measurement errors in all three sets of estimates, and the real wage series are still provisional. However, there are obvious conceptual differences between the series for average real wages and for per capita real GDP, and it is necessary to consider how these might affect the comparison. The differences can be expressed in terms of the following identity:

$$\frac{e}{P_w} \equiv \frac{\dfrac{Y}{P_y.N} \cdot \dfrac{W}{Y} \cdot \dfrac{P_y}{P_w}}{\dfrac{N_w}{N}}$$

The term on the left-hand side is average money earnings per worker (e) deflated by the cost of living index (P_w). On the right-hand side, the first term of the numerator is GDP (Y) deflated by the GDP deflator (P_y) and divided by the total population (N) to give real per capita GDP. This is differentiated from the average real wage by the three remaining terms.

The first is W/Y, the share of the total wages bill ($W=e.N_w$) in national income. Any given rate of growth of real wages would be consistent with more rapid growth of per capita real GDP if this ratio had fallen over the period, i.e. if other components of national income had increased more rapidly than wages. It is possible that there was such a redistribution of income, with landowners and businessmen gaining relative to wage-earners during a period of swift advances in rents and profits, especially during the war-time years. However, it seems unlikely that any such shift would have moved labour's share downward by more than a few percentage points.[16]

The second factor is the relative price, P_y/P_w. Average real wages could increase less rapidly than per capita real income if the price of all goods and services were falling over the period relatively to those making up the cost of living index. This would have occurred if, for example, there had been an unfavourable movement in the net barter terms of trade so that export prices fell more rapidly than those of imported and home-consumed goods. There is considerable uncertainty about the movements in the terms of trade, but it seems likely that there was such a deterioration, at least for second period covered in Table 8.7, from 1801 to 1831.[17] Given the rapid growth in exports of the products of the revolutionary cotton industry it is likely that an appreciable part of the gains from technological advances in British industry was enjoyed by foreign consumers.

The third term, the denominator on the right-hand side, is the ratio of the number of wage-earners (N_w) to the total population (N). A rise in this participation rate would also make a given rate of growth of average wages consistent with a more rapid increase in per capita GDP. In fact, however, this particular trend went the other way. The proportion of the population of working age was falling during the period of rapid increase in birth rates and – even though there was probably a rise in the proportion of women in the occupied labour force – the number of dependants per worker was rising in these years, not falling.[18]

If the evidence of the real-wage series is accepted, it would thus only be possible to reinstate the pattern of rapid GDP growth indicated by the Deane and Cole estimates if it could be demonstrated that there was a substantial fall in the share of wages in the national income and/or a substantial rise in the relative price of wage-goods. The extent of such changes would have to be sufficient both to offset the adverse effect on per capita incomes of the rising number of dependants, and to raise the rate of growth of real earnings by a substantial margin. The research necessary to measure these effects has still to be completed, but preliminary indications do not suggest that they were sufficiently powerful to close the gap between the present growth rates and those calculated by Deane and Cole.

Thus the implication for the overall growth of the economy of these income-based estimates of real wages is that they are broadly consistent with the results derived by Crafts and Harley from completely independent output-side data. They do not support the attempt to re-establish the classic view of the Industrial Revolution involving a sharp acceleration to a high rate of growth in per capita real GDP before 1830. This does not, of course, preclude either dramatic social changes or rapid growth in individual sectors of the economy.

Appendix 8A. Estimates of full-employment weekly earnings, Great Britain, 1770–1881

The aim in this appendix is to provide brief notes on the sources and methods of the estimates of annual earnings over the period 1770–1881.

Mining

The index is based on a series for coal hewers' shift earnings. This is taken as representative of the trends in all mining and quarrying. For 1800–81 I have used the estimates by Mitchell (1984, pp. 194–5). To interpolate for the years in the early part of the nineteenth century not covered by Mitchell's data, and to carry the series back to 1770, I have relied on scattered and very imperfect indications in Bowley (1900, pp. 101–9), Hamilton (1926, pp. 312–16), Jenkin (1927, pp. 132–40, 171, 199 and 205), Ashton and Sykes (1929, pp. 134–41), Dodd (1933, pp. 337–44), Langton (1979, pp. 117 and 201–9), and Flinn (1984, pp. 386–95).

Building

This covers the main building trades and also work on the construction of the railways. For the former, Bowley (1901, pp. 107–12) gives annual estimates from 1830 for wages of both craftsmen and labourers in a range of towns, and makes an allowance for changes in the relative importance of the different towns included in the index. For earlier years his overall index is given only in the form of average levels for four sub-periods from 1795 to 1830, though more information is given for individual towns. The present index is based on Bowley for the period from 1795, and was extrapolated to 1770 by making a weighted average of indices for building craftsmen (weight 1) and labourers (weight 2). The former is based on series for London, Lancashire, Kent, Gloucester and the Midlands; the latter includes these regions and also the North Riding. These series were taken from Gilboy (1934, pp. 254–87) and Eccleston (1976).

For railway construction labour, I have used an unpublished index generously made available by Brian Mitchell. This was compiled in connection with his estimates of railway capital formation (Mitchell, 1964).

Engineering and shipbuilding

From 1794 onwards it is possible to rely on the enormous mass of information assembled from trade unions, employers, and official and private enquiries by Bowley and Wood (1906, pp. 185–90). Their index covers a wide range of skilled, semi-skilled and unskilled labourers in engineering and machine-shops, iron foundries, boiler-shops and shipyards in a large number of inland and maritime centres. It allows for changes in the composition of the labour force and for the effects on weekly earnings of various piece rate systems.

For the late eighteenth century the few comparable estimates which I could find point to an increase in weekly earnings for millwrights and mechanics from about 12 or 13 shillings in the 1770s and 1780s to around 18 shillings to £1 in the late 1790s. For shipwrights the level of pay was higher, but the increase was also roughly 50% or a little more (PP, 1887, p. 33; Bowley, 1900, p. 60; Bowley and Wood, 1905, pp. 115 and 136; Ashton, 1924, pp. 189–93; Mantoux, 1928, pp. 432–3; Daniels, 1929, p. 593; Rule, 1981, p. 18). This rise is broadly in line with the increase in the series for building craftsmen described above, and the index was extrapolated back to 1770 by means of this series.

Clothing and footwear

Two indices were compiled in order to cover at least part of this large industry, one for tailors and the other for boot and shoemakers. It is likely that both provide a broadly acceptable measure of the overall trend in earnings, but there is insufficient information to make accurate estimates of short-term changes or of the changing importance of the trade in different centres.

The index for tailors is intended to cover the average earnings of both men and boys, but is based largely on figures for journeymen tailors. The main sources are Galton (1896, p. 147), Porter (1847, p. 457); George (1925, pp. 163–5 and 368), Palgrave (1926, pp. 634–5), Mayhew (1980, 2, pp. 72–149) and the *Returns of Wages* (PP, 1887, LXXXIX, p. 392). The series for boot and shoe makers covers both men and women. The main source for the period after 1830 is the information for a number of towns given in the *Returns of Wages* (PP, 1887, LXXXIX, pp. 253–9) and Department of Employment (1971, p. 37). For earlier years the index is based mainly on the wages quoted in Porter (1847, p. 457), Palgrave (1926, pp. 634–5) and Mayhew (1980, 3, pp. 111–203).

Printing

Bowley and Wood (1899, pp. 708–15) give an index based on the weekly time wages of compositors employed on book and jobbing work from 1777 to the end of our period. It is a weighted average of the various towns for which figures are available at different dates, but makes no allowance for any changes in the structure of the printing industry, for example, between book and jobbing work and newspaper printing, though the effect of such changes was thought to be small before the 1880s.

Pottery

An index of money earnings of skilled potters in North Staffordshire has been compiled by Botham (1982; see also Hunt and Botham, 1987). It is based on information drawn from surviving account books and firm records, parliamentary enquiries, newspapers, trade union records, and arbitration proceedings. There is a gap in the series between 1770 and 1790 and this was bridged by assuming a linear increase.

Merchant Seamen

The index is based on the wages in cash and kind of able seamen, and it is assumed that there were no significant changes in the composition or age structure of the crews. For 1840, 1850 and 1861–81 Bowley (1895, pp. 266–9; 1898, p. 482) constructed an index of cash earnings weighted to allow for the gradual transition from sail to steam. Interpolation for the intervening years was based on the rates for seamen on foreign-going vessels from London and Liverpool given in the unpublished collection of data assembled by Wood for the Board of Trade (1908, p. 290). For 1817 to 1833 the index relies on continuous series for three voyages, reported by a shipowner to a Select Committee (PP, 1833, VI, p. 480). These are broadly consistent with the later figures.

Starting at the other end of the period we can obtain good estimates for the eighteenth century from the research into shipping records by Davis

(1962, pp. 137–45), supplemented by figures quoted by Bowley (1900, pp. 77–9) and Ashton (1955, p. 226). The main source for the extent of the very large movements in earnings during the war years is the evidence of shipowners and brokers to the 1833 Select Committee (PP, 1833, VI, Qs 3597–601, 6175–82, 7864–5).

The value of the food supplied to seamen was estimated by Giffen to be worth about 33 shillings per month in the 1880s.[19] If this is adjusted to 1770 prices it comes to some 23 shillings, whereas the figure given for that period by Davis (1962, 145) is only 17 shillings, presumably reflecting the lower standard of the ordinary seamen's victuals in the late eighteenth century. An annual estimate was obtained by interpolating between the 1770 and 1880 benchmarks on the basis of the cost of living index, with the improvement in standards introduced gradually over the course of the intervening years.

Railways

This index covers porters, guards, shunters, drivers, firemen and other wage-earners employed in railway occupations in goods and passenger traffic. Other employees of the railways (for example, building or engineering workers or carters) are included with those occupations; railway clerks and station masters are treated as salaried workers. The main source for the movements in pay on the railways is the data assembled by Kingsford (1970, pp. 88–115); there is also an unpublished return submitted by the railwaymen's trade union, which gives scales for a few towns for the 1870s and 1880s.[20] The various categories were weighted according to the numbers employed in England and Wales as given in the 1886 census of earnings (PP, 1893–4, pp. 266–7).

Other transport and storage

This very crude index covers a variety of wage-earners employed on canals and docks; as carters, carmen, coachmen and other workers in road transport; as warehouse men and women; and as messengers. A very rough measure of the wages paid at various dates in each of these occupations was derived from the *Returns of Wages* (PP, 1887) and other sources (George, 1927, pp. 246–7; Oram, 1970, pp. 84–5, 189). The separate series were then combined in a single index for the period from 1800, and this was extrapolated back to 1770 by means of the index for building labourers described above.

Army

The estimate covers the pay and allowances of privates and non-commissioned officers in the infantry, cavalry and artillery. The pay includes deferred and good-conduct pay, and the allowances cover clothing, provisions, accommodation, fuel and medical attendance so far as these were not paid for by deductions from pay. The starting point was a figure of £48 9s in 1878 based on an official estimate (PP, 1878, p. 2).

This was then extrapolated by an index based on movements in the pay and allowances of infantry privates. The basic pay was static for long periods, and the main changes are noted in parliamentary reports and enquiries (see especially PP, 1830, pp. 96–7; PP, 1871, p. 37; PP, 1892, Q14,317), and a very informative paper by Tulloch (1863).

Navy

This series covers the pay and allowances of seamen, stokers, artisans, and others below the rank of warrant officer, including petty officers (for example, gunners, carpenters and boatswains). The starting point is an estimate prepared by the Admiralty for the *Final Report* on the 1886 wage census (PP, 1893–94, pp. xxiii–xxiv). This gives benchmarks of £42 13s for the average annual pay of some 39,000 men in the Royal Navy, and of £22 2s for the estimated annual cost of allowances including provisions.

The figure for pay was extrapolated by means of a weighted average of three series for able seamen (weight 3), ordinary seamen (3) and petty officers (2). These were based on information about the relatively infrequent improvements in pay, with adjustments to cover the introduction of good-conduct bonuses and the reduction involved in the switch from lunar to calendar pay-months in 1852 (Lewis, 1960, pp. 293–305 and 1965, pp. 210–5; Lloyd, 1968, pp. 248–50, 271).

The series for provisions was compiled from estimates of the expenditure per man derived from parliamentary reports (see especially, PP, 1817, IV, pp. 183 and App. 17) and the *Navy Estimates*. No evidence was found for the years before 1792, and the series was extrapolated from there back to 1770 by reference to the cost of living index.

General unskilled labour

This index is designed to cover the large number of unskilled labourers who were not assigned to specific occupations in the occupational censuses. The majority were probably employed in manufacturing industries and are included with that sector in Table 8.3. A rough index was constructed on the basis of information included in the *Returns of Wages* (PP, 1887) for labourers employed in a large range of different towns and manufacturing industries, and on data in Eden (1795), Young (1770) and other sources.

Notes

I am grateful to the editors and to Anne Digby, Stan Engerman, Patrick O'Brien and Keith Snell for their helpful suggestions, and to Philip Grover for his admirable research assistance.

1 Notable contributions include Hoppit (1990), Jackson (1992), Berg and Hudson (1992, 1994), Crafts and Harley (1992, 1995), Cuenca Esteban (1994, 1995).

2 Bowley and Wood (1906) p. 148; the named industries to which he referred included agriculture, engineering, and building.

3 Further details of the construction of these estimates of the occupied labour force are available on request from the author.

4 The addition of a series for Irish agricultural earnings would effectively extend the present index to cover the United Kingdom; however, the available estimates for Ireland are not altogether comparable with those for Great Britain, and the issues will be dealt with separately in another paper.

5 See further, Feinstein (1990) p. 616.

6 For those not familiar with pre-decimal currency, one shilling was the equivalent of 5p and there were 12 pennies in a shilling; 3s 6d thus equals 17.5p.

7 See also Bowley (1900) pp. 110-13 and Unwin (1924) pp. 110-14.

8 See Bowley (1902) but note the partial retraction in Bowley (1937) p. 9. Wood published his own indices for Huddersfield and Bradford in a number of papers, but without ever describing his sources and methods; see, for example Wood (1909a; 1909b). It is possible that they were based in part on information collected from 50 firms in a Labour Department enquiry with which Wood was associated but which was never published; see Woollen and Worsted Wage Enquiry, 1839-1907, PRO, LAB 41/61. On occasion Wood also reproduced Bowley's series for Leeds, but its absence from his 1909 table, and thus presumably from his own overall index, suggests that he may not have fully endorsed it; see Wood (1910), p. 618.

9 Keith Snell has advised me that this series includes but is not limited to domestic servants, and that some of the variation may reflect age differences and payments of board wages. I have tried to minimise these problems by using the series only for the period 1766-1820 when the average sample size in each five-year period is 24 women.

10 I was also able to consult the wage books of an Oxford college.

11 Wood noted that each year in his index should be considered as the average of a three-year period, and corresponding averages have been taken for comparison.

12 The substantial disagreement in the 1840s is not significantly reduced when the present estimates are corrected to allow for cyclical unemployment in industry

and seasonal unemployment in agriculture; these adjusted estimates will be presented in a separate paper.

13 See Deane (1956, 1957) and Lindert and Williamson (1982, pp. 395–8). In particular, the latter treat the estimates given by Massie (1760) as family earnings, and consider that as such they are too either too low or else assume a very short working week. It is perfectly true that the logic of the exercise Massie was undertaking in relation to the consumption of sugar required estimates for all breadwinners in the family. Nevertheless, it seems clear from his other writings that his 1760 estimates refer only to the adult male wage-earners. Elsewhere, for example (Massie, 1758, p. 104), he explicitly raised the husband's earnings of 7s 6d per week by 4s 6d to cover income earned by a wife and two children.

14 The one marked disagreement is with Smee's figure for 1846, but this stands out as low in comparison with those by his predecessors and successors.

15 For this purpose the present index of nominal earnings was deflated by a new cost of living index. This is a revised version of the index presented in Feinstein (1995); the main change affects the component for the price of clothing. Details of the revision will be published in a forthcoming paper; they are at present available on request from the author.

16 Deane and Cole (1962) p. 251.

17 Imlah (1958) pp. 93–109; Deane and Cole (1962) pp. 82–8.

18 Wrigley and Schofield (1981) p. 529; Horrell and Humphries (1995).

19 PP, 1893–94, LXXXIII, Pt II, p. xxii; Giffen's estimate of £20 p.a was based on the difference between seamen's wages paid with and without food.

20 Railway Wages, PRO, LAB 41/25. A representative of the Labour Department of the Board of Trade recorded his uncomplimentary view of this data with the comment: 'I thoroughly distrust this scrappy return', but the figures are broadly consistent with those given by Kingsford.

9 Company failure and hysteresis

Andrew Goudie and Geoff Meeks

9.1 Introduction

This chapter combines two strands which have run through the work of the DAE for most of its life. The first is the disaggregated modelling of the UK economy which originated in the research of Dick Stone's team in the early days of the DAE and flourishes still, under the direction of Terry Barker. The second is the construction and analysis of a large databank of UK company accounts which the second Director of the DAE, Brian Reddaway, helped to launch in the sixties with Geoffrey Whittington, and which has been completed just this year.

Here we combine this UK model with the company databank to analyse a piece of economic history located part way through the DAE's lifetime: the spate of failures of large listed UK companies in the 1979–83 recession. From the time of the DAE's birth until that recession, company failure was relatively rare among larger listed British companies – probably around the rate of one per thousand per year calculated by Mueller (1986) for their counterparts in the US. But then, suddenly, between 1979 and 1983, 30 of them failed.

The following sections explore the contribution to these failures of certain exogenous, policy-related macroeconomic shocks. Sections 9.2 and 9.3 outline the modelling framework: section 9.2 presents a macro–micro model which generates financial accounts for each company contingent on the setting of exogenous macroeconomic variables; section 9.3 presents a model of company failure in which pre-failure company accounts provide the explanatory variables. Then section 9.4 combines these models in a counterfactual exercise re-running the history of the period 1977–83. It asks which of the 30 failing companies would have survived if the exchange and interest rates had not departed from their 1977 level. The final section draws some conclusions for hysteresis and other wider issues.

The literature suggests several mechanisms for hysteresis, where a short-run change in the rate of unemployment affects the rate of unemployment which is sustainable in the medium or long run. Some (Lindbeck and Snower, 1986 and Blanchard and Summers, 1986) focus on the actions of 'insiders' in the labour market; Layard and Nickell (1986) emphasise the role of the long-term unemployed; while Soskice and Carlin (1989) argue that lower investment induced by lower short-run rates of capacity utilisation leads in the medium run to a decline in the capital stock, and this feeds through to pricing behaviour.

The mechanism considered below is closest to that of Soskice and Carlin. A macroeconomic change precipitates the failure of companies. This often leads to an immediate loss of capacity and jobs which is not readily reversed, even in the medium term.

9.2 The macro–micro model of the effect of alternative macroeconomic conditions upon the financial statements of individual companies

The way in which alternative states of the world affect the company in our model can be traced using the funds flow identity:

$$e_{iy} \equiv (g_{iy} + s_{iy} + c_{iy}) - (p_{iy} - t_{iy} - d_{iy} - n_{iy} + r_{iy}) \tag{9.1}$$

where e = external finance requirement
g = fixed investment
s = growth of inventories
c = growth of net liquid assets
p = gross profit
t = taxation
d = dividends
n = interest payments
r = interest receipts
i = ith company
y = year.

The terms in the first bracket of (9.1) are the usual components of (fixed and current) capital expenditure; the second bracket gives an income and appropriation account; and the difference between the two, e_{iy}, is the company's external finance requirement. A closing balance sheet can readily be obtained by combining (9.1) with the opening balance sheet.

Within our model, t_{iy}, n_{iy} and r_{iy} are contingent upon macroeconomic variables in an obvious and easily modelled way: t depends upon the tax rates set by government, n and r upon the interest rates set by the capital market (their precise determination is given in Goudie and Meeks, 1981, 1984).

It is in making p, g, s and c contingent upon exogenous developments that the model is more unusual. It uses the large-scale disaggregated macroeconomic model initiated by Dick Stone and the Cambridge Growth Project and now maintained by Cambridge Econometrics Ltd. The determination of the company value of, for example, p for a given year and state of the world is shown by equation (9.2):

$$p_{iy} = \sum_j u_{ij}^p P_{jy} + p_i^B(1 + w_y) \qquad (9.2)$$

where p_{iy} = profits of company i

P_{jy} = profits of industry j determined by the Cambridge Econometrics model

u_{ij}^p = share of company i in domestic industry j for variable p (profits) in the base year B (the classification converter – from companies' annual reports)

p_i^B = value of profits of company i attributable to overseas operations in the base year B (from companies' annual reports)

w_y = growth in world industrial production between base year B and year y.

The three capital expenditure variables, g, s and c, are derived analogously from the industry projections in the Cambridge Econometrics model.

The Cambridge Econometrics model lends itself to this use because of its extensive disaggregation: for many of the economic relations in the model (e.g. price, investment and inventory functions) industries are treated as the behavioural agents: the respective variable is estimated econometrically using past data for the industry and inter-industry supply relations are expressed in input–output coefficients.

With some 40 industries, 500 exogenous and 5,000 endogenous variables, the model is too large to document fully here (a thorough account is provided, for example, in Barker and Peterson (eds), 1987). At the macro-economic level, the model is driven by demand in the market for goods and services. One major exogenous component of demand and character-istic of the state of the world is government spending, and for projections into the future this, along with tax rates, is derived from published information on government plans. The growth of demand in export markets is another characteristic of the state of the world which has a major influence on the model, feeding through to export demand *via* equations for individual industries. Projections of growth overseas, along with certain other variables such as the exchange rate, are set by the model user in the version we have employed here.

Using the systems of equations underpinning (9.1) and (9.2), then, we are able to estimate for an individual company in our model a set of finan-cial statements contingent on the 'state of the world' defined by our set-tings of the exogenous variables in the Cambridge Econometrics model.

9.3 Modelling company failure in alternative states of the world[1]

The contingent financial statements generated by our macro–micro model are combined with a discriminant model of company failure in order to identify which companies are at risk of failure in any particular state of the world. The discriminant model classifies companies on the basis of their financial statements into probable survivors on the one hand and, on the other, companies which are liable to failure within a year. In principle, a discriminant model can be estimated and employed for any forewarning period, and previous researchers concerned in year t with forecasting failure in, say, year $t+5$ have used actual financial statements for year t as input to a 5-year discriminant model. But usually, the shorter the forewarning period, the higher the success rate in forecasting failure. And our model enables us (in this example) to use contingent financial statements for year $t+4$ as input to the more successful 1-year version of the discriminant model.

The actual 1-year discriminant model we have used is of the conventional type which has emerged from the empirical literature (see, e.g., Foster, 1986). Goudie (1987) describes and justifies the model in detail: only its key features are sketched here.

This classification is carried out using five discriminating variables, profitability, liquidity, cash flow and two indicators of gearing, combined in the discriminant function:

$$Z = a_1\pi + a_2h + a_3f + a_4b_1 + a_5b_2 \tag{9.3}$$

where π=post-tax rate of return on equity assets

h=working capital as a proportion of gross assets

f=current year's retentions plus depreciation as a proportion of total net assets

b_1=post-tax income less interest payments as a proportion of post-tax income

b_2=percentage change in the capital gearing ratio from the previous year (income and assets are measured throughout using the historic cost convention).

Historically, the higher Z is for a company, the lower is the probability that it will fail. In forecasting, companies with a value of Z above a certain critical value (explained below) are regarded as probable survivors, those below as at risk of failure. The choice of discriminating variables follows the previous literature which began with the wide range of variables typically reviewed by bankers in assessing firms' credit-worthiness and then carried out experiments to select from among them the most efficient predictors (see Beaver, 1966; Blum, 1974; Marais, 1979).

The values of the coefficients were found by using a sample of failing companies and a random sample of survivors in the period 1960–74 drawn from the population of larger listed companies in the Cambridge/DTI Databank (see Goudie and Meeks, 1986) for details of the population).[2]–Forty-eight members of the population failed in the period 1960–74 (on a narrow definition of failure: they were liquidated or had receivers appointed). Of these, 24 (selected randomly) were used as the estimation sample, and the other half were reserved for *ex-post* validation tests. Details of the estimation procedure for the coefficients, which is designed to maximise the discriminating power of the function in identifying companies liable to failure, are provided in Anderson (1958). Details of the usual statistical tests and the precise estimates of the coefficients and of the relative contribution of the discriminating variables are available from the authors. In round figures, the relative contribution of income gearing is 40%, of profitability and cash flow 20% each, and of liquidity and capital gearing 10% each (the figures given by the Mosteller and Wallace (1963) approach, representing the contribution of each variable to the Mahalanobis distance).

The critical value of Z used to classify companies as at risk of failure or as sound again reflects the previous literature. This recognised that the losses from type I and type II errors are highly asymmetric: failing to identify a prospective failure is more costly to, say, the bankers who use such models than including prospective survivors on the list of possible casualties. Inevitably, there is some subjectivity in determining the loss ratio which is required when loss minimisation is the criterion for establishing the critical level of Z.[3] Again we have relied upon the existing literature which has explored the views of users of discriminant models: we adopt the same loss ratio as Altman *et al.* (1977) and Taffler (1982) based on the judgement of bankers and stockbrokers respectively. As a consequence, the resulting critical Z deliberately errs on the side of including several prospective survivors on the danger list for each actual failure – in order to reduce the risk of 'failure without warning'.

In testing the model and in the counterfactual exercise of section 9.3, values for profitability, etc. drawn from companies' actual financial statements or from contingent statements predicted by our macro–micro model of companies have been used in the estimated discriminant function to calculate Z scores for each company. The resulting Z scores have been compared with the predetermined critical value of Z: companies above the critical Z have been classified as 'probable survivors', those below as 'liable to failure'.

The model has been tested in various ways. Tests of the 1-year model for the cross-validation sample for 1960–74 and for a sample of failures and survivors in the post-estimation period 1975–7 are available from the

214   Andrew Goudie and Geoff Meeks

authors. Both suggest an encouraging level of predictive success compared with the previous literature (e.g. Altman, 1968; Deakin, 1972; Taffler, 1982). One example, reported in Goudie and Meeks (1991), gives orders of magnitude for the model's success which are helpful when interpreting the later results. The 1-year model is used to classify members of our population of companies at the beginning of the post-estimation period. As against a failure rate for the whole population of 4% (on a broad definition of 'failure'), the death rate was calculated as 25.6% amongst those classified as potential failures, but only 0.6% among those classified as probable survivors.

Goudie and Meeks (1991) report corresponding tests of predictive performance as the forewarning period is extended to 5 years and the macro-micro model of contingent financial statements is employed. The type I errors are 33% and 30% respectively (albeit for very small samples); the type II errors are 16% and 12%. Whilst a direct comparison is not at all straightforward (see Goudie, 1987), corresponding type I errors[4] which have been obtained from discriminant analysis alone, without the contingent financial statements generated by our macro–micro model, have generally been substantially higher for such long forewarning periods: for a 4-year period Altman (1968) reports 71% and Taffler 65%.

Previous contributors to the literature have in fact often been sceptical of using their models for such long forewarning periods. They expected a deterioration in forecasting performance as the forecast period was extended, partly because in the medium term a greater role is likely to be played by factors external to the firm – many of them macroeconomic – the influence of which may differ between companies with the same initial accounting characteristics (see Foster, 1986, p. 549). Our tests give substance to that conjecture: type I errors were halved when intervening macroeconomic developments were incorporated in the model. Parallel with this improvement in *forecasting* corporate failure, the tests have implications for the *explanation* of failure. Comparing our results with earlier work which leaves out macroeconomic influences suggests a substantial role for external factors, a role which section 9.4 explores further.

9.4 The contribution of exchange rate changes to particular failures of UK companies

We now use the modelling framework of the earlier sections to analyse particular company failures. We focus on the shock to the corporate sector caused by the sharp rise in the British exchange rate in the late 1970s and beginning of the 1980s: Table 9.1 charts a rise of over one-third in the nominal exchange between 1977 and 1980, after which it falls, by 1983, to

Table 9.1. *Macroeconomic characteristics of the UK economy, 1977–83*

	Exchange rate[a]	Gross domestic product[b]	Manufacturing production[c]
1977	1.00	1.00	1.00
1978	1.10	1.03	1.01
1979	1.23	1.05	1.00
1980	1.37	1.03	0.92
1981	1.19	1.02	0.86
1982	1.05	1.03	0.86
1983	0.97	1.07	0.89

Notes:
[a] Nominal exchange rate: overseas currency/pound.
[b] Constant prices: HMSO, *Economic Trends.*
[c] Constant prices: HMSO, *Monthly Digest of Statistics.*

roughly its original level. Whether the exchange rate movement was the product of developments unique to the British economy (such as its switch to self-sufficiency in oil) has been the subject of some debate; but some researchers see it primarily as a classic overshooting response to sharp rises in interest rates as the UK authorities experimented with tight monetary policies (see Niehans, 1981). Whatever the cause, the rise was accompanied, as Table 9.1 also shows, by modest declines in gross domestic product and much sharper falls in the output of the key trading sector, manufacturing.

In order to quantify the impact on company failure of this specific external development, we compare two states of the world – actual conditions resulting from the exogenous shock, on the one hand, and, on the other, conditions had the exchange rate remained unchanged. For each year from 1978 to 1983 our model has generated financial statements contingent upon the state of the world where the exchange rate (and the interest rate)[5] are held at their 1977 level. All other exogenous variables take on their actual value for the respective year. The resulting financial statements can then be compared with statements contingent upon actual exogenous values throughout: the difference between the two sets of financial statements represents our estimate of the *ceteris paribus* effect of the exchange rate shock.

The estimates of contingent financial statements were constructed for all companies in manufacturing and certain service industries which:

- had a full UK Stock Exchange listing
- were of sufficient size to warrant inclusion in the panel of companies analysed by the UK Department of Industry (assets $\geq£5$ million or income $\geq£0.5$ million in 1973)
- failed in the years 1979–83 (liquidated or receivers appointed). A list of the 30 companies which belong to this population is provided in the appendix to this chapter.

They represent the full spectrum of larger listed companies, ranging from the leaders of their respective industries (such as Alfred Herbert) to more modest organisations. Their aggregate UK employment in 1977 was some 63,000.

Table 9.2. *The combined profits which would have been earned by the 30 members of the sample had they continued trading in the counterfactual regime as a proportion of their corresponding value under actual conditions*

1978	1979	1980	1981	1982	1983
1.0	1.15	1.35	2.60	1.45	0.94

Source: Own calculations using the macro–micro model.

Table 9.2 summarises one result of our comparison of contingent financial statements: the aggregate profits of the population of 30 failed companies in the state of the world where the exchange rate was unchanged relative to profits in the actual state of the world. (Of course, as the Appendix Table 9.A1 shows, members of the population were dying off through the period, so actual financial statements are not available throughout: figures for the actual state of the world represent instead projections from the model contingent on actual settings of the exogenous variables.) There are many channels through which the rise in the exchange rate might affect profits: in export markets profit margins would typically have to be squeezed or market share would be lost; in domestic markets exposed to foreign competition the same forces would operate; and even home markets sheltered from foreign competition would suffer as a result of the generally depressed conditions induced by the higher exchange rate and recorded in Table 9.1. Whatever the underlying mechanisms, the profit consequences for the population of failed companies of the alternative state of the world are very serious: the movement of the relative profits measure in Table 9.2 mirrors but also magnifies the movement of the

Table 9.3. *A comparison of contingent financial statements in the two macroeconomic states of the economy*

Z scores reveal	
(a) Higher Z score (reduced probability of failure) if exchange and interest rates held constant	
Total	12
of whom	
(i) raised above critical Z for≥1 yr	4
(ii) substantial increase in Z – almost in (i) above	4
(iii) other (more modest improvement in Z)	4
(b) Liable to failure under both regimes	7
(c) Not captured by the discriminant approach: not recorded as liable to failure in either regime	<u>11</u>
	<u>30</u>

exchange rate in Table 9.1. A sharp decline in profits is attributed to the higher exchange rate.

Of course, other components of the companies' financial statements would have been affected too by the alternative state of the world. In terms of equation (9.1) above, the higher exchange rate might be expected to depress profits but also to result in lower capital expenditure, taxation and dividends: the net effect on, say, gearing or liquidity is ambiguous *a priori*. Capturing the collective impact of these movements in practice and condensing them into a single indicator of viability is the purpose of the discriminant function ((9.3) above). Z scores have therefore been computed for each company, year, and state and compared with the critical value of Z we adopted earlier to classify companies either as probable survivors or else as liable to failure.

Implicitly, we are testing the null hypothesis that these exogenous macroeconomic developments have no impact on the survival prospects of members of the population. This is the hypothesis implicit in the literature on financial statement analysis which (however reluctantly) omits from its predictive models macroeconomic variables which could change between the issue of the observed financial statement and the death or survival of the company.

Table 9.3 reports our test of this hypothesis not as a formal statistical test but through a case by case description of the experience of the 30

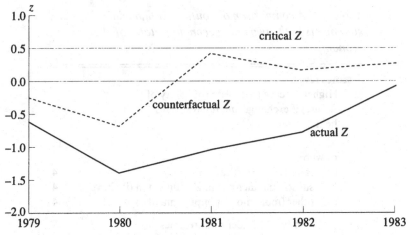

Figure 9.1 Actual and counterfactual Z scores for Alfred Herbert

failing companies as summarised in the comparative levels of their Z scores. In 12 of the 30 cases the results contradict the null hypothesis: the effect of the lower exchange rate assumption is to raise the company's Z score (i.e. reduce its probability of failure). The remaining cases are consistent with the null hypothesis: seven would have been classified on the basis of their Z score as liable to failure in both states of the economy; whilst the remaining 11 were not captured by the discriminant analysis we adopted: their financial statements did not indicate in either state that the companies were at risk of failure.

Of the 12 companies for whom lower exchange and interest rates would have reduced the probability of failure, four saw their Z score rise above the critical level of Z in at least one year: if the exchange rate had not risen, our estimates suggest, they would have escaped classification as potential failure. A further four are reported by our model to experience a substantial improvement in Z, almost sufficient to raise them above the critical level of Z. An example of a company in this category is provided in Figure 9.1. This charts Z scores derived from the two sets of contingent financial statements for Alfred Herbert, the UK's leading producer of machine tools at the time, which collapsed during the period. Z scores under actual conditions fall consistently and substantially below the critical level of Z throughout the period; but the alternative macroeconomic conditions feed through the model to improve the company's financial statements and raise Z almost above the critical level at which the probability of failure is not counted as material.

The external developments or changes in the state of the world on which we have focused are then estimated to have had a major impact on the survival prospects of a substantial minority of our population.

9.5 Summary and conclusion

This chapter asks to what extent macroeconomic factors can be held responsible for the failure of large companies in the turbulent exchange rate regime of 1977–83. It uses a macro–micro model which generates financial statements for individual companies contingent on exogenous macroeconomic developments. On the basis of these contingent financial statements companies are classified using a discriminant model as likely survivors or likely failures.

The model was used to construct financial statements for two states of the world for each large listed UK company which failed in the years 1979–83. One of these states represented actual conditions in the years 1977–83 when the economy experienced a major exchange rate rise. The other was constructed on the counterfactual assumption that interest and exchange rates had remained unchanged at their previous levels through this period. Our estimates suggest that for a substantial minority of the population the probability of failure would have been decisively or substantially reduced had the economy not experienced this interest rate rise and currency appreciation.

This conclusion is relevant to both hysteresis and economic natural selection. As to the former, it offers another mechanism for hysteresis: unless these failures are promptly reversed by the re-birth of the old companies *via* receivership or by the entry of replacement companies, capacity and jobs will disappear: sustainable employment levels decline. As to natural selection, if factors outside the control of management often play a substantial role in failure, it may be appropriate to question the efficiency of this mechanism of economic natural selection: the results offer a corrective to the 'wide or even universal agreement that the prime cause of failure is bad management' (Argenti, 1976, p. 123).

Appendix 9A: The sample of larger listed failing companies

Table 9.A1: *The sample of larger listed failing companies*

Company	Year of failure
Airfix	81
Amalgamated Industries	81
Austin (F) Leyton	82
Berwick Tempo	82
Blackwood Morton & Sons (Holdings)	81
Brittain	79
Brocks Group of Companies	81
Burrell & Co.	80
Caravans International	82
Carron Company (Holdings)	82
Cawdaw Industrial Holdings	82
Clark Son & Morland	83
Dundee-Combex-Mar	80
Dykes J Holdings	80
Fodens	80
Gieves Realisations	80
Herbert (Alfred)	80
Homfray & Co.	81
Inveresk Group	81
Lesney Products	82
Lockwoods Foods	81
Oxley Printing Group	81
Pickles (William) & Co.	82
Richards & Wallington Industries	81
Sanger (JE)	80
Southern Construction (Holdings)	80
Stone Platt Industries	82
Viners	82
Whiteley (BS & W)	81
Wyatt (Woodrow) Holdings	82

Note:
Companies are included which were members of the
Department of Trade and Industry population of larger listed
companies in 1977 and which were liquidated or went into
receivership in the years 1979–83. Information on liquidations
and receivership was obtained from successive editions of the
Stock Exchange Official Yearbook.

Notes

We are grateful to the Leverhulme Trust for sponsoring this research and to ICAEW for subsequent support, to Cambridge Econometrics Ltd for the use of their macroeconomic model and to the UK Business Statistics Office for financial statement data.

1 This section draws very heavily on Goudie and Meeks (1991).
2 This truncated historical period is chosen so that estimation ends before the start of the historical case studies of section 9.4 in which the models are used to predict a subsequent set of failures.
3 The critical level, λ, depends on the odds ratio and the loss ratio:
$$\lambda = \ln (q_1.C_{21}/q_2.C_{12})$$
where q_1 and q_2 are the priors for failing (group 1) and surviving (group 2) corporations respectively, C_{12} is the cost of classifying a corporation in group 1 when it is actually in group 2.
4 With a comparable critical value for Z.
5 Because of the intimate relationship between exchange and interest rates in macroeconomic theory (see e.g. Dornbusch and Fischer, 1990) and in practice.

Part Three

Using models to guide policy

10 On the equilibrium properties of macroeconomic models

Andrew Britton and Peter Westaway

10.1 Introduction

Macroeconomic models were first estimated as an aid to understanding the behaviour of the economy in the short to medium term, that is, over a horizon of about six months to about two or three years. But there has been some shift of attention in the past ten years or so away from relatively short-term demand stabilisation policy questions to supply-side issues which require a more extended view. The Government has a medium-term financial strategy. The behaviour of financial markets has drawn attention to the way in which expectations about the distant future can have immediate effects. The result for macroeconomic modellers has been rather more attention paid to the long-term properties of models. These issues were addressed specifically in Hargreaves (ed.) (1992).

In Britain there is a long tradition of using estimated macroeconomic models in the design of macroeconomic policy. The research has been undertaken, continuously since the 1950s, at the National Institute of Economic and Social Research, the London Business School and the Department of Applied Economics at Cambridge, to mention just three of the many institutions involved. The practical use of models has been the responsibility of the Treasury and the Bank of England, where some innovative model-building has also taken place. In this paper we concentrate mainly on the use of models to describe the consequences of monetary policy changes. For this purpose it is, of course, essential to use a model which has appropriate theoretical properties and a sensible definition of equilibrium conditions.

The first requirement of any model which claims to represent the long-term behaviour of the economy is that its solution should be computable and defensible when projected indefinitely into the future. Estimated models are often complex systems which even their proprietors find difficult to understand, so this test is not a trivial one. The second requirement is that the model should fit the facts. The third requirement is that the long-run behaviour of the model should conform to a coherent theory of economic behaviour. In this paper we assume that model-builders know their craft and that the first and second requirements are met. The third requirement raises issues of more general interest.

The paper begins with a discussion of theory and methodology, centring on the so-called neoclassical synthesis (which applies different theories to the short run and the long run), and on the concept of equilibrium. After that, two simple algebraic models are presented: the first is a Walrasian model and the second corresponds to the equilibrium solution of a macro-economic model similar to that used at the Institute and elsewhere. The point of the comparison is to show how similar they are, but some important differences are also identified. The next section applies this theoretical framework to the Institute's model. It is shown to possess a well-defined equilibrium both in the short run (with wealth and capital stocks effectively fixed) and in the long run (as wealth and capital stocks adjust). Simulations with the model demonstrate that the short-run equilibrium is approached within a few years, but that the long run is very remote indeed. The final section identifies some conclusions.

10.2 Economic theory and methodology

Since the 1960s, many macroeconomic models have been constructed along the lines suggested by the neoclassical synthesis, the attempt to reconcile Keynesian economics with the classical tradition, beginning with Hicks and continued by Patinkin and by Klein. 'The way is open for the re-integration of the Keynesian message into a more general system of interpretation. The model becomes sufficiently eclectic to be able to produce both Keynesian and monetarist results—monetarist in the long period and Keynesian in the short period' (Fitoussi, 1983, pp. 4–5; see also Blanchard, 1987). The contribution of Keynes to this synthesis is to provide an explanation of fluctuations in output corresponding to variation in the 'pressure of demand' as recorded by unemployment, capacity use or the responses to business surveys, that is to behaviour over the cycle. Within that time scale, it is assumed that markets do not all clear, so that excess or deficient demand can persist for goods and services or for labour. The Keynesian short period is treated as a disequilibrium state.

The 'monetarist' component of the synthesis is the standard classical or neoclassical theory against which Keynes rebelled. It means that the equilibrium properties of the model are based on the assumption of market clearing, in the traditions of general equilibrium theory. The key figure is Walras, although the synthesis does not have to follow his assumption of perfect competition. The crucial point is that price adjustment will always tend to bring the economy back towards an equilibrium in which excess supply or demand is eliminated.

This synthesis is by no means universally accepted. The new classical school insists that agents behave in a rational way in the short term as well as in the long term, so that market transactions which are mutually beneficial will be made continuously, at prices acceptable to all parties. On this reasoning the cycle itself is an equilibrium phenomenon. Some Keynesians, on the other hand, would find 'co-ordination failure' even in the long term—see for example Weintraub (1979).

There are two quite different ways of characterising equilibrium: it can be defined in relation to a theory of economic behaviour, or in relation to a mathematical representation of the economy. A theory-based definition of equilibrium has been suggested as follows: 'An economy is in equilibrium when it generates messages which do not cause agents to change the theories which they hold or the policies which they pursue' (Hahn, 1974). This broader definition would not only apply to a Walrasian general equilibrium model with perfect competition but could also apply to models of imperfect competition and incomplete markets.

In looking at the properties of macroeconomic models, however, we have the option of defining equilibrium in quite different terms, by reference to mathematics rather than economic theory. The definition can be quite straightforward, at least in a linear system.

The concept of equilibrium in its dynamic sense may be explored through an apt semantic interpretation of the procedure for solving a basic dynamic equation. The general solution is obtained by summing a particular solution with the general solution of the homogeneous equation. The particular solution is the equilibrium path, in that by definition it represents the behaviour of the system when one excludes the endogenous dynamics. (Vercelli, 1991, p. 13)

(This definition is similar to but not identical with, the 'collapsing' or 'telescoping' of adjustment lags often adopted by model-builders as a means of exhibiting the equilibrium properties of their models.) This mathematical definition may be wider than that which is typically assumed by general equilibrium theory. The 'endogenous dynamics' of the economy will include quantity and price alignments, and the adjustment of expectations, but they may include other kinds of adaptation as well. Suppose that the structure of competition between firms evolves gradually in response to opportunities for new entrants into monopolistic industries. Suppose that the behaviour of trade unions, and their success in attracting or holding membership, evolves gradually in response to labour market conditions. These processes of adjustment would most naturally be treated as exogenous in a general equilibrium model, but they might well be subsumed into the 'endogenous dynamics' of an estimated macroeconomic model. Any definition of equilibrium rests on the choice of variables to be represented as exogenous or endogenous (as the definition quoted above makes clear). One must think of equilibrium as a property of a particular model or level of explanation.

In macroeconomic modelling there is another very important reason for gradual adjustment towards equilibrium relating to the life-cycle of individual households and their age distribution in the population as a whole. A 'technology shock' for example will have a different effect on workers of different ages. Its full effect will not be felt until all those who were in the workforce at the time it occurred have reached the age of retirement. Similar considerations apply to consumer behaviour, in response for example to the abolition of restrictions on borrowing (for a detailed discussion, see Ermisch and Westaway, 1994).

By holding some variables constant one can explore a variety of different concepts of equilibrium within the same model. Models will possess a hierarchy of 'short-period' and 'long-period' concepts of equilibrium, since their mathematical form corresponds to a difference equation of a very high order. Since Marshall if not before, economists have made this distinction: the capital stock is assumed constant in short-run equilibrium, which determines the level of output, but variable in long-run equilibrium. The same distinction must be made in a macroeconomic model, and will be used extensively in this paper. (It is not to be confused with the distinction between long-period equilibrium and short-period disequilibrium which is made in the neoclassical synthesis described above.)

But the adjustment processes will all overlap and interact. It may take longer to adjust some prices than it takes to approach the desired level of some kinds of capital stock, so in a sense long-run equilibrium could be approached more rapidly than short-run equilibrium. In a reasonably complex model there will be a great variety of adjustment processes, which each involves a rapid or slow approach to some concept of equilibrium. 'Clearly a short-period equilibrium generally turns out to be a disequilibrium from the long-period point of view. Confusion and misunderstanding arise unless one precisely establishes the type of "period" one is referring to' (Vercelli, 1991, p. 19).

The question remains whether it is appropriate for a macroeconomic model to possess any unique and well-defined equilibrium properties of this kind. Should the equilibrium solution of the model, whether for the flow of output or for the stock of capital, in fact be independent of the path by which it is approached?

10.3 Economics and history

Neoclassical theory describes economic behaviour as the consequence of a continuous process of rational decision-making. The equilibrium state of the economy depends on today's preferences and possibilities, not on past history. History takes place 'off-stage', determining the exogenous variables: population, technology, tastes, institutions, endowments and so on. The process of history is not endogenous to the economic system itself.

The implication of this theory is that transitory economic events cannot have permanent consequences. Equilibrium, to be sure, is not maintained continuously, so the economy exhibits persistence, of higher or lower degree. Nevertheless, if we are concerned only with processes that involve conscious decisions taken afresh from first principles every day, then persistence is finite. In the end bygones are bygones. If we stay within the neoclassical framework then the exceptions to this rule will reflect externalities of some kind. One possible example is endogenous technical progress – discussed in Lucas (1988). Knowledge is a public good and does not in general depreciate. If the state of the economy in the short term influences the rate of increase or dissemination of useful knowledge, then the history of economic disequilibrium will influence the subsequent development of the economy in perpetuity.

Other examples abound. The attitude of individuals to unemployment may depend on their own experience of it, and on the way it is viewed by the community in which they live. Changes in social attitudes, resulting from experience, may be inevitable and be passed on from one generation to another. Cross (ed.) (1988) provides a collection of papers on hysteresis in the labour market and a useful discussion of the broader issue of the relationship of historical events to economic analysis.

History includes many relationships between events which cannot be reasonably approximated by any linear equations. Some historical situations are like watersheds: once they are crossed there is no going back. There are ratchet effects, such that movement in one direction is inhibited but not in the other. If we allow for all these possibilities the potential for 'path dependence' is unlimited.

A broader definition of the subject matter of economics would embrace the evolution of institutions—for example how persistent inflation leads to indexation or a shortening of contract periods. Social norms and the framework of law are clearly influenced by economic events—the legal or conventional age of retirement is influenced, for example, by experience of the demand for labour. This is a rich field for further research, which could perhaps eventually be reflected in the long-run properties of estimated macroeconomic models. There can be little doubt that the course of history does change the behaviour of the economy; the question is rather whether the process is sufficiently regular to be represented by mathematical equations.

10.4 The equilibrium structure of a Walrasian macroeconomic model

We now proceed to specify the long-run behaviour of a model which would accord with the neoclassical synthesis, that is to say, an equilibrium macroeconomic model in the classical tradition.

The starting point is a Walrasian general equilibrium system, but to transform this into a macroeconomic model requires aggregation over commodities and over agents. The definition of a commodity is always rather obscure: no two apples are exactly the same. If we need to think of very broadly defined commodities like 'output' or 'labour' then we have to begin our theorising by supposing that individual agents are able to make choices at this level of generality. Equally, we must assume that the production technology requires inputs which are not specified at a level to which our analysis does not discriminate: goods are produced using labour and capital, not labour with particular skills or machines of a particular kind.

Conventionally, aggregation is often done by applying the theory to a 'representative' firm or household, and by assuming that all firms and all households conform to that norm. A fairly typical example of this procedure can be found in Sargent (1979, p. 7): 'it is assumed that all firms share the same production function. ... Our assumptions about the identity of firms' production functions and their profit maximising behaviour in the face of perfectly competitive markets for output and labour imply that there is a useful sense in which there exists an aggregate production function'. This approach to aggregation comes in for heavy criticism in Granger (1990, p. 25): '[These] results provide an implied criticism of the "typical decision-maker" theory used to suggest macroeconomic relationships from a micro theory. A behavioural equation for a typical consumer, say, is derived from basic micro theory, all consumers are considered to be identical, and the macro relationship is just N times the micro one. It is seen that a badly misspecified macro relationship can occur'. Granger shows that successful aggregation across large numbers of individuals depends rather on 'common factors' in the movements of the independent variables in the micro-equations. If all consumers have income movements in common, then it will be possible to trace out an aggregate relationship between income and consumption, although different households necessarily have very different marginal propensities to consume. The aggregation issue is fundamental to the choice of specifications for macroeconomic models. It is, indeed, fundamental to the existence of a meaningful subject called macroeconomics.

A recent history of macroeconomic modelbuilding (Bodkin, Klein and Marwah, 1991) includes an interesting chapter on their 'antecedents'. This gives an account of the general equilibrium models devised by Walras, and contrasts them with the structure of macroeconomic models of the Klein school. The debt of all model-builders to Walras is acknowledged, especially as the originator of the idea of general equilibrium. The aesthetic appeal of that idea is recognised by a quotation from Walras himself: 'The system of the economic universe reveals itself, at last, in all its grandeur and complexity, a system at once vast and simple, which, for sheer beauty, resembles the astronomic universe' (Walras, *Eléments d'économie politique pure*; quoted by Bodkin *et al.*, 1991, p. 5).

We begin by specifying a system of macroeconomic equations consistent with Walras.

The commodities specified might be: domestic output (y with a price p), foreign output (y^* with a price p^*), labour (l with a wage w), domestic investment, including stockbuilding, ($K-K^0$) which produces future output (with a return of r) and net investment overseas (n, with a return of r^*). The economy consists of firms which use labour, capital (K^*) and net imports to produce domestic output, and households which consume output, supply labour and own capital. Here we are concerned with equations for supply and demand, but behind these one must assume that there exist functions which describe the utility of individual households and the production of individual firms.

For the present we shall assume that all contracts are specified in real terms, and that the return to all asset holders includes full compensation for changes in the price level. It is a familiar result of Walrasian models that the equilibrium price level depends on monetary policy, changing in proportion to changes in the money supply or the exchange rate, according to the regime in operation. With full indexation, the equilibrium of the real economy will be unaffected by such monetary policy. (We shall discuss below the implications of nominal inertia in wages and prices, and of the existence of assets on which the return is not indexed.)

The foreign price level and the rate of return on overseas investment are exogenous. To keep things simple we do not specify exports and imports separately, or distinguish between trade in materials and finished goods. Such distinctions must be made in a useful macroeconomic model, but they add little to a purely theoretical discussion of the kind presented here.

The model consists of equations for the flow of supply and demand of four quantities (y, n, DK and l) to determine three relative prices (w/p, p/p^*, $r-r^*$). It is a model of flow equilibrium in which all markets clear. It implies a long-run model of stock equilibrium towards which the economy will move.

For each firm there are equations of the form:

$$l^d = f_1(K^0, T, y^*; p/p^*, w/p, r) \tag{10.1}$$

$$K^d = K^0 + f_2(K^0, T, y^*; p/p^*, w/p, r) \tag{10.2}$$

$$y^s = f_3(K^0, T, y^*; p/p^*, w/p, r) \tag{10.3}$$

where K^0 is the initial quantity of capital and T is a parameter defining technical progress. It is assumed that there are increasing costs to the adjustment of the capital stock, and that the second equation determines the flow of investment demand. For simplicity it is assumed that firms do not invest or borrow overseas. All profits are distributed to households. Demand for net imports of foreign output is defined by the budget constraint of the firm:

$$(p^*/p)n = -y^s - w/p \; l^d + K^d - K^0$$

For each household there are equations of the form:

$$l^s = g_1(W^0, D; w/p, r, r^*) \tag{10.4}$$

$$K^s = g_2(W^0, D; w/p, r, r^*) \tag{10.5}$$

$$C = g_3(W^0, D; w/p, r, r^*) \tag{10.6}$$

where W^0 is the initial quantity of wealth and D is a parameter defining population growth (or the tax and benefit system). By identity $W = W^0 + w/p \; l^s + rK + r^*(W - K) - C$, where C is consumption. Consumer behaviour implies a long-run demand for wealth, but the wish to spread consumption equally across time periods prevents the immediate adjustment of wealth to its long-run target level. The budget constraint for the household defines its demand for overseas assets.

The supply and demand equations for individual firms or households can be aggregated with reasonable confidence since all face the same set of relative prices. This, indeed, is the beauty of the Walrasian model. (In practice, however, the price indices appropriate to each household or firm would have different weights, so that the aggregation problem is not entirely avoided. What matters is that the movements of price indices are dominated by factors which are common to all households and all firms.) The conditions for market equilibrium are:

$$l^s = l^d, \; K^s = K^d, \; y^s = C + K^d - K^0 - n$$

The market for overseas transactions also clears, in accordance with

Walras' Law, so the current and capital accounts of the balance of payments are necessarily equal.

The solution of this model determines the levels of prices and quantities. In general, all prices and all quantities will be influenced by all the variables which define the behaviour of households and firms. It would be misleading to speak of a 'supply-side' equilibrium, except in special cases. Thus the level of output in this very classical model depends on demand as well as on supply, on tastes as well as on technology. If demand for output rises, this will be reflected in relative prices, including in general a rise in real wages, which will provide the incentive for an increased supply of labour. In the long run, the supply of capital will also respond to higher rates of return.

The model determines output, employment and investment, conditional on initial values of wealth and the capital stock. The firms' investment decisions will take account of the costs of adjusting the capital stock and the households' spending decisions will take account of the benefit of smoothing consumption over time. The model could be solved period by period to show the approach to a full stock equilibrium, that is to a long-term equilibrium in the Marshallian sense of the word. Because of the inter-temporal nature of saving and investment decisions, all the supply and demand equations should be specified in terms of expected prices for all relevant time periods as well as the prices which clear spot markets. There are no future markets for products or for factors of production.

The prices expected in all future periods will reflect expectations about the future path of the exogenous variables, together with perceptions of the structure and parameters which define the behaviour of the economy. Such expectations will be discounted and, to the extent that goods or assets are durable, will be reflected in their current prices. If perceptions about the behaviour of the economy are correct then the expectations will be consistent with the outcome predicted by the model itself. We can, if we wish, define such a condition as necessary for equilibrium, although it is quite separate from the notion of market clearing. The system will not be at rest so long as agents can perceive systematic errors in their predictions and take steps to correct them.

The long-term or stock equilibrium of the model is implied by equations (10.1) to (10.6). It could be defined by a similar system of equations in which K^0 and W^0 were omitted from all the supply and demand functions. We know from consideration of the production functions of individual firms that a unique equilibrium for the stock of fixed capital should exist, given the availability of technology, population and land. We also know from the intertemporal budget constraint which applies to the behaviour of each individual household that the stock of wealth should also converge towards a unique equilibrium, given the productive capacity of the economy and the return available on all forms of investment, as well as the age structure of the population and all sorts of other exogenous conditions.

In this long-term equilibrium all prices and all endogenous quantities will be uniquely determined by the current state of technology, tastes and other exogenous variables. Neither the past, nor the expected future, is of any relevance, except to the extent that it is imprinted in those exogenous variables. The long-term stock equilibrium model would be purely static. This does not mean, of course, that the economy itself would be static. The exogenous variables have their own exogenous dynamics to which the economy responds.

10.5 Imperfect competition

Walrasian general equilibrium models assume perfect competition. Individual agents base their decisions on market prices, which they cannot themselves influence at all. Most macroeconomic models, however, assume imperfect competition, as being a much better approximation to the market structure of most sectors in advanced industrial countries. Suppliers, generally speaking, are assumed to set prices. It is natural, therefore, to specify some equations with quantities on the right-hand side and prices on the left. In some equations also it is appropriate to have one quantity dependent on another quantity as well as on relative prices. This is not just a renormalisation; it is a different view of the way the aggregate economy works.

There are many ways of combining the first-order conditions for profit maximisation to give equations that describe the behaviour of individual firms, although none of them will be strictly appropriate as a basis for specifying aggregate relationships. Amongst the alternatives often used are the following:

- the production function itself
- an equation to determine the 'mark-up' of prices over costs
- factor demand equations conditional on output.

Although none of these relationships provides a strictly valid basis for aggregation, any of them may be a useful basis for aggregation in practice. Thus the production function of individual firms may be very different, yet a rise in aggregate output (with a given aggregate capital stock) may as a rule be associated with a rise in aggregate demand for labour. In this context it is interesting to note that the behaviour of an individual firm in response to a rise in its own sales may not be the same when that rise in sales reflects its own competitive success as when it reflects an upturn in the economy as a whole. Indeed, the aggregate response of firms, especially in setting prices, may rest mainly on the way that individual firms respond to their perceptions of aggregate demand. If so, aggregation across firms is less of a problem.

It may be useful to set out briefly how the assumption of imperfect competition might change the six-equation algebraic model set out above. Demand for factors of production is conditional on output. Hence we replace equations (10.1) and (10.2) from the Walrasian system with:

$$l^d = h_1(K^0, T, y^*, y; w/p^*, w/r) + u_1 \tag{10.1'}$$

$$K^d = K^0 + h_2(K^0, T, y^*, y; w/p^*, w/r) + u_2 \tag{10.2'}$$

The equation for the supply of output is then replaced with an equation for the price level. To preserve homogeneity in nominal variables, the variable on the left-hand side is the inverse of the real wage.

$$p/w = h_3(K, T, y^*, y; w/p^*, r) + u_3 \tag{10.3'}$$

Equation (10.3') could be replaced by an equation for the mark-up on marginal costs, that is for prices relative to unit labour costs and to import prices.

$$p/w = (K^0, y, y^*, l; w/p^*) + u_5 \tag{10.3'}$$

The behaviour of households is also re-specified. Equation (10.4) for the supply of labour is inverted to become an equation for the real wage, conditional on employment.

$$w/p = j_1(l, D) + v_1 \tag{10.4'}$$

The supply of capital could be seen as resulting from sequential decisions on how much to save and how to allocate the stock of wealth. This would justify replacing W^0, w/p and D in equation (10.5) with W, and replacing separate terms in r and r^* with the difference between them:

$$K^s = j_2(W, r - r^*) + v_2 \tag{10.5'}$$

The remaining equation is the consumption function, which is specified to depend on income as well as initial wealth.

$$c = j_3(W^0, y', r') + v_3 \tag{10.6'}$$

where $y' \equiv lw/p + r'W^0$ is private sector income, and $r' \equiv ar + (1-a)r^*$ is an average rate of return on wealth.

The equilibrium conditions cannot be written in exactly the same form as they were in the Walrasian system since l^s and y^s do not appear in this model explicitly. Instead we should write $l=l^d$, $k^s=k^d$ and $y=c+k^d-k^0-n$, conditions which will in fact hold even when markets do not all clear. The process of market adjustment would be represented by the dynamic relationships for which equations (10.3') and (10.4') are the equilibrium conditions. Firms set prices and their employees bargain for nominal wages: the result is an aggregate real wage, which (in conjunction with the cost of capital and the real exchange rate) should be consistent with all the relationships modelled by equations (10.1') to (10.6').

This summary treatment of equilibrium in a model of imperfect competition does not do justice to the complexities beneath the surface. If individual firms and unions have market power, then their interactions must include strategic behaviour, which can be modelled in a variety of ways using game theory. However, such interactions have no place in a macroeconomic model which depicts aggregate behaviour, since agents do not co-ordinate their strategies at the sectoral level. We must assume that the outcome can be represented by a set of aggregate functional relationships similar in most respects to the aggregate supply and demand equations appropriate under perfect competition.

10.6 Nominal inertia and the determination of prices

Up to this point we have assumed that the absolute price level, and the monetary policy which fixes it, have no effect at all on the real economy, because all contracts and the return on all assets are index-linked. The real world, of course, is not like that at all. In this section we consider how the discussion of equilibrium in macroeconomic models should be modified to take account of nominal inertia or non-indexation.

Consider first the very long-term equilibrium behaviour of the model when all stock adjustment is completed. That equilibrium clearly must be invariant to the price level, as it has been in our discussion so far. The equations which determine the level of all real variables are derived from the rational choices of individual agents, and the price level as such makes no difference to tastes or technology.

At the other extreme, it is equally clear that the behaviour of the economy in Keynesian short-period disequilibrium will not be invariant to monetary policy. If nominal wages and prices take time to adjust to market-clearing levels, then real wages and relative prices will change in the immediate aftermath of an unexpected change in monetary policy – for example, a devaluation of the exchange rate.

An interesting question concerns what we have referred to as the short-term equilibrium, that is, the levels of output and expenditure flows at which the market clears consistent with given stocks of fixed capital and other assets. The point to emphasise is that this flow equilibrium is not invariant to monetary policy, if some assets and liabilities are not indexed. An unexpected devaluation, for example, will reduce the real value of nominal debt and hence the flow of net saving by debtors in short-term equilibrium, and that effect will persist until the desired relationship is restored between the stock of net assets and the flow of income. Such an adjustment may take a very long time to complete.

No model is complete without a representation for monetary policy to explain the price level in the long run. (In a model solved under the assumption of rational expectations even a short-run solution is impossible unless the equilibrium price level is clearly defined.) The representation of monetary policy must include an exogenous nominal variable – the exchange rate, the money supply or a target for the price level itself would all be appropriate under different regimes. The policy instrument determined by this relationship would normally be a nominal rate of interest. In the long run, however, nominal interest rates must be equal to the real rate of return determined by the capital market plus the rate of inflation, which will necessarily be in line with the rate of change of the exogenous equilibrium price level.

It may be convenient at this point also to mention the representation of fiscal policy. The equilibrium conditions of the model must be such that the stock of public sector debt tends to some finite level relative to the tax base. At least one dimension of tax or government expenditure must be represented by a rule which will tend to preserve stability. Some countries have for many years followed fiscal policies which do not have this stability property. However, they can do so only because financial markets believe that eventually they will change their behaviour. The choice of stabilising rule to include in the model depends on the purpose for which it is being used. It is unusual for the rule to be estimated from past data, although it might, for some countries at least, be possible to do so.

10.7 The National Institute model

A full description of the most recent version of the National Institute macroeconomic model is given in NIESR (1995). In reconciling its properties with the stylised model just outlined, the key features are as follows;

10.7.1 Production technology, labour demand and investment

Unlike the simple one-good production technology of the stylised model, the fully specified model is disaggregated into a number of sectors: manufacturing, distribution, business services, other non-manufacturing, public sector and oil. The first four sectors are explicitly based on a CES production technology. The long-run desired capital stock is specified accordingly and is guaranteed by the specification of the relevant forward-looking investment equations which drive the respective capital–output ratios to their required long-run level as a function of relative factor prices, as described in Young (1992). The labour demand curves are defined in terms of hours with separate equations determining the number of people employed.

10.7.2 Wages and prices

As in the stylised model, the key wage and price setting equations are determined at the aggregate level. Econometric details and the implications for model properties are given in Soteri and Westaway (1993), extending the earlier work of Joyce and Wren-Lewis (1991). The long-run solution for whole economy domestic prices (the GDP deflator) is determined as a mark-up on whole economy unit labour costs, where the mark-up itself is found to depend on the role of capacity utilisation, the cost of stockbuilding and the real exchange rate. Price dynamics are determined by intertemporal optimisation in the face of quadratic adjustment costs, thus introducing forward-looking 'New Keynesian' effects into the price equation. Wages are also determined in a forward-looking manner with overlapping wage contracts based on Taylor (1980), (see Mogadham and Wren-Lewis, 1994). Equilibrium real wages are determined according to the 'reduced form' bargaining framework of Layard et al. (1991).

10.7.3 Consumer spending and the housing market

The consumption function described in Pain and Westaway (1994) incorporates explicit effects from the flow of consumer credit and mortgage equity withdrawal. As with all conventional consumption functions derived from the original Hendry and von Ungern Sternberg (1981) approach, it contains an integral correction term which determines the long-run ratio of total wealth (financial and housing) to income for the personal sector.

10.7.4 Government spending and taxation

In exactly the same way that the consumption function guarantees long-run stock-flow equilibrium for the personal sector, so too is government policy determined with a view to long-run government solvency. In our simulations, we hold government spending fixed and choose the rate of income tax to move so as to ensure that the public sector deficit to income ratio achieves its target value in the long term.

10.7.5 Company sector finances

In the stylised model, we assume that all financial wealth is held by persons. In fact, companies are very important as financial intermediaries. The company sector behavioural equations must therefore embody some form of financial stock equilibrium. In the Institute model, this is achieved by a quasi-buffer stock system whereby any disequilibrium between desired and actual liquid assets is assumed to feed back into company sector real and financial decisions, affecting dividend payments for example (see Westaway and Young, 1993; Young, 1993).

10.7.6 Trade and the overseas sector

The demand for UK-produced goods by overseas customers is determined by sectoral export equations depending on world trade and relative prices (see NIESR, 1995, for details). The demand for imports by UK residents is determined by a demand system whereby total final demand is allocated between domestic and overseas output according to the expenditure composition of demand and by relative prices (see Pain and Westaway, 1996). In terms of overall model properties, the overseas sector may be seen as the residual sector since there is no behavioural equation which will determine the "desired" current account of the balance of payments. However, since the financial balances of the other sectors of the model (personal, corporate and government) are tied down by behavioural relationships which target the respective long-run sectoral wealth to income ratios, this should guarantee that the long-run balance of payments should stabilise relative to output. Importantly, this property of the model would still hold even if the nominal exchange rate were held fixed, as in a monetary union, for example.

10.8 Short-run and long-run equilibrium in the Institute model

A convenient way of demonstrating some of the equilibrium properties of the model is to simulate the effects of a permanent change in the price level. This can be achieved in a number of ways; we compare two different methods. First, we illustrate the effects of a devaluation of the sterling exchange rate, which for simplicity we assume occurs exogenously. Since domestic prices will eventually adjust completely to a change in overseas prices deflated by the exchange rate, a devaluation of 4.76% should produce a long-run increase in domestic prices of 5%. Alternatively, and perhaps more relevantly in a policy context, we show how an interest rate feedback rule can be used to drive the price level up by 5%.

The results of the simulations are shown in Figures 10.1 to 10.14. The model is solved under the assumption of model-consistent expectations but the price-level change itself is assumed to be unexpected. The model is solved over the period 1995Q1 to 2028Q4.

Figure 10.1 shows that the adjustment of the price level for domestic output is relatively rapid, being virtually completed after three years in the case of the rule-based response. The devaluation case is quicker but more oscillatory and takes longer to settle down at the same equilibrium. The difference is mainly explained by Figure 10.2 which shows the nominal exchange rate which falls immediately by 4% in the rule-based case, but then gently approaches the long-run devaluation over the next five years. Figure 10.3 shows the movement in nominal interest rates required by the simple feedback rule to raise the price level, an immediate cut of 0.5% followed by an immediate increase of around the same amount before returning approximately to base values after ten years or so. Although nominal interest rates are held fixed in the devaluation case, the resulting change in real interest rates, which is the more important channel of influence on real activity in the model, is very similar across the two simulations, both showing an initial fall in real rates of slightly more than 2% before returning to base values after seven years in the rule-based case, slightly more in the devaluation case (Figure 10.4). Figure 10.5 shows that the competitiveness gain from the devaluation disappears within a slightly longer time scale. These two effects are the main cause of the stimulus to real activity which rises by a maximum of between 0.75 and 1%, before asymptoting towards base values over the later years of the simulation (Figure 10.6). The difference between the two simulations can be explained by the response of the income tax rate (Figure 10.7) which is used to stabilise the public sector deficit to GDP ratio. This tax rate is required to fall more in the devaluation case because of the larger increase in prices which causes a greater public sector surplus. The increase in consumption (Figure 10.8) is correspondingly larger. Although the public sector deficit (Figure 10.9) is controlled relatively quickly, the stock of public sector debt relative to GDP (Figure 10.10) takes much longer to be returned to base values, and stock equilibrium is still not fully restored by the end of the simulation after 35 years. As a consequence, the full stock–flow equilibrium of the model is not achieved either, for example because tax rates are still slowly returning towards base values. This explains why consumption and hence GDP are still away from their long-run equilibrium values but nevertheless are clearly tending towards them.

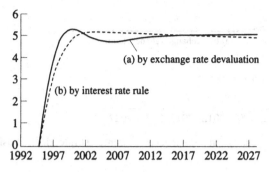

Figure 10.1 Effect of 5% change in price level on RPI excluding mortgage interest component

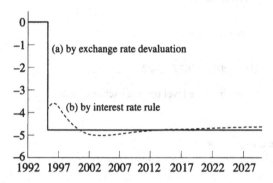

Figure 10.2 Effect of 5% change in price level on effective exchange rate

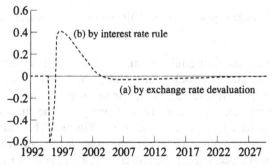

Figure 10.3 Effect of 5% change in price level on base rate interest

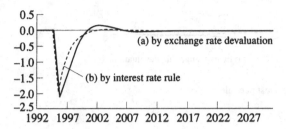

Figure 10.4 Effect of 5% change in price level on real interest rate (defined using RPIX)

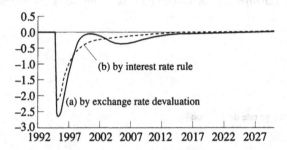

Figure 10.5 Effect of 5% change in price level on real exchange rate

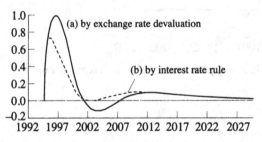

Figure 10.6 Effect of 5% change in price level on GDP (expenditure estimate) at factor cost

This distinction between the flow equilibrium, which is usually achieved within five to seven years, and the stock equilibrium, which takes decades to reach, can equally well be illustrated by the financial positions of the other sectors. For companies, investment rises strongly for the first five years but is back around base levels after seven years (Figure 10.11), while the net capital stock, in manufacturing for example, while returning towards base levels, is still much higher even after 35 years (Figure 10.12). Similarly, while consumption is trending back towards base (Figure 10.8),

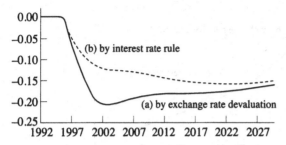

Figure 10.7 Effect of 5% change in price level on standard rate of income tax

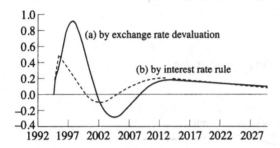

Figure 10.8 Effect of 5% change in price level on consumers' expenditure

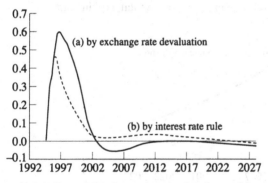

Figure 10.9 Effect of 5% change in price level on public sector NAFA to GDP ratio

it is still higher because of the lower income tax rate and the corresponding stock of wealth (including housing assets) relative to income, shown in Figure 10.13, is still away from its equilibrium value at the end of the simulation period.

Finally, it is interesting to confirm that the current account of the

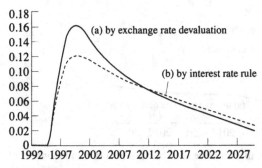

Figure 10.10 Effect of 5% change in price level on public sector net wealth to GDP ratio

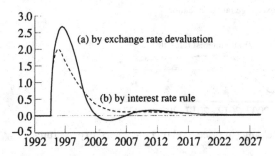

Figure 10.11 Effect of 5% change in price level on total fixed investment

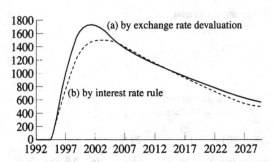

Figure 10.12 Effect of 5% change in price level on net capital stock in manufacturing sector

balance of payments relative to GDP does indeed return to base levels in the long run (Figure 10.14) as explained in the broad overview of the model given above, even in the case when the nominal exchange rate is fixed. This 'self-correcting' feature of the balance of payments should be a feature of any macroeconomic model which embodies behavioural

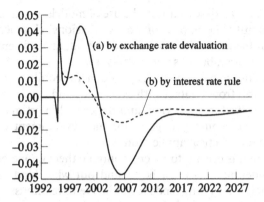

Figure 10.13 Effect of 5% change in price level on total personal sector wealth (including housing) relative to income

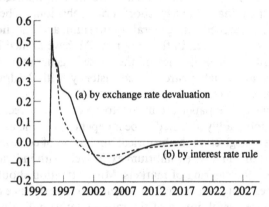

Figure 10.14 Effect of 5% change in price level on overseas sector NAFA to GDP ratio

stock–flow consistency in the personal, company and public sectors of the model. As such, this can be used as an important check on the theoretical coherence of the long-run properties of the model.

10.9 Conclusions

At the end of his survey of developments in macroeconomics, Stanley Fischer bewailed the fashionable tendency for serious macroeconomists in the United States to abdicate from making policy recommendations, leaving the field open to 'those either ignorant or unscrupulous enough to claim full understanding of the issues'. He added: 'Macroeconomists will not be able to participate seriously in such analyses without the use of models, small or large, that attempt to quantify the impact of policy decisions' (Fischer, 1988). This remains one of the main motives for model-building, sufficient on its own to justify the enterprise, but it is not the only one.

It is all too easy to discuss macroeconomics and general equilibrium theory in a vacuum, sealed off from contact with experience and empirical research. The discipline involved in specifying, and better still in estimating, a complete model of the economy is good for the development of theoretical ideas as well as for practical application.

The concept of equilibrium is central to macroeconomic theory. One of the main concerns of model-builders must be to find out what kind of equilibrium (if any) the macro-economy tends towards. We have discussed that issue in this paper making use of the neoclassical synthesis, and appealing to the elegant framework of Walrasian market-clearing. Estimated macroeconomic models were originally Keynesian, and concerned mainly with explaining relatively short-term behaviour. Their inventors were not much concerned with general equilibrium, and may not have believed it was approached even in the long run. We have argued in this paper that the equilibrium properties of the present generation of macroeconomic models are much nearer to consistency with Walras, although important differences remain.

Some of the reflections in the paper are meant to be critical of recent practice. Equilibrium is too readily assumed to be independent of the path by which it is approached, neglecting the historical dimension of economics. This neglect arises from equating equilibrium exclusively with individual choice behaviour and the clearing of markets. More attention should be paid to issues of aggregation, which are fundamental to the existence of macroeconomics. The once useful notion of the representative individual has been used to make credible the absurd assumption that all individuals are alike. Aggregation should not be based on that fallacy, but on common factors that influence the behaviour of all individuals.

The Walrasian system deals with the issue of aggregation better than any other specification we have considered. But it is unrealistic in assuming perfect competition. There is no uniquely correct way of representing a market system with imperfect competition, and several alternatives have been discussed. On the whole the ones closest to Walras seem more attractive – but that may just be a personal preference. The more urgent question concerns the speed of adjustment towards equilibrium, on which turns the relevance of the whole equilibrium analysis both to theory and to the policy debate.

Note

The views expressed in this paper do not represent those of the Bank of England.

11 Empirical analysis as an underpinning to policy

John Llewellyn

11.1 Introduction

Whether by accident or design, I have worked practically all of my professional life at or around, as the lawyers say, the interface between economic analysis and economic policy-making. Life at an interface tends to be turbulent, with a propensity to throw up the sorts of events which are not easy to explain. Nor does it sufficiently often provide the time to draw breath and reflect, so I am grateful to Iain Begg not only for giving me the opportunity to write this paper, but also for imbuing me with a certain sense of obligation. For as E. M. Forster, I understand it was, observed, how can I know what I think until I see what I write?

The structure of the paper is something of an Odyssey; but that is how my experience of this subject came to me, and I can see no better way to set it down.

11.2 Theory or applied?

Some months after I joined the Department of Applied Economics, in 1970, I had the opportunity to ask the august Joan Robinson what was to me, a young man newly arrived from doing an applied economics DPhil at Oxford, a particularly important, if personal, question. The opportunity arose because, late for the next train to London, she had graciously accepted my offer to drive her to Cambridge station.

Emboldened, as we sped from Sidgwick Avenue in the pride of my life, my open top, wire-wheeled, British racing green MGB, by Joan's tossing of her mane of white hair and her observation that 'This takes me back to when I was a girl,' I put the question. 'Joan,' I asked (she always insisted that students and young members of staff should call her Joan), 'Joan, if you were a young girl today, starting out in economics, what would you elect to be, a theorist or an applied economist?'

247

A set of issues, or rather perhaps emotions, lay behind the question. Cambridge – Sidgwick Avenue – was an impressive place, to the point of being overwhelming. The Faculty list was a veritable roll call of the great and the good, and then of course there was all that history. 'Maynard' was omnipresent. His name was incessantly evoked: scarcely a day went by without Austin Robinson, Joan, Lord Kahn, Nicky Kaldor (with whom Roger Tarling and I had just come to work as research assistants) and others invoking his name almost as if they had only just been speaking with him. One almost had the feeling that the great man was not there to speak for himself only because he was down in London for the day, expected back that evening. But more important than the frequent uttering of that famous name was the hard to define, but nevertheless real, underlying cult of the theorist, something that the younger neoclassicals, and particularly Frank Hahn, were clearly keen to perpetuate.

If the Faculty was living in a penumbra, the DAE was living, or at least so it felt, in full shadow. It was almost received wisdom within the DAE at the time that the Faculty view was that really bright people did theory, the less bright did applied work. I thought this rather silly; and it has to be said that it was principally the applied economists, rather than the theorists, who propounded this supposed view. Indeed, there was counter evidence. Frank Hahn once told me, in tones almost of the confessional, that the economist he most admired was – guess – Brian Reddaway. And there were various young theorists – David Newbery was probably the most evident, but Geoff Heal and Gordon Hughes were others – who went out of their way to show that they had no truck with any such distinction.

That said, there was no avoiding the fact that what we applied economists were doing was less glamorous than, say, it would be to write a General Theory, and perhaps by extension than to work in other areas of theory too. So had we chosen wrong? Were we missing the boat? Would we come to regret our decision? I know that a number of us asked ourselves those questions, and I remember particularly vivid discussions with Mervyn King and Angus Deaton, both of whom too had recently joined the DAE.

Hence the question to Joan. Imagine therefore my surprise when, without a moment's hesitation, almost as if she had been reflecting upon that very subject herself and had been waiting only for me to put the question, she replied 'Oh, an applied economist, no doubt about that.'

She explained. I can remember the words almost perfectly to this day. 'When I was a young girl,' she said, 'there were not many theories about how the economy worked, and those that there were were absolutely dotty. So we had to come up with theories that made sense.' 'But today', she continued, 'there are lots and lots of theories. Too many in fact. What we really need today is to find out which ones are right.'

With that we arrived at Cambridge station, Joan got her train, and I my reassurance.

11.3 Whole-economy modelling

I tell that story because it captures much of where many of us were at the time. If not the sole purpose, then at least a major purpose of economics was taken to be to figure out how the economy worked. The theorists, following the powerful example set by Keynes, did this essentially by thinking. If it was possible in the process to stand conventional wisdom on its head, an art form that Nicky Kaldor in particular had refined to perfection, so much the better. Then, in a partnership with the theorists, the applied economists were supposed to look at the numbers, apply fancy tests, and determine who actually was right. Popper, more or less.

In practice, however, it did not work out quite like that. Just as truth may be stranger than fiction, so did the applied macroeconomic research generate its own stories, its own issues, its own conundra. Thus while Dick Stone and Angus Deaton worked on the (interesting to the theorists) linear consumption function, or Roger Tarling worked on what exactly the relationship was between output and employment, so did Terry Barker and Francis Cripps work at putting the whole systems of equations together. And they found, as they took the clever equations estimated by the various members of their respective teams, that there was a whole further raft of questions about how these individual equations interacted when they were assembled into a complete model of the economy.

Indeed, the behaviour of the simulated economy was often affected as much by decisions taken 'for practical reasons' by model managers Francis and Terry as it was by the empirical findings of the theory-inspired applied researcher. This is not to criticise the model managers. Somebody has to do the job, and that somebody has to do it somehow. It is simply to observe that the properties of the models were determined as much by equations about which we had little or no evidence as by those in respect of which we had a statistically well-founded view. So we never did find out, for example, whether savings determine investment, or whether causality runs the other way: in respect of what the theorists most wanted from us, we never really did deliver the goods.

11.4 Gaining self-confidence

As our research progressed, however, we gained in self-confidence. We learned to worry progressively less that we were not answering the questions that the theorists considered important: indeed, we increasingly came to the view that our research was throwing up both more interesting discoveries and more important questions about how the economy worked than those which came out of the heads of the theorists. And perhaps even more importantly we were, with Wynne Godley at the helm, addressing real (macroeconomic) policy issues, the answers to which stood to influence at least somewhat how the government set the macroeconomic policy levers. As researchers, it seemed to us, we were pulling our weight.

At the same time there were problems. Perhaps the biggest – certainly I thought so – was that both Dick Stone's and Wynne Godley's groups were working on models of only a single economy (the United Kingdom). At least two major difficulties flowed from this. First, President Nixon had taken the United States off the Gold Standard in 1971, and generalised floating followed in 1973, introducing a fundamental structural change into the way that economies interacted. The exchange rate in this new world could no longer be taken as a given: it had to be modelled. And this was not just a matter of estimating a few simple equations and putting them in. The subject was both intellectually difficult and involved, at a minimum, modelling the rest of the world as the counterparty.

Second, it was evident that, where single-country economic forecasting was concerned, the largest error now very frequently derived not from an incorrect forecast or understanding of domestic variables or relationships, but from an incorrect forecast of export volumes and prices, the result in turn of an incorrect forecast of, or assumption about, developments abroad and/or exchange rates. Hence, just as British weather forecasters were finding that the most important improvement that they could make in forecasting British weather would come from modelling and forecasting the hitherto ignored weather system in the southern hemisphere, so did several of us conclude that the most cost-effective strategy to improve the accuracy of the UK economic forecast would very likely be to model and forecast the non-UK economy. This stood, however, to be a large and expensive task.

11.5 Multi-country modelling

By lucky chance, the opportunity to do serious work along these lines came my way, in the shape of an offer in 1977 from the Organisation for Economic Co-operation and Development (OECD) to take charge of its Economic Prospects Division, the group which, together with its Econometric Unit, was responsible for co-ordinating the Organisation's international forecasting and policy analysis. There had been criticism from the US Administration that the Organisation's forecasting methods were out of date, too literary, and insufficiently econometric and scientific.

What really made the task feasible, as well as a pleasure, was the presence of the learned and industrious Lee Samuelson who, as head of the Econometric Unit, was already the proprietor of a small world model, INTERLINK, which he had built with Franciscus Meyer zu Schlochtern. We teamed up, and in the space of just a few years we had built and were running a practical, larger international linkage model designed specifically to assist the OECD semi-annual projection exercise, as well as to illuminate by model simulation a number of the pressing economic policy problems of the day. Our thinking was that, while it was clearly necessary to have individual models of each of the OECD economies – the so-called Major 7 first, and then progressively the smaller ones – this was not where we should put our major effort. Country by country, therefore, we sought merely to construct sensible country models of modest size that exhibited middle of the road properties, wherever possible closely representative of the single-country models used in national administrations.

What we concentrated on was modelling the system as a whole, and in particular on understanding and modelling how economic shocks were transmitted from one country or region to another. The pioneering work had of course been undertaken by Lawrence Klein at Wharton, who in Project LINK had sought to link together different (private sector) national models. The vision was right; but the models were very different from one another; linking them was technically difficult; and the results were often not easy to interpret. As far as OECD governments' own models were concerned, even the large member countries generally had models only of their own individual economies. Hence to show each member country administration broadly how its individual-country model would interact if only it could have been joined up to run in linked mode with its partner countries' national models was clearly an OECD Secretariat comparative advantage, and we sought to exploit that. Art imitated life.

As earlier with single-country models, the modellers learned not only from building INTERLINK, but also from playing with it, just as they then learned further by having its properties, its projections and its forecasts tested by the vigorous, and at times interestingly confident, members of national administrations.

If it was the case at the single-country level that the properties of the model typically were determined as much by the decisions of the model manager as by the properties of the better equations, this was even more the case with INTERLINK. The difference for me at least was that by now I knew and – largely – accepted the fact, not least because of Lee Samuelson's wise and patient explanations. Thus it is, I think, true to say that it had become more and more clear to a number of us that the Joan

Robinson-type hopes, that we would through estimation and modelling 'find out which theories were right,' was almost certainly too ambitious a hope for the foreseeable future. The data, the estimation techniques, and the modelling methods just could not take us that far. But, nevertheless, they could take us a lot further than it was possible to go without them, and we made – rightly in my view – no apologies for our modelling efforts.

What we sought to do, principally, was to enrich the policy debate: to ensure that as much as possible of the (largely empirical) knowledge that the economics profession had was brought to bear on the macroeconomic policy discussions in various of the OECD committees. Sometimes this took the form of model-supported forecasts; more frequently it took the form of policy simulations.

My judgement is that, on balance, the applied economic research as embodied in INTERLINK played, and continues to this day to play, a reasonably important role both in the international policy debate and, sometimes, in consequent policy formulation. At the very least it was generally agreed in the OECD Secretariat that the discipline of having to take all the main relationships into account, both qualitatively and quantitatively, usually led to a more informative policy document, provided – and this is an important proviso – that enough time was available for the writing up to be done well. A bad text, which presents results but does not explain them convincingly, generally does more harm than good.

11.6 Two principal roles

Within any policy-oriented bureaucracy there are two principal roles for a model. The first and perhaps the most continuingly useful feature of any large and reasonably complete model is that it represents a library, or repository, of all the behavioural relationships that its researchers have considered to be important over the model's life. Once a behavioural relationship has been identified, quantified, and incorporated in the model it does not later get casually overlooked; it remains in place, continuing faithfully to play its part, unless or until an explicit decision is taken to remove it.

The late Chris Higgins, a first-rate academic economist and excellent bureaucrat, who after his time as a Director at OECD was to become the Secretary of the Australian Treasury, always used to emphasise particularly this aspect of models. An extremely thorough man with a deep policy experience, he appreciated more than most the professional as well as political obligation that every serious policy advisor has not to overlook any dimension that could reasonably be considered to be important.

The second – related – role of largish models is that of logic machine. I remember Max Corden – my thesis supervisor – impressing on me in 1967, shortly after he arrived at Nuffield College in Oxford, his surprise at the extent to which his Sociology colleagues placed their faith in relatively simple, uni-directional, single-stage theories. He contrasted this with the situation in economics, where it is widely understood that in principle almost everything influences almost everything else, and where even in practice there are many quite well understood relationships which simply have to be taken into account before it can become even remotely credible to offer policy advice.

The point is well made although, as so often, actually applying it can call for nice judgement. I would cite just one episode to illustrate the point (a number of other examples are given in Llewellyn et al., 1985).

11.7 The third oil shock

This episode was what is sometimes called the third oil shock, the virtual halving of the dollar price of internationally traded oil between the end of 1985 and mid 1986. Oil and its effects – at least for large price rises – were relatively well modelled in INTERLINK, being a phenomenon of world economic importance, and with the evidence of the two large rises, of 1973/74 and 1978/79, from which to draw behavioural relationships. As always, we ran an array of simulations, some with unchanged nominal money growth, others with unchanged real money; some with unchanged nominal interest rates, others with unchanged real rates; some with unchanged real government expenditure, others with a (targeted) unchanged final budget position. The interesting thing was that nearly half the runs suggested that, at least in the first two years following the large oil price fall, OECD real GDP would fall below baseline.

We did not fully track down why this should be so, and given the limited time available – the more important the issue, the less time there tends to be to present it properly – we put a write-up of a representative selection of the results before the committee in question, Working Party No. 3 of the Economic Policy Committee. None of the delegates really liked the paper, but one in particular – let him be called Sir G – was scathing. It was intuitively obvious, he stated, that a large fall in oil prices would stimulate output. The two large rises had caused OECD GDP to fall; obviously a large fall would cause it to rise. When his econometricians came out with such garbage, he told them to go away and run their models again. If they must. Harrumph.

Admittedly the results had not been well written up. But the interesting thing, as smarting with indignation we came to realise somewhat later, was that the model had been seeking to tell us all something rather important.

Quite simply, it was the following. Large changes in the price of internationally traded oil, whether up or down, make one group in the world better off, and the other worse off. The group that is made worse off (oil consumers in the case of a price rise, oil producers in the case of a price fall) typically have quite quickly to adjust their expenditure downwards in line with their now-reduced income. The gainers, however, are under no such constraint. They can put their new income in the bank, to spend as and when they wish. Hence, for a large fall in oil prices as for a large rise, the world's propensity to save rises for a year or two, and world aggregate demand dips below baseline. QED.

I wish only that we could have recognised, and put, the point so simply at the time. The lesson, however, is clear. The repository of knowledge and the logic machine roles of largish models are all very well and useful. But unless the results that they produce are fully, simply and clearly explained, the policy masters will ignore them at best, and at worst get positively hostile. Had we done a more convincing job with the write-up in 1986, we might have retained our confidence, and not found ourselves a year later having to write in the June 1987 *OECD Economic Outlook:*

The economic situation is less favourable than expected last year. The assessment then was that lower oil prices and the associated falls in inflation and interest rates had created an opportunity to achieve faster growth accompanied by both low inflation and an unwinding of major current account imbalances. It now appears that the oil-price fall may have improved performance by somewhat less than originally projected...

11.8 But be careful

It is not always thus, however. To trust a model simply because it has been put together from a large number of relationships, each of which is believed in individually, and has been solved by a computer doing a job that the human brain is not powerful enough to accomplish, is to court disaster. The most elegant demonstration of this that I have ever seen was the devastating critique that William Nordhaus made in the *Economic Journal* of the Forrester/Meadows study '*The Limits to Growth*' (Nordhaus, 1973). In essence, Nordhaus raised a strong presumption that the odd, or at least extreme, results that Forrester and Meadows obtained were due not to the supposedly impressive size or complexity of their model, but rather to just a handful of equations that embodied relationships that, to the economist at least, looked to be fundamentally at odds with either theory or the empirical evidence. Flows being functions of stocks, rather than of other flows, peculiar or perverse price elasticities, and that sort of thing. To make his point, Bill built a small model of their model – in a neat jibe, he argued that their model was too complex to understand – using just the handful of relationships that he took to be key. Lo and behold, the Nordhaus model behaved basically like Forrester/Meadows – but the difference was that Nordhaus knew why.

11.9 So empirical models are useful

My experiences therefore lead me to the following conclusions. Of course they are only one person's conclusions: others may have had a different experience.

Whether at the single or at the multi-country level, the researchers and modellers with whom I worked probably never proved, disproved, or even raised particularly strong presumptions about most of the matters of particular concern to economic theorists. The data and the techniques available simply will not bear that weight. But applied research and modelling do assist the policy debate, nationally and internationally, and perhaps thereby policy formulation too, at least on occasions, even if the number of instances of genuinely co-ordinated policy action is disappointingly small. Certainly I and those with whom I worked, both at the DAE and at the OECD, considered that as a result of our models we overlooked less; that our thought processes were better; and that we gave better advice.

11.10 But the issues move on

Most of the research and modelling that I have described so far was concerned with demand-side effects – the modelling of fiscal and monetary shocks, together with the demand-side effects of such other phenomena as oil price shocks and, increasingly, large exchange-rate movements. This was in line with the broad policy preoccupations up to that time, particularly in treasuries and ministries of economics: the manipulation of aggregate demand, particularly through fiscal policy, so as to keep unemployment low through the minimisation of the economic so-called cycle.

Issues, however, move on. As the size of the government sector and government debt broadly doubled as a proportion of GDP; as the economic stabilisers became more important; and as restrictions on international trade and on international financial flows were progressively lifted, so did both the scope and to some extent also the need for demand-smoothing single-country macroeconomic policy action become smaller.

The most important policy problem, on the other hand, namely how to achieve high employment, became ever more pressing. The one thing that was clear was that the solution was unlikely to be found wholly in faster growth; and certainly not in single-country demand-side action to achieve such faster growth. Progressively there developed the view, the realisation, that demand-side economics had for too long been asked to do too much of the work, that over the longer term – and unemployment had been building up in Europe over more than two decades – it was the supply side of the economy which had to be fundamentally at fault if the economy was unable to employ anything like all of its labour force.

For my part, I was accordingly keen to move my focus, and this happened in 1986 when the Secretary General of the OECD moved me to the post of Deputy Director for Manpower, Social Affairs and Education, which served the relevant ministries in much the same way that the Economics Department served treasuries and ministries of economics.

Perhaps all well-trained economists of today know the situation for what it is; but for me at least, educated in the 1960s, and having trained and practised thereafter as a macroeconomist, it came as a rude and fundamentally unsettling shock to find out basically three things, namely that:

- the number of (micro-level) policy influences on employment was enormous
- the contribution that each one made was almost certainly very small
- while there was a huge and truly valiant literature, much of it was inconclusive.

The result of all of this was that it was necessary for me to study a vast amount of applied labour market literature in order to develop any sort of feel – judgement would probably be too strong a word – for the minimum list of structural policies that would be necessary to start to bring about a marked improvement in the employment and unemployment situation in many of the countries of Europe. This view was confirmed for me when, two years ago, I chaired the OECD group that, with the powerful help of John Martin, Mike Feiner, Bengt Åke Lundvall, Carolyn Ervin and others, wrote the Organisation's *Jobs Study* (OECD, 1994–5), in turn drawn from a massive work by a team led by Peter Schwanse that reviewed as far as we could tell all of the relevant theoretical and empirical work on the subject, as well as undertaking some original work in the most needed areas.

11.11 Final conclusion

The results of that work have been published in succinct form for all to see in the OECD *Jobs Study*, and I do not attempt here to summarise the 67 detailed policy recommendations that, if implemented, would do much to reduce this modern day scourge of unemployment.

The more general conclusion that I wish to draw, in line with the basic thrust of this paper, is that in my judgement disproportionate effort continues to be put today, whether in government or in private sector research, including importantly in the banks, into researching, modelling and forecasting the transmission of macroeconomic demand impulses. This is not where the policy debate is at; and increasingly it is not where the prime concerns of financial markets lie.

I am not yet 67 years old, as Joan Robinson was in 1970; and I most certainly will never be Joan. Should it ever be the case however that some young researcher takes me to the station in her sports car, and puts to me the question that I put to Joan, my reply will be that, were I starting out in today's world as an economist, I would, as I did in the 1960s, elect to be an applied economist. I would not, however, today start out down the path of macroeconomic research and modelling; not because that was the wrong place at which to start in 1967 – it was not – but simply because the world, and more importantly the nature and cause of its major problems, have moved on.

Unemployment remains the priority problem, in my view, and much more work and policy effort has to be put into reducing it. But the work that needs to be done today, it seems to me, is to design much better policies than the ones that we currently have. The task is really twofold. First, governments have to continue to provide, within affordable limits, the social protection that all modern civilised countries wish to provide. But second, this must be achieved without doing undue damage to incentives, so that the policies do not, in a globalised and highly competitive world, hinder the otherwise natural tendencies of economies to tend towards high employment.

Note

Many helpful comments on the first draft of this chapter were received, and have been incorporated with many thanks into this revised version, from Terry Barker, Max Corden, Angus Deaton, Gordon Hughes, Mervyn King, David Newbery, Andrew Sentance (who chaired the session at which this paper was read), Stephen Potter, Brian Reddaway, Lee Samuelson, and Franciscus Meyer zu Schlochtern.

12 Using figures to guide macroeconomic policy

Wynne Godley

12.1 Context

Soon after Mrs Thatcher came to power, the Cambridge Economic Policy Group forecast that the policies of her government would cause the worst slump of the post-war period; simultaneously, Patrick Minford forecast that they would cause a boom. Angus Deaton (privately) made a 'semi-serious' forecast that, whatever else happened, we should all still be in business two years later.

Deaton's semi-joke raises profound questions. What framework of thought is appropriate for making judgements about macroeconomic policy and can it be rationalised, codified, and taught? How is work of this kind to be evaluated?

Before trying to answer these questions, let me describe what it is that I actually do and why.[1]

12.2 Perspective

Any methodology for policy analysis obviously has to be conditional on a view about how the economy works and about what can be achieved by policy. My view is that fiscal and monetary policy can and should be used to keep aggregate demand growing fairly steadily at a level which is always well within the limits of the economy's productive potential; that net export demand as well as 'capacity' sets limits to the permissible growth rate, and therefore that domestic demand cannot be allowed to grow by more than is warranted by foreign trade performance. I do not rule out the use of incomes policy if inflation threatens.

12.3 Brass tacks

The macroeconomic conjuncture, with its attendant strategic problems, changes so drastically from period to period that it is difficult to say anything general about procedure: different circumstances call for different methods. But an important and firm foundation, at least for clear thinking, is to be found in the laws of logic; for every buyer there is a seller, for every financial asset there is a financial liability, and corresponding to every financial imbalance there is a change in financial assets or liabilities. This is a good moment to pay tribute to the genius of Richard Stone and affirm, following him, a very strong belief in the importance, and powerful implications, of rigorous accounting, since this extends the ability of the mind to absorb and manipulate large quantities of information in a succinct and consistent way.

The model I am using for policy analysis is based on a double entry system of accounts, in which all flows appear as transactions between six sectors. As every row sums to zero and every column sums either to zero or to a net change in the stock of financial assets, logical coherence is ensured; everything visibly comes from somewhere and goes somewhere. The flow matrices have, as their counterpart, a consistent system of balance sheets. The whole stock flow system is then inflation accounted – that is, a consistent system of real stocks and flows is derived using appropriate deflators. While constructing this system of accounts, the standard economic statistics are to some extent re-organised and massaged. For instance, oil is given a sector all to itself because otherwise the analysis of trade, the fiscal stance and corporate profit is impossible. Again, the analysis of indirect taxation, consumer prices and consumption requires that the poll tax be treated in a way that does not involve meaningless discontinuities; and similar considerations apply to privatisation and the changing frontier between the public and private sectors. Statistical discrepancies are a perpetual source of torment which, particularly with double entry accounts, must be faced and dealt with courageously.

I have about 25 equations which describe behaviour. Regressions (usually two-stage least squares) 'explain' the main expenditure series (including exports and imports), prices, wages, employment and unemployment. Homogeneity is built into the price equations, ensuring that prices eventually respond in full proportion to costs and that profits never become negative. However I do not assume that the long-run Phillips curve is vertical because I do not think this is justified either in theory or by evidence implying plenty of scope for demand management. Taxes are estimated as proportions of the relevant flow variables (this is a weak link in the chain) and interest payments by reference to interest rates and accumulated asset stocks. In all, there are 140 equations, of which about 100 are accounting equations. The main exogenous variables are world trade, the world terms of trade measured in foreign currency, tax, interest and exchange rates, the price of houses and equities and the flow of credit to the household and business sectors.

The software I use[2] enables me to display, simultaneously, as many time series as I wish, either in their naked state or as growth rates, first differences, ratios of one another, scatter diagrams and so on. A complete resolution of the model and display of selected results takes less than fifteen seconds – so the opportunity cost of trying out alternatives is zero.

The main part of any 'forecasting' exercise resides (for me) in making a careful analysis of the present economic situation, always seen in the context of the last two decades or so. First I scan the figures for what they tell me, taking particular care to check for anomalies of measurement. What were the residual errors in the national accounts and in the balance of payments and what do these mean? What happened to non-oil trade and the non-oil terms of trade, to general government investment, to the gap between the population of working age and the working population? Next, I try to identify what it is about the recent past which is the same and what is different compared with earlier periods. To some extent this may be ascertained by inspection of the sign and size of the residuals in the model's equations. But this is never very illuminating because regression residuals tend by their very nature to be inexplicable. Of greater significance is the performance of the Great Ratios which no-one, so far as I know, models directly: the terms of trade; the private sector's net acquisition of financial assets as a share of GDP; the financial deficit of general government as a share; the share of tax receipts; the share of consumption, private and personal disposable income and profits; real wages and productivity; and the ratios of the deflators of all the main components of expenditure to one another.

I think the idea of an econometric model which in any real sense thinks for one is anomalous. The purpose of a model is rather to enlarge the capacity of the mind to encompass a far more complex system of interrelationships than would otherwise be possible. So, having gathered *in my mind* a picture of what has been going on in the recent past, I feed in alternative configurations of exogenous variables. In the case of inexact, behavioural relationships I do not follow any fixed rule as to how residuals should be treated, but try out a huge range of adjustments ('fudge factors') to the raw output of regression equations.

Then I make the model simulate the next four or five years and display the results in the form of growth, inflation and unemployment rates, together with those Great Ratios. I would expect, in any one exercise, to try out about a hundred alternatives using different exogenous variables, fudge factors and equation specifications. As I put it in a recent article in the *Financial Times*, 'gradually, an ordered series of logically and behaviourally possible scenarios forms in the mind. Some of these are plausible others are not. Some carry strong implications for policy, albeit of a conditional nature'. And while there has to be an element of forecasting, my object is not to produce a forecast as such but (again in the words of my *Financial Times* article) to 'provide a navigational chart which lays down alternative courses to desirable destinations [and which] should make it possible to skirt hazards and be prepared for surprises'.

12.4 Comment

The kind of analysis I have described, to answer one of the questions I asked in the second paragraph of this note, can never be codified because the essence of it is to discover what is unique about the present – what is the same and what is different from what happened on previous occasions. To make such an evaluation it is necessary to bring a store of local knowledge and expertise to the operation. It is, for instance, an advantage to have a fairly detailed knowledge of the history of the post World War II period – to remember what happened to inflation in the fifties, what exactly was the succession of events leading to great boom periods such as 1963, 1973 or 1987 or how long it was before such and such a policy gesture had perceptible consequences? Moreover, the choice of values for the model's 'exogenous' variables cannot be reduced to an arid list of logical possibilities. It is here, in particular, that imagination is required. And the end result will follow no standard format. For instance, in some past periods (1973 perhaps, or 1980) the most important thing, if one could only have got it right, was indeed to make a short-term forecast because the immediate prospect was so unpleasant and the need to simply reverse direction so compelling. On other occasions (1975 or 1990?) the important thing was to draw attention to the extremely difficult strategic predicament which threatened the medium term.

Any power I have to persuade others resides not in model 'runs', let alone in single point forecasts, but in the verbal argument deployed. Although I work with a computer model, I aspire to the tradition of the great quantitative political economists such as Keynes, Kaldor or, for that matter, Samuel Brittan, who argue their case with reason and rhetoric,[3] supported with whatever evidence they think appropriate for the particular purpose in hand.

12.5 Some negative views

It follows from what I have said that the results of this kind of analysis cannot properly be summarised in a single table, which shows unemployment, inflation, and GDP one year from now with no verbal commentary at all. Yet that, by implication, is what Christopher Huhne of the *Guardian* newspaper was doing when he made his coveted Golden Guru awards, ignoring all conditionality and restricting attention to a narrow range of topics and time spans. Apart from the fact that forecasting in this sense is, as I believe, impossible (and there is no evidence that it has improved significantly over the years or that one method is better than another) it is never going to tell the policy-maker what to do. I do not think that the more serious statistical evaluations of econometric forecasts, for instance by the Warwick Bureau, are much better. They are all trying to find something which will always elude them – a model which can predict, without fudging (or with it for that matter), the future with any acceptable degree of reliability. In my opinion the quest is foolish one.

12.6 Evaluation

I expect my work to be judged by whether the short-term and medium-term policy problems seem, after the event, to have been correctly identified, whether the policy recommendations look right and whether the case was clearly and convincingly argued.

How well did we do, my Cambridge colleagues and I? I think our strategic evaluation in 1989 and in the period up to September 1992 served the public discussion very well (see Coutts *et al.*, 1990; Godley, 1992). We clearly perceived that consumption would have to be severely restrained for several years and that with sterling in the ERM at $2.95 there would be a very deep and prolonged recession but that (provided fiscal policy remained restrictive) a devaluation of about 12.5% might, we thought, eventually produce a tolerable outcome. When I joined the Treasury's panel of independent forecasters in the autumn of 1992 I was quite emphatic, as I put it, that 'the government is now essentially on the right track. It should on no account be panicked into changing course. Conceivably we have unique opportunity for breaking out of the deeply entrenched and self-reinforcing process of decline which has afflicted the country for so long'. I still think that was the right thing to say at the time and I have continued to support the government policy stance ever since, correctly as I at present believe. But while my policy evaluation was, I believe, pretty good, my work for the Treasury was initially blemished by being far too pessimistic about all the major objectives of policy, in particular, inflation and unemployment.

I hesitate to say, at this stage, more than a word about the seventies and early eighties. I believe that during this time we made an important contribution to the public discussion even if we had no influence over the course of events. The scale and unsustainability of the Heath–Barber boom were clearly foreseen and before the end of 1973 we correctly pointed out that commodity prices could interact with the unfortunate 'threshold' scheme in a way that might generate inflation of 20% or more. (This was important because the inflation in 1974 was not, so far as I know, foreseen by anyone else, but was later attributed to the growth of the money stock which had taken place in 1972.)

And I think the public discussion was well served by the Cambridge Economic Policy Group between 1979 and 1982, when we correctly foresaw that the attempt to subordinate all macroeconomic policy to controlling the stock of M3 would cause an extremely large rise in unemployment from which no recovery would occur without a drastic change in policy. (It should not be necessary to point out that the deregulation of all financial institutions did amount to a policy change of enormous size, for the growth of credit and therefore money turned out to be far in excess of the target which had been the main, if not sole, plank of the government's policy.)

There was much that was wrong with what we wrote in the mid-seventies, partly because, like everyone else, we did not understand inflation accounting properly. And I now think we were probably wrong to back protection in such a (relatively) unqualified way. At least we tried, with integrity and without fear, to think through the consequences of Britain's progressive failure to compete successfully in international trade at that time and subsequently. And we doggedly resisted the abandonment of full employment as a valid target of macroeconomic policy, by a Labour government, in 1976.

Notes

1 The methodology described here is the same as that which has always been used by the Cambridge Economic Policy Group. But my present model is impoverished compared with the models which Francis Cripps made in the seventies.
2 MODLER, supplied by Alphametrics.
3 'The whole art of using language so as to persuade others' (Chambers Dictionary).

Bibliography

Abel-Smith, B., 1960. *A History of the Nursing Profession*, London: Heineman

Adams, S. and S., 1825. *The Complete Servant*, London: Knight and Lacey

Aitchison, J. and Brown, J. A. C., 1957. *The Lognormal Distribution*, Department of Applied Economics Monograph No 5, Cambridge: Cambridge University Press

Almon, C., 1991. 'The INFORUM approach to interindustry modelling', *Economic Systems Research* 3(1), 1–7

Altman, E. I., 1968. 'Financial ratios, discriminant analysis and the prediction of corporate bankruptcy', *Journal of Finance* 22, 589–609

1983. *Corporate Financial Distress*, New York: John Wiley

Altman, E. I., Haldeman, R. G. and Narayanan, P., 1977. 'Zeta analysis: a new model to identify bankruptcy risk of corporations', *Journal of Banking and Finance* 1, 29–54

Amemiya, T., 1985. *Advanced Econometrics*, Cambridge MA: Harvard University Press

Amihud, Y. and Lev, B., 1981. 'Risk reduction as a motive for conglomerate mergers', *Bell Journal of Economics* 12, 605–17

Anderson, T. W., 1948. 'The asymptotic distributions of the roots of certain determinantal equations', *Journal of the Royal Statistical Society*, Series B, 10(1)

1958. *An Introduction to Multivariate Statistical Analysis*, New York: Wiley

Andrés, J., Dolado, J. J., Molinas, C., Sebastián, M. and Zabalza, A., 1988. 'The Influence of Demand and Capital Constraints on Spanish Unemployment', Working Paper SGPE-D-88005, Ministerio de Economía y Hacienda, Madrid

Arellano, M. and Bond, S., 1991. 'Some tests of specification for panel data: Monte-Carlo evidence and an application to employment equations', *Review of Economic Studies* 58, 277–97

Argenti, J., 1976. *Corporate Collapse: The Causes and Symptoms*, London: McGraw Hill

Armington, P., 1969. 'A theory of demand for products distinguished by place of production', *IMF Staff Papers* 16, 159–78

Armstrong, W. A. and Huzel, J. P., 1989. 'Labour II: Food, shelter and self-help, the Poor Law and the position of the labourer in rural society', in J. Thirsk (ed.), *The Agrarian History of England and Wales, VI, 1750–1850*, Cambridge: Cambridge University Press

Arrow, K. J. and Debreu, G., 1954. 'Existence of and equilibrium for a competitive economy', *Econometrica* 22(3), 265–90

Arrow, K. J. and Kehoe, T. J., 1994. 'Distinguished fellow: Herbert Scarf's contributions to economics', *Journal of Economic Perspectives* 8, 161–81

Ashton, T. S., 1924. *Iron and Steel in the Industrial Revolution*, Manchester: Manchester University Press

    1955. *An Economic History of England, The Eighteenth Century*, London: Methuen

    1959. *Economic Fluctuations in England, 1700–1800*, Oxford: Oxford University Press

Ashton T. S. and Sykes, J., 1929. *The Coal Industry of the Eighteenth Century*, Manchester: Manchester University Press

Auerbach, A. J. and Kotlikoff, L. J., 1987. *Dynamic Fiscal Policy*, Cambridge: Cambridge University Press

Baines, E., 1970. *Baines's Account of the Woollen Manufacture of England*, edited by K. G. Ponting, Newton Abbot: David and Charles

Ballard, C. L. and Goulder, L. H., 1985. 'Consumption taxes, foresight, and welfare: a computable general equilibrium analysis', in J. Piggott and J. Whalley (eds), *New Developments in Applied General Equilibrium Analysis*, Cambridge: Cambridge University Press

Baltagi, B. H. and Griffin, J. M., 1983. 'Gasoline demand in the OECD: an application of testing and pooling procedures', *European Economic Review* 22(2), 117–37

Banks, J. A., 1954. *Prosperity and Parenthood*, London: Routledge and Kegan Paul

Barker, T. S., 1977. 'Making the Cambridge Growth Project model dynamic', in W. F. Gossling (ed.), *Medium-term Dynamic Forecasting*, London: Input-Output Publishing

    1978. 'Towards strategic paths in economic planning', in R. Stone and A.W. A. Peterson (eds), *Econometric Contributions to Public Policy*, London: Macmillan

    1993. 'MEGEVE-E3ME: Approaches to Long-Run E3 Modelling and Preliminary Specification', MEGEVE-E3ME Working Paper No. 11, Cambridge Econometrics

    1995. 'Taxing pollution instead of employment: greenhouse gas abatement through fiscal policy in the UK', *Energy and Environment* 6(1), 1–28

Barker, T. S. (ed.), 1976. *Economic Structure and Policy*, London: Chapman and Hall

Barker, T. S., Ekins, P. and Johnstone, N. (eds), 1995. *Global Warming and Energy Demand*, London: Routledge

Barker, T. S. and Gardiner, B., 1996. 'Employment, wage formation and pricing in the European Union: empirical modelling of environmental tax reform', in C. Carraro and D. Siniscalco (eds), *Environmental Fiscal Reform and Unemployment*, Amsterdam: Kluwer

Barker, T. S., Gardiner, B. and Dieppe, A., 1995. *E3ME Version 1.1 User's Manual*, Cambridge: Cambridge Econometrics

Barker, T. S. and Pesaran, M. H. (eds), 1990. *Disaggregation in Economic Modelling*, London: Routledge

Barker, T. S. and Peterson, A. W. A. (eds), 1987. *The Cambridge Multisectoral Dynamic Model of the British Economy*, Cambridge: Cambridge University Press

Barker, T. S., Peterson, A. W. A. and Winters, A., 1984. 'IDIOM an international dynamic input-output model', in UNIDO (ed.), *Proceedings of the Seventh International Conference on Input-Output Techniques*, New York: United Nations

Barns, D. W., Edmonds, J. A. and Reilly, J. M., 1992. 'Use of the Edmonds-Reilly Model to Model Energy-related Greenhouse Gas Emissions', OECD Economics Department Working Paper No. 113, Paris

Barro, R. and Sala-i-Martin, X., 1995. *Economic Growth*, New York: McGraw Hill

Baxter, R. D., 1868. *National Income*, London: Macmillan

Beaver, W. H., 1966. 'Financial ratios as predictors of failure', *Empirical Research in Accounting*, supplement to *Journal of Accounting Research*, 71–111

Beeke, H., 1800. *Observations on the Produce of the Income Tax*, new edition, London: Wright

Bell, B., 1802. *Essays on Agriculture*, Edinburgh: Bell and Bradfute

Berg, M. and Hudson, P., 1992. 'Rehabilitating the Industrial Revolution', *Economic History Review* 45, 24–50

1994. 'Growth and change: a comment on the Crafts–Harley view of the Industrial Revolution', *Economic History Review* 47, 147–9

Bergman, L., Jorgenson, D. W. and Zalai, E. (eds), 1990. *General Equilibrium Modelling and Economic Policy Analysis*, Oxford: Basil Blackwell

Berndt, E. R., 1991. *The Practice of Econometrics*, Reading MA: A. Wesley

Bierens, H. J., 1984. *Topics in Advanced Econometrics. Estimation, Testing and Specification of Cross-section and Time Series Models*, Cambridge: Cambridge University Press

Bischoff, J., 1842. *A Comprehensive History of the Woollen and Worsted Manufactures*, London: Smith, Elder

Blanchard, D., 1987. 'Neo-classical synthesis', in J. Eatwell, M. Milgate and P. Newman (eds), *New Palgrave Dictionary*, London and New York: Macmillan

Blanchard, O. J. and Summers, L., 1986. 'Hysteresis and the European unemployment problem', *NBER Macroeconomics Annual*, 15–78

Blum, M., 1974. 'Failing company discriminant analysis', *Journal of Accounting Research* 12, 1–25

Board of Trade, 1908. *Rates of Wages and Hours of Labour in Various Industries in the United Kingdom for a Series of Years*, London: HMSO

Bodkin, R. G., Klein, L. R. and Marwah, K., 1991. *A History of Macroeconomic Model-building*, Aldershot: Edward Elgar

Boero, G., Clarke, R. and Winters, L. A., 1991. *The Macroeconomic Consequences of Controlling Greenhouse Gases: A Survey*, UK Department of the Environment, Environmental Economics Research Series, London: HMSO

Botham, F. W., 1982. 'Working-class Living Standards in North Staffordshire, 1750–1914', unpublished PhD dissertation, University of London

Bowen, A., Buxton, T. and Ricketts, M., 1991. 'The Economics of Innovation: Setting the Scene', paper presented at the NEDO Policy Seminar, 12–13 September 1991

Bowley, A. L., 1895. 'Changes in average wages (nominal and real) in the United Kingdom between 1860 and 1891', *Journal of the Royal Statistical Society* 58, 223–85

1898. 'Comparison of the changes in wages in France, the United States and the United Kingdom from 1840 to 1891', *Economic Journal* 8, 474–89

1899. 'The statistics of wages in the United Kingdom during the last hundred years', Part II, 'Agricultural wages in Scotland'; Part III, 'Agricultural wages in Ireland' and Part IV, 'Agricultural wages, earnings and general averages', *Journal of the Royal Statistical Society* 62, 140–51, 399–404 and 555–70

1900. *Wages in the United Kingdom in the Nineteenth Century*, Cambridge: Cambridge University Press

1901. 'The statistics of wages in the United Kingdom during the last hundred years: wages in the building trades', *Journal of the Royal Statistical Society* 64, 102–12

1902. 'The statistics of wages in the United Kingdom during the last hundred years: wages in the worsted and woollen manufactures of the West Riding of Yorkshire', *Journal of the Royal Statistical Society* 65, 102–26

1937. *Wages and Income in the United Kingdom since 1860*, Cambridge: Cambridge University Press

Bowley, A. L. and Wood, G. H., 1899. 'The statistics of wages in the United Kingdom during the last hundred years: printers', *Journal of the Royal Statistical Society* 62, 708–15

1905. 'The statistics of wages in the United Kingdom during the last hundred years: engineering and shipbuilding', *Journal of the Royal Statistical Society* 68, 104–37

1906. 'The statistics of wages in the United Kingdom during the last hundred years: engineering and shipbuilding', *Journal of the Royal Statistical Society* 69, 148–92

Boyer, G., 1990. *An Economic History of the English Poor Law, 1750–1850*, Cambridge: Cambridge University Press

Bracke, I. and Brechet, T., 1994. 'The Estimation of an Allocation System for Consumption: Progress Report and First Simulations for Belgium', MEGEVE-E3ME Working Paper No. 38, Cambridge Econometrics

Breiman, L. W., Meisel, A. and Purcell, E., 1977. 'Variable kernel estimates of multivariate densities', *Technometrics* 19, 135–44

Briggs, F. E. A., 1962. 'The influence of errors on the correlation of ratios', *Econometrica* 30, 1, 162–77

Britton, A. and Westaway, P., 1992. 'On the Equilibrium Properties of Macroeconomic Models: with special reference to Black Wednesday', paper presented to an ESRC Conference on 'The Future of Macroeconomic Modelling in the United Kingdom', London, 30 November–2 December 1992

Brown, J. A. C., 1965. *Exploring 1970: Some Numerical Results*, Volume 6 in the series edited by R. Stone, 'A Programme for Growth', London: Chapman and Hall

Brown, J. A. C., Houthakker, H. S. and Prais, S. J., 1953. 'Electronic computation in economic statistics', *Journal of the American Statistical Association* 48, 263, September

Buiter, W. H. and Miller, M., 1982. 'Real exchange rate overshooting and the output costs of bringing down inflation', *European Economic Review* 18, 85–123

Burniaux, J.-M., John, P., Martin, G. N. and Martins, J. O., 1992. 'GREEN – A Multi-region Dynamic General Equilibrium Model for Quantifying the Costs of Curbing CO_2 Emissions: A Technical Manual', Working Paper No 116, OECD Department of Economics and Statistics, Paris

Business Monitor, various dates. *Business Monitor M7 Acquisitions and Mergers of Industrial and Commercial Companies*, London: HMSO

Cambridge Econometrics, 1995. *IDIOM International Dynamic Input-Output Modelling Language User's Guide*, Cambridge: Cambridge Econometrics

Cappelen, Å., 1991. 'MODAG A Medium Term Macroeconometric Model of the Norwegian Economy', Discussion Paper No. 67, Central Bureau of Statistics, Oslo

Capros, P., 1992. 'The SOLFEGE/GEM-E3 Computable General Equilibrium Approach in Modelling Economy-Energy-Environment Interactions in Europe', paper presented at an international workshop on 'Modelling Economy-Environment Linkages', Fondazione ENI Enrico Mattei, Milan, 3–4 December 1992

Carlson, J. A. and Parkin, M., 1975. 'Inflation expectations', *Economica* 42, 123–38

Carraro, C., 1992. Presentation on the MERGE model at an International Workshop on 'Modelling Economy-Environment Linkages', Fondazione ENI Enrico Mattei, Milan, 3–4 December 1992

Caves, R. E., 1989. 'Mergers, takeovers, and economic efficiency', *International Journal of Industrial Organization* 7(1), March, 151–74

CBI various dates. *Quarterly Industrial Trends Survey*, various issues

Central Plan Bureau, 1990. *ATHENA Een bedrijfstakkenmodel voor de Nederlandse economie*, Monograph No. 30, The Hague: Central Plan Bureau

Central Statistical Office, 1993. *Financial Statistics* 372, April

Charkham, J., 1995. *Keeping Good Company*, Oxford: Oxford University Press

Charnes, A., Cooper, W. W. and Rhodes, E., 1978. 'Measuring the efficiency of decision making units', *European Journal of Operations Research* 3, 392–444

Clapham, J. H., 1934. 'Work and wages', in G. M. Young (ed.), *Early Victorian England, 1830–1865*, Oxford: Oxford University Press

Clifton, J. A., 1977. 'Competition and the evolution of the capitalist mode of production', *Cambridge Journal of Economics* 1(2), June, 137–51

Cline, W. R., 1992. *The Economics of Global Warming*, Washington DC: Institute of International Economics

Collier, F., 1964. *The Family Economy of the Working Classes in the Cotton Industry, 1784–1833*, Manchester: Manchester University Press

Colquhoun, P., 1806. *A Treatise on Indigence*, London: Hatchard

'Controversy' 1995. *Economic Journal* 105(433), November, 1594–1648

Cosh, A. D. and Hughes, A., 1987. 'The anatomy of corporate control: directors, shareholders and executive remuneration in giant US and UK corporations', *Cambridge Journal of Economics* 11(4), December, 285–313

Cosh, A. D. and Hughes, A., 1994a. 'Acquisition activity', in A. Hughes and D. J. Storey (eds), *Finance and the Small Firm*, London and New York: Routledge

Cosh, A. D. and Hughes, A., 1994b. 'Size, financial structure and profitability: UK companies in the 1980s', in A. Hughes and D. J. Storey (eds), *Finance and the Small Firm*, London and New York: Routledge

Cosh, A. D. and Hughes, A., 1995. 'Failures, Acquisitions and Post-merger Success: The Comparative Performance of Large and Small Firms', Working Paper 19, ESRC Centre for Business Research, University of Cambridge

Cosh, A. D., Hughes, A. and Kambhampati, U. 1993. 'Size, Gowth and Failure: An Analysis of the UK Quoted and Unquoted Company Sectors', Working Paper 32, Small Business Research Centre, University of Cambridge

Cosh, A. D., Hughes, A., Lee, K. and Singh, A., 1989. 'Institutional investors, mergers and the market for corporate control', *International Journal of Industrial Organization*, March, 73–100

Cosh, A. D., Hughes, A. and Singh, A., 1980. 'The causes and effects of takeover in the UK: an empirical investigation for the late 1960s at the microeconomic level', in D. C. Mueller (ed.), *The Determinants and Effects of Mergers*, Cambridge MA: Oelgeschlager, Gunn and Hain

Cosslett, S. R., 1983. 'A distribution-free maximum likelihood estimator of the binary choice model', *Econometrica* 51, 765–782

Coutts, K. J., 1976. *CEPG Model of the UK Economy, Technical Manual*, Cambridge: Department of Applied Economics, University of Cambridge

Coutts, K. J., Godley, W., Rowthorn, B. and Zezza, G., 1990. *Britain's Economic Problems and Policies in the 1990s*, IPPR Economic Study 6, London: Institute for Public Policy Research

Cox, D. and Harris, R., 1985. 'Trade liberalization and industrial organization: some estimates for Canada', *Journal of Political Economy* 93, 115–45

Crafts, N. F. R., 1976. 'English economic growth in the Eighteenth Century: a re-examination of Deane and Cole's estimates', *Economic History Review* 29, 226–35

1980. 'National income estimates and the British standard of living debate: a reappraisal of 1801–1831', *Explorations in Economic History* 17, 176–88

1983. 'British economic growth, 1700–1831: a review of the evidence', *Economic History Review* 36, 177–99

1985. *British Economic Growth during the Industrial Revolution*, Oxford: Oxford University Press

Crafts, N. F. R. and Harley, C. K., 1992. 'Output growth and the British Industrial Revolution: a re-statement of the Crafts–Harley view', *Economic History Review* 45, 703–30

1995. 'Cotton textiles and industrial output growth during the Industrial Revolution', *Economic History Review* 48, 133–44

Cross, R. (ed.), Oxford: 1988. *Unemployment, Hysteresis and the Natural Rate Hypothesis*, Oxford: Blackwell

CSO, 1994. *Shareownership: The Share Register Survey Report end 1993*, London: HMSO

Cubbin, J. S. and Geroski, P. A., 1990. 'The persistence of profits in the United Kingdom' in D. C. Mueller (ed.), *The Dynamics of Company Profits*, Cambridge: Cambridge University Press

Cuenca Esteban, J., 1994. 'British textile prices, 1770–1831: are British growth rates worth revising once again?', *Economic History Review* 47, 66–105

1995. 'Further evidence of falling prices of cotton cloth, 1768–1816', *Economic History Review* 48, 145–50

Data Resources Incorporated (DRI), 1991. *The Economic Impact of a Package of EC Measures to Control CO_2 Emissions*, Final Report prepared for the EC, November

DRI, 1992. *Impact of a Package of EC Measures to Control CO_2 Emissions on European Industry*, Final Report prepared for the EC, January

Daniels, G. W., 1929. 'A "turn-out" of Bolton machine makers in 1831', *Economic Journal, Economic History Supplement* I, 591–602

Davies, S. W. and Lyons, B. R., 1982. 'Seller concentration: the technological explanation and demand uncertainty', *Economic Journal* 92, 903–19

Davis, R., 1962. *The Rise of the English Shipping Industry*, Newton Abbot: David and Charles

Deakin, E. B., 1972. 'A discriminant analysis of predictors of business failure', *Journal of Accounting Research* 10, 167–79

Deane, P., 1956. 'Contemporary estimates of national income in the first half of the Nineteenth Century', *Economic History Review* 8, 339–54

1957. 'Contemporary estimates of national income in the second half of the Nineteenth Century', *Economic History Review* 9, 451–61

Deane, P. and Cole, W. A., 1962. *British Economic Growth, 1688–1959*, Cambridge: Cambridge University Press

Deaton, A., 1975. *Models and Projections of Consumer Demand in Post-War Britain*, London: Chapman and Hall

1987. 'Stone, John Richard Nicholas', in J. Eatwell, M. Milgate and P. Newman (eds), *The New Palgrave Dictionary of Economics*, Vol. IV, London and New York: Macmillan

1989. 'Rice prices and income distribution in Thailand: a non-parametric analysis', *Economic Journal* 99, 1–37

1993. 'Stone, John Richard Nicholas 1913–1991', *Proceedings of the British Academy* 82, 475–92

de Marchi, N. and Gilbert, C. (eds), 1989. *The History and Methodology of Econometrics*, Oxford: Oxford University Press

Demsetz, H., 1983. 'The structure of ownership and the theory of the firm', *Journal of Law and Economics* 26, 375–90

Department of Applied Economics, 1948. *First Report: Activities in the Years 1946–1948*, Cambridge: University of Cambridge, Department of Applied Economics

1952. *Second Report: Activities in the Years 1948–1951*, Cambridge: University of Cambridge, Department of Applied Economics

1954. *Third Report: Activities in the Years 1951–1953*, Cambridge: University of Cambridge, Department of Applied Economics

1958. *Fourth Report: Activities in the Years 1954–57*, Cambridge: University of Cambridge, Department of Applied Economics

1965. *Fifth Report: Activities in the Years 1958–64*, Cambridge: University of Cambridge, Department of Applied Economics

1967. *Sixth Report: Activities in the Period January 1965 to September 1966*, Cambridge: University of Cambridge, Department of Applied Economics

1968. *Seventh Report: Activities in the Period October 1966 to September 1967*, Cambridge: University of Cambridge, Department of Applied Economics

1969. *Eighth Report, Activities in the Period October 1967 to September 1968*, Cambridge: University of Cambridge, Department of Applied Economics

1970. *Ninth Report: Activities in the Period October 1968 to September 1969*, Cambridge: University of Cambridge, Department of Applied Economics

1971. *Tenth Report: Activities in the Period October 1969 to September 1970*, Cambridge: University of Cambridge, Department of Applied Economics

1972. *Eleventh Report; Activities in the Period October 1970 to September 1971*, Cambridge: University of Cambridge, Department of Applied Economics

Department of Employment, 1971. *British Labour Statistics, Historical Abstract, 1886–1968*, London: HMSO

Dervis, K., de Melo, J. and Robinson, S., 1982. *General Equilibrium Models for Development Policy*, Cambridge: Cambridge University Press

Desai, M. and Montes, A., 1982. 'A macroeconomic model of bankruptcies in the British economy', *British Review of Economic Issues* 4, 1–14

Dixon, P. B., Parmenter, B. R., Powell, A. A. and Wilcoxen, P. J., 1992. *Notes and Problems in Applied General Equilibrium Economics*, Amsterdam: North-Holland

Dixon, P. B., Parmenter, B. R., Sutton, J. and Vincent, D. P., 1982. *ORANI: A Multisectoral Model of the Australian Economy*, Amsterdam: North-Holland

Dodd, A. H., 1933. *The Industrial Revolution in North Wales*, Cardiff: University of Wales Press

Don, H., van de Klundert, T. and van Sinderen, J. (eds), 1989. *Applied General Equilibrium Modelling*, Dordrecht and Boston: Kluwer

Dornbusch, R. and Fischer, S., 1990. *Macroeconomics*, fifth edition, New York: McGraw-Hill

Downie, J., 1959. *The Competitive Process*, Duckworth, London

Dunne, J. P. and Hughes, A., 1992. 'Age, Size, Growth and Survival Revisited', Small Business Research Centre Working Paper No. 24, Department of Applied Economics, University of Cambridge

1994. 'Age, size, growth and survival: UK companies in the 1980s', *Journal of Industrial Economics* 42, 115–40

Eccleston, B., 1976. 'A Survey of Wage Rates in Five Midland Counties, 1750–1834', unpublished PhD dissertation, University of Leicester

Eden, F. M., 1797. *The State of the Poor*, 3 vols, London: B. and J. White

Edinburgh Review, 1862. 'Modern domestic service', *Edinburgh Review* 115, 409–39

Ekins, P., 1996. 'The secondary benefits of CO_2 abatement: how much emission reduction do they justify?', *Ecological Economics* 16, 13–24

Engle, R. F. and Granger, C. W. J., 1987. 'Cointegration and error correction: representation, estimation and testing', *Econometrica* 55, 251–76

    1991. *Long-run Economic Relationships (Readings in Cointegration)*, Oxford: Oxford University Press

Epstein, R. J., 1987. *A History of Econometrics*, Amsterdam: North-Holland

Ermisch, J. and Westaway, P. F., 1994. 'The dynamics of aggregate consumption in an open economy life cycle model', *Scottish Journal of Political Economy* 41, 113–27

European Commission (ed.), 1993. *HERMES: Harmonised Econometric Research for Modelling Economic Systems*, Amsterdam: North-Holland

Evans, D. S., 1987a. 'Tests of alternative theories of firm growth', *Journal of Political Economy* 95(4), 657–74

    1987b. 'The relationship between firm growth, size and age: estimates for 100 manufacturing industries', *Journal of Industrial Economics* 35, 567–81

Evans, H. D., 1972. *A General Equilibrium Analysis of Protection*, Amsterdam: North-Holland,

Fama, E. F. and Jensen, M. C., 1983. 'Separation of ownership and control', *Journal of Law and Economics* 26, 301–26

Fare, R., Grosskopf, S. and Lovell, C. A. K., 1985. *The Measurement of Efficiency of Production*, Boston: Kluwer Nijhoff

Farrell, J. and Shapiro, C., 1990. 'Horizontal mergers: an equilibrium analysis', *American Economic Review* 80, March, 107–26

Farrell, M., 1957. 'The measurement of productive efficiency', *Journal of the Royal Statistical Society*, Series A, 120(3), 253–81

Feinstein, C. H., 1990. 'New estimates of average earnings in the United Kingdom, 1880–1913', *Economic History Review* 53, 603–11

    1995. 'Changes in nominal wages, the cost of living and real wages in the United Kingdom over two centuries, 1780–1990', in P. Scholliers and V. Zamagni (eds), *Labour's Reward, Real Wages and Economic Change in 19th and 20th Century Europe*, Aldershot: Edward Elgar

Fischer, S., 1988. 'Recent developments in macroeconomics', *Economic Journal* 98, 294–339

Fisher, G. R., 1957. 'Maximum likelihood estimators with heteroscedastic errors', *Review of the International Statistical Institute* 25(1/3), 52–5

Fisher, M. R., 1976. 'The economic contribution of Michael James Farrell', *Review of Economic Studies* 43(3), 371–82

Fitoussi, J.-P., 1983. *Modern Macroeconomic Theory: An Overview*, Oxford: Blackwell

Flinn, M. W., 1984. *The History of the British Coal Industry, II, 1780–1830: The Industrial Revolution*, Oxford: Clarendon Press

Foster, G., 1986. *Financial Statement Analysis*, second edition, Englewood Cliffs: Prentice Hall

Fox, A. Wilson, 1903. 'Agricultural wages in England and Wales during the last fifty years', *Journal of the Royal Statistical Society* 66, 273–348

Frisch, R., 1933. 'Editorial', *Econometrica* 1, 1–4

Fullerton, D., Shoven, J. B. and Whalley, J., 1983. 'Replacing the US income tax with a progressive consumption tax: a sequenced general equilibrium approach', *Journal of Public Economics* 20, 3–23

Gabler, S., Laisney, F. and Lechner, M., 1993. 'Seminonparametric estimation of binary-choice models with an application to labor-force participation', *Journal of Business and Economic Statistics* 11, 61–80

Gallant, A. R. and Nychka, D. W., 1987. 'Semi-nonparametric maximum-likelihood estimation', *Econometrica* 55, 363–90

Galton, F. W., 1896. *Select Documents Illustrating the History of Trade Unionism, I, The Tailoring Trade*, London: Longmans, Green

Geary, R. C., 1948. 'Studies in the relations between economic time series', *Journal of the Royal Statistical Society*, Series B, 10(1), 140–58

George, D., 1925. *London Life in the Eighteenth Century*, London: Kegan Paul

1927. 'The London coalheavers, attempts to regulate waterside labour in the Eighteenth and Nineteenth Century', *Economic Journal, Economic History Supplement* 1, 229–48

Geroski, P. A. and Mueller, D. C., 1990. 'The persistence of profits in perspective', in D. C. Mueller (ed.), *The Dynamics of Company Profits*, Cambridge: Cambridge University Press

Gilbert, C. L., 1986. 'The Development of British Econometrics 1945–85', Applied Economics Discussion Paper, Institute of Economics and Statistics, Oxford

Gilboy, E., 1934. *Wages in Eighteenth Century England*, Cambridge MA: Harvard University Press

Ginsburgh, V., 1994. 'In the Cournot–Walras general equilibrium model, there may be "more to gain" by changing the numéraire than by eliminating imperfections: a two-good economy example', in J. Mercenier and T. N. Srinivasan (eds), *Applied General Equilibrium and Economic Development*, Ann Arbor: University of Michigan Press

Ginsburgh, V. and Waelbroeck, J. L. (eds), 1981. *Activity Analysis and General Equilibrium Modelling*, Amsterdam and New York: North-Holland

Godley, W. A. H., 1992. *The Godley Papers*, London: New Statesman and Society

Goudie, A. W., 1987. 'Forecasting company failure: the use of discriminant analysis within a disaggregated model of the company sector', *Journal of the Royal Statistical Society*, Series A, 150, 69–81

Goudie, A. W. and Meeks, G., 1981. 'Medium-term projections of individual companies' financial flows', *Accounting and Business Research* 11, 291–302

1984. 'Individual agents in a macroeconomic model', *Journal of Policy Modelling* 6, 289–309

1986. *Company Finance and Performance*, Cambridge: University of Cambridge, Department of Applied Economics

1991. 'The exchange rate and company failure in a macro-micro model of the UK company sector', *Economic Journal* 101, 444–57

Goulder, L. H., 1994. 'Environmental Taxation and the "Double Dividend": A

Reader's Guide', unpublished paper, Department of Economics, Stanford University

Goulder, L. H. and Summers, L. H., 1989. 'Tax policy, asset prices, and growth: a general equilibrium analysis', *Journal of Public Economics* 38, 265–96

Granger, C. W. J., 1990. 'Aggregation of time-series variables: a survey', in T. Barker and M. H. Pesaran (eds), *Disaggregation in Economic Modelling*, London: Routledge

Greene, W. H., 1993. *Econometric Analysis*, New York: Macmillan

Hahn, F., 1974. 'On the Notion of Equilibrium in Economics', reprinted in F. Hahn, 1984, *Equilibrium and Macroeconomics*, Oxford: Blackwell

Hall, B. H., 1987. 'The relationship between firm size and firm growth in the manufacturing sector', *Journal of Industrial Economics* 35(4), 583–606

Hamilton, H., 1926. *The English Brass and Copper Industries to 1800*, London: Longmans Green

Hammond, J. L. and B., 1919. *The Skilled Labourer 1760–1832*, London: Longmans Green

Han, A. K., 1987. 'Non-parametric analysis of a generalised regression model, the maximum rank correlation estimator', *Journal of Econometrics* 35, 303–16

Hannah, L. and Kay, J. A., 1977. *Concentration in Modern Industry*, London: Macmillan

Hansen, L. P., 1982. 'Large sample properties of generalized method of moments estimators', *Econometrica* 50, 1029–54

Harberger, A., 1955. 'Review of R. Stone, *The Measurement of Consumers' Expenditure and Behaviour in the United Kingdom, 1920–1938*, Vol. I', *Econometrica* 23, 217–18

    1962. 'The incidence of the corporate income tax', *Journal of Political Economy* 70, 215–40

Harcourt, G. C., 1987. 'Reddaway, William Brian', in J. Eatwell, M. Milgate and P. Newman (eds), *The New Palgrave Dictionary of Economics*, Vol. IV, London and New York: Macmillan

Härdle, W., 1990. *Applied Nonparametric Regression*, Cambridge: Cambridge University Press

Hargreaves, C. (ed.), 1992. *Macroeconomic Modelling of the Long Run*, Aldershot: Edward Elgar

Harley, C. K., 1982. 'British industrialization before 1841: evidence of slower growth during the industrial revolution', *Journal of Economic History* 42, 267–89

Harris, R., 1984. 'Applied general equilibrium analysis of small open economies with scale economies and imperfect competition', *American Economic Review* 74, 1016–32

Hart, P. E., 1965. *Studies in Profit, Business Saving, and Investment in the United Kingdom 1920–62*, I, London: George Allen and Unwin

Hasbach, W., 1908. *A History of the English Agricultural Labourer*, London: P. S. King and Son

Hausman, J. A. and Wise, D. A., 1979. 'Attrition bias in experimental and panel data: the Gary income maintenance experiment', *Econometrica* 47, 455–73

Hecht, J. J., 1956. *The Domestic Servant in Eighteenth-Century England*, London: Routledge and Kegan Paul

Heckman, J. J., 1974. 'Shadow prices, market wages and labour supply', *Econometrica* 42, 679–94

1979. 'Sample selection bias as a specification error', *Econometrica* 47, 153–61

Hendry, D. F., 1994. *Dynamic Econometrics*, Oxford: Oxford University Press

1996. 'A Theory of Co-breaking', unpublished manuscript, Institute of Economics and Statistics, University of Oxford

Hendry, D. F. and Morgan, M., 1989. 'A reanalysis of confluence analysis', in de Marchi and Gilbert (eds) (1989)

Hendry, D. F. and Clements, M. P., 1994. 'On a theory of intercept corrections in macroeconomic forecasting', in S. Holly (ed.), *Money, Inflation and Employment: Essays in Honour of Sir James Ball*, London: Edward Elgar

Hendry, D. F., Pagan, A. and Sargan, J. D., 1984. 'Dynamic specification', in Z. Griliches and M. D. Intriligator (eds), *Handbook of Econometrics*, Vol. II, Amsterdam: North-Holland

Hendry, D. F. and von Ungern Sternberg, T., 1981. 'Liquidity and inflation effects on consumers' expenditure', in A. Deaton (ed.), *Essays in the Theory and Measurement of Consumer Behaviour*, Cambridge: Cambridge University Press

Hoeller, P., Dean, A. and Hayafuji, M., 1992. 'New Issues, New Results: The OECD's Second Survey of the Macroeconomic Costs of Reducing CO_2 Emissions', Working Paper No. 123, OECD Economics Department, Paris

Hoffmann, W. G., 1955. *British Industry, 1700–1950*, Oxford: Blackwell

Hoppit, J., 1990. 'Counting the industrial revolution', *Economic History Review* 43, 173–93

Horn, P., 1986. *The Rise and Fall of the Victorian Servant*, Gloucester: Alan Sutton

Horowitz, J. L., 1992. 'A smoothed maximum score estimator for the binary response model', *Econometrica* 60, 505–31

1993. 'Semiparametric estimation of a work-trip mode choice model', *Journal of Econometrics* 58, 49–70

Horrell, S. and Humphries, J., 1992. 'Old questions, new data and alternative perspectives: families' living standards in the industrial revolution', *Journal of Economic History* 52, 849–80

1995. 'Women's labour force participation and the transition to the male-breadwinner family, 1790–1865', *Economic History Review* 48, 89–117

Houthakker, H. S., 1951. 'Some calculations on electricity consumption in Great Britain', *Journal of the Royal Statistical Society*, Series A, No. 114, III, 351–71

Hughes, A., 1989. 'Small firms, merger activity and competition policy', in J. Barber, J. S. Metcalfe and M. Porteous (eds), *Barriers to Growth in Small Firms*, London: Routledge

1993. 'Mergers and economic performance in the UK: a survey of the empirical evidence 1950–90', in M. Bishop and J. A. Kay (eds), *European Mergers and Merger Policy*, Oxford: Oxford University Press

Hughes, A. and Singh, A., 1987. 'Takeovers and the stock market', *Contributions to Political Economy*, March, 73–85

Hunt, E. H. and Botham, F. W., 1987. 'Wages in Britain during the Industrial Revolution', *Economic History Review* 40, 380–99

Hunt, J. W., Lees, S., Grumbar, J. J. and Vivian, P. D., 1987. *Acquisitions – The Human Factor*, London: Egon Zehnder International

Ichimura, H. 1993. 'Semiparametric least squares (SLS) and weighted SLS estimation of single-index models', *Journal of Econometrics* 58, 71–120

Instituto Nacional de Estadística, 1983. *Encuesto de Presupuestos Familiares, 1980–81*, Madrid: Instituto Nacional de Estadística

1986. *Contabilidad Nacional de España, Base 1980, Cuentas Nacionales y Tabla Input–Output*, Madrid: Instituto Nacional de Estadística

1987a. *Contabilidad Nacional de España, Base 1980, Serie 1980–84 Definitivos, 1985 Provisional y 1986 Avance*, Madrid: Instituto Nacional de Estadística

1987b. *Indice de Precios de Consumo, Boletín Trimestral, Octubre–Diciembre 1986*, Madrid: Instituto Nacional de Estadística

1988a. *Contabilidad Nacional de España, Base 1980, Serie 1985 Definitivos, 1986 Provisional y 1987 Avance*, Madrid: Instituto Nacional de Estadística

1988b. *Indice de Precios de Consumo, Boletín Trimestral, Octubre–Diciembre 1987*, Madrid: Instituto Nacional de Estadística

Jackson, R. V., 1992. 'Rates of industrial growth during the Industrial Revolution', *Economic History Review* 45, 1–23

Jenkin, A. H. H., 1927. *The Cornish Miner*, London: Allen and Unwin

Jensen, M. C. 1986. 'Agency costs of free cash flow, corporate finance and takeovers', *American Economic Review* 76, 323–9

Johansen, L., 1960. *A Multi-sectoral Study of Economic Growth*, Amsterdam: North-Holland

Johansen, S., 1988. 'Statistical analysis of co-integrating vectors', *Journal of Economic Dynamics and Control* 12, 231–54

John, A. H., 1989. 'Statistical appendix', in J. Thirsk (ed.), *The Agrarian History of England and Wales, VI, 1750–1850*, Cambridge: Cambridge University Press

Jorgenson, D. W., 1984. 'Econometric methods for applied general equilibrium analysis', in H. E. Scarf and J. B. Shoven (eds), *Applied General Equilibrium Analysis*, Cambridge: Cambridge University Press

1989. 'Capital as a factor of production', in D. W. Jorgenson and R. Landau (eds), *Technology and Capital Formation*, Cambridge MA: MIT Press

Jorgenson, D. W. and Wilcoxen, P. J., 1990. 'Global Change, Energy Prices and US Economic Growth', Discussion Paper No. 1511, Harvard Institute of Economic Research, Cambridge MA

1992. 'Energy, the Environment and Economic Growth', Discussion Paper No.1604, Harvard Institute of Economic Research, Cambridge MA

1993. 'Reducing US carbon emissions: an econometric general equilibrium assessment', *Resource and Energy Economics* 15(1), 7–25

Jorgenson, D. W. and Yun, K.-Y., 1990. 'Tax policy and US economic growth', in L. Bergman, D. W. Jorgenson and E. Zalai (eds), *General Equilibrium Modeling and Economic Policy Analysis*, Oxford: Basil Blackwell

Joyce, M. and Wren-Lewis, S., 1991. 'The role of the real exchange rate and capacity utilisation in convergence to the NAIRU', *Economic Journal* 101, 497–507

Kehoe, P. J. and Kehoe, T. J., 1994. 'A primer on static applied general equilibrium models', *Federal Reserve Bank of Minneapolis Quarterly Review* 18(2),
2–16

Kehoe, P. J. and Kehoe, T. J. (eds), 1995. *Modeling North American Economic
Integration*, Boston: Kluwer Academic Publishers

Kehoe, T. J., Manresa, A., Noyola, P. J., Polo, C. and Sancho, F., 1988. 'A general
equilibrium analysis of the 1986 tax reform in Spain', *European Economic
Review* 32, 334–42

Kehoe, T. J., Manresa, A., Noyola, P. J., Polo, C., Sancho, F. and Serra-Puche, J.,
1985a. 'Modelos de equilibrio general aplicado (MEGA): Un análisis del
impacto del impuesto sobre el valor addido (IVA) sobre la economía
Española', unpublished manuscript, Instituto de Estudios Fiscales

1985b. 'A Social Accounting System for Spain: 1980', Working Paper 63.86,
Departament d'Economia i d'Història Econòmica, Universitat Autònoma de
Barcelona

1986a. 'A General Equilibrium Analysis of the Indirect Tax Reform in Spain',
Working Paper 66.86, Departament d'Economia i d'Història Econòmica,
Universitat Autònoma de Barcelona

1986b. 'Política econòmica i equilibri general. Quins són els efectes de l'IVA?',
Revista Econòmica de Catalunya 2, 76–81

Kehoe, T. J., Manresa, A., Polo, C. and Sancho, F., 1988. 'Una matriu de contabilidad social de la economía española', *Estadística Española* 30, 5–33

1989. 'Un análisis de equilibrio general de la reforma fiscal de 1986 en España',
Investigaciones Económicas 13, 337–85

Kehoe, T. J., Polo, C. and Sancho, F., 1995. 'An evaluation of the performance of
an applied general equilibrium model of the Spanish economy', *Economic
Theory* 6, 115–41

Kehoe, T. J. and Serra-Puche, J., 1983. 'A computational general equilibrium model
with endogenous unemployment: An analysis of the 1980 fiscal reform in
Mexico', *Journal of Public Economics* 22, 1–26

1991. 'A general equilibrium appraisal of energy policy in Mexico', *Empirical
Economics* 16, 71–93

Kenway, P., 1994. *From Keynesianism to Monetarism: The Evolution of UK
Macroeconometric Models*, London: Routledge

Keuzenkamp, H. A. and Magnus, J. R. (eds), 1995. *The Significance of Testing in
Econometrics*, Special Issue of the *Journal of Econometrics* 67(1)

Keynes, J. M., 1940. *How to Pay for the War*, London: Macmillan

Kim, K. and Pagan, A. R., 1995. 'The econometric analysis of calibrated macroeconomic models', in M. H. Pesaran and M. Wickens, *Handbook of Applied
Econometric Macroeconomics*, London: Routledge

Kingsford, P. W., 1970. *Victorian Railwaymen, The Emergence and Growth of
Railway Labour 1830–1870*, London: Frank Cass

Kitching, J., 1967. 'Why do mergers miscarry?', *Harvard Business Review*,
November–December, 84–101

1973. *Acquisition in Europe: Causes of Corporate Successes and Failures*,
Geneva: Business International

Klein, L., 1952. 'Review of R. Stone, *The Role of Measurement in Economics*', *Econometrica* 52, 104–5

Klein, R. W. and Spady, R. H., 1993. 'An efficient semiparametric estimator for binary response models', *Econometrica* 61, 387–421

Knight, J. 1987. 'Top companies in the DTI Company Accounts Analysis', *Statistical News* 76, February, 16–19

Koenker, R. and Bassett, G., 1978. 'Regression quantiles', *Econometrica* 46, 33–50

Kumar, M. S., 1984. *Growth, Acquisition and Investment*, Department of Applied Economics Occasional Paper No. 56, Cambridge: Cambridge University Press

Kuznets, S., 1937. *National Income and Capital Formation, 1919–1935*, New York: National Bureau of Economic Research

Langton, J., 1979. *Geographical Change and Industrial Revolution: Coalmining in South West Lancashire, 1590–1799*, Cambridge: Cambridge University Press

Laroui, F. and Velthuijsen, J. W., 1992. *The Economic Consequences of an Energy Tax in Europe: An Application with HERMES*, Amsterdam: SEO Foundation for Economic Research of the University of Amsterdam

Layard, R. and Nickell, S., 1986. 'Unemployment in Britain', *Economica* 53, S121–S169

Layard, R., Nickell, S. and Jackman, R., 1991. *Unemployment: Macroeconomic Performance and the Labour Market*, Oxford University Press

Layton, W. T., 1908. 'Changes in the wages of domestic servants during fifty years', *Journal of the Royal Statistical Society* 71, 515–24

Lee, K. C., 1992. 'Modelling supply-side adjustment and changing industrial structure', in C. Driver and P. Dunne (eds), *Structural Change in the UK Economy*, DAE Occasional Paper No. 58, Cambridge: Cambridge University Press

    1994. 'Formation of cost and price inflation expectations in British manufacturing industries: a multisectoral approach', *Economic Journal* 104, 372–385

    1995. 'Expectations Formation and Business Cycle Fluctuations: An Empirical Analysis of Actual and Expected Output in UK Manufacturing, 1975–1993', DAE Working Paper No. 9524, Department of Applied Economics, University of Cambridge

Lee, K. C. and Pesaran, M. H., 1993. 'The role of sectoral interactions in wage determination in the UK economy', *Economic Journal* 103, 21–55

Lee, K. C., Pesaran, M. H. and Pierse, R. G., 1990. 'Aggregation bias and labour demand equations for the UK economy', in T. S. Barker and M. H. Pesaran (eds), *Disaggregation in Econometric Modelling*, London: Routledge

Lee, K. C., Pesaran, M. H. and Smith, R., 1997. 'Growth and convergence in a multi-country empirical stochastic Solow model', *Journal of Applied Econometrics* 12(4), 357–92

Leontief, W. W., 1941. *The Structure of American Economy, 1919–1929: An Empirical Application of Equilibrium Analysis*, Cambridge MA: Harvard University Press

Levi, L., 1885. *Wages and Earnings of the Working Classes*, London: John Murray

Lewis, C., 1979. 'Constructing a sampling frame of industrial and commercial companies', *Statistical News* 44, February, 6–11

Lewis, M., 1960. *A Social History of the Navy 1793–1815*, London: Allen and Unwin
1965. *The Navy in Transition, 1814–1864, A Social History*, London: Hodder and Stoughton
Lindbeck, A. and Snower, D., 1986. 'Wage setting, unemployment and insider outsider relations', *American Economic Review* 101(75), Papers and Proceedings, May, 235–39
Lindert, P. H. and Williamson, J. G., 1982. 'Revising England's Social Tables, 1688–1912', *Explorations in Economic History* 19, 385–408
Lipson, E., 1921. *The History of the Woollen and Worsted Industries*, London: A. and C. Black
Llewellyn, J., Potter, S. and Samuelson, L. W., 1985. *Economic Forecasting and Policy: The International Dimension*, London: Routledge and Kegan Paul
Lloyd, C., 1968. *The British Seamen 1200–1860, A Social Survey*, London: Collins
Lucas, R. E., 1976. 'Econometric policy evaluation: a critique', in K. Brunner and A. Meltzer (eds), *The Phillips Curve and Labour Markets*, Supplement to *Journal of Monetary Economics*
1988. 'On the mechanics of economic development', *Journal of Monetary Economics* 22, 3–42
Mabey, N., 1995. 'Macroeconomic Modelling of Carbon Taxes', Discussion Paper No. DP 11–95, Centre for Economic Forecasting, London Business School
McKenzie, L., 1959. 'On the existence of general equilibrium for a competitive market', *Econometrica* 27, 54–71
McKibbin, W. J., 1992. 'Integrating Macroeconomic and Multisectoral Computable General Equilibrium Models', paper presented to an ESRC Conference on 'The Future of Macroeconomic Modelling in the United Kingdom', London, 30 November–1 December 1992
McKibbin, W. J. and Wilcoxen, P., 1992. 'GCUBED: A Dynamic Multisectoral General Equilibrium Growth Model of the Global Economy', Brookings Discussion Papers in International Economics, No. 97, Washington DC
Mann, H. B. and Wald, A., 1943. 'On the statistical treatment of linear stochastic difference equations', *Econometrica* 11, 173–220
Manne, A. S. (ed.), 1985. *Economic Equilibrium: Model Formulation and Solution*, Mathematical Programming Study 23, Amsterdam: North-Holland
Manne, A. S. and Rutherford, T. F., 1994. 'International trade in oil, gas and carbon emission rights: an intertemporal general equilibrium model', *Energy Journal* 15(1), 31–56
Manne, H. G., 1965. 'Mergers and the market for corporate control', *Journal of Political Economy* 73, 693–706
Manski, C., 1975. 'Maximum score estimation of the stochastic utility model of choice', *Journal of Econometrics* 27, 313–34
Mansur, A. H. and Whalley, J., 1984. 'Numerical specification of applied general equilibrium models: estimation, calibration, and data', in H. E. Scarf and J. B. Shoven (eds), *Applied General Equilibrium Analysis*, Cambridge: Cambridge University Press

Mantoux, P., 1928. *The Industrial Revolution in the Eighteenth Century*, revised edition, London: Jonathan Cape

Marais, D. A. J., 1979. 'A Method of Quantifying Companies' Relative Strength', Bank of England Discussion Paper No. 4, London

Massie, P., 1758. *A Plan for the Establishment of Charity Houses*, London: T. Payne
   1760. *A Computation of the Money that hath been exorbitantly Raised upon the People of Great Britain by the Sugar Planters, in one year from January 1759 to January 1760*, London: T. Payne

Mathias, P., 1957. 'The social structure in the Eighteenth Century: a calculation by Joseph Massie', *Economic History Review* 10, 30–45

Mayhew, H., 1980. *The Morning Chronicle Survey of Labour and the Poor: The Metropolitan Districts*, new edition, 6 vols, Firle: Caliban Books

Meade, J. E. and Stone, J. R. N., 1941. 'The construction of tables of national income, expenditure, savings, and investment', *Economic Journal* 51, 216–33

Meeks, G., 1977. *Disappointing Marriage: A Study of the Gains from Merger*, Department of Applied Economics Occasional Paper No. 51, Cambridge: Cambridge University Press

Mercenier, J. and Srinivasan, T. N. (eds), 1994. *Applied General Equilibrium and Economic Development*, Ann Arbor: University of Michigan Press

Ministerio de Agricultura, 1990. *Anuario de Estadística Agraria 1987*, Madrid: Ministerio de Agricultura

Mitchell, B. R., 1962. *Abstract of British Historical Statistics*, Cambridge: Cambridge University Press
   1964. 'The coming of the railway and United Kingdom economic growth', *Journal of Economic History* 24, 315–36
   1984. *Economic Development of the British Coal Industry*, Cambridge: Cambridge University Press

Mogadham, R. and Wren-Lewis, S. 1994. 'Are wages forward-looking?', *Oxford Economic Papers* 46(3), 403–24

Morgan, M. S., 1990. *The History of Econometric Ideas*, Cambridge: Cambridge University Press

Mors, M., 1991. 'The Economics of Policies to Stabilize or Reduce Greenhouse Gas Emissions: the Case of CO_2', EC Economic Papers No. 87, Luxembourg

Mosteller, F. and Wallace, D. L. K., 1963. 'Inference in the authorship problem', *Journal of the American Statistical Association* 58, 275–309

Moyle, J., 1971. *The Pattern of Ordinary Share Ownership 1957–70*, DAE Occasional Paper No. 31, Cambridge: Cambridge University Press

Moyle, J. and Revell, J., 1966. *The Owners of Quoted Ordinary Shares: A Survey for 1963*, No. 7 in the series 'A Programme for Growth', London: Chapman and Hall

Mueller, D. C., 1969. 'A theory of conglomerate merger', *Quarterly Journal of Economics* 83, 643–59
   1986. *Profits in the Long Run*, Cambridge: Cambridge University Press

Meuller, D. C. (ed.), 1990. *The Dynamics of Company Profits*, Cambridge: Cambridge University Press

Myrdal, G., 1957. *Economic Theory and Underdeveloped Regions*, London: Duckworth

A New System of Practical Domestic Economy, 1825. London: H. Colburn

Nickell, S. J., 1981. 'Biases in dynamic models with fixed effects', *Econometrica* 49, 1417–26

Nicoletti, G. and Oliveira-Martins, J., 1992. 'Global Effects of the European Carbon Tax', Working Paper No. 125, OECD Economics Department, Paris

NIESR, 1995. 'National Institute Domestic Economic Model', National Institute for Economic and Social Research, London

Niehans, J., 1981. 'The Appreciation of Sterling: Causes, Effects and Policies', Centre Symposia Series 11, Graduate School of Management, University of Rochester

Nordhaus, W., 1973. 'World dynamics: measurement without data', *Economic Journal* 83, December, 1156–83

O'Donnell, R., 1995. 'Keynes and formalism', in G. C. Harcourt and P. A. Riach (eds), *A 'Second Edition' of the General Theory*, London: Routledge

OECD, 1994–5. *The OECD Jobs Study*, Paris: Organisation for Economic Cooperation and Development

Oliveira-Martins, J., 1995. 'Unilateral emission control, energy-intensive industries and carbon leakages', Annex B in *Global Warming Economic Dimensions and Policy Responses*, Paris: OECD

Oliveira-Martins, J., Burniaux, J.-M. and Martin, J. P., 1992. 'Trade and the effectiveness of unilateral CO_2 abatement policies: evidence from Green', *OECD Economic Studies No.19*, Winter, 123–40

Oram, R. B., 1970. *The Dockers' Tragedy*, London: Hutchinson

Orcutt, G. H., 1948. 'A study of autoregressive nature of the time series used for Tinbergen's model of the economic system of the United States', *Journal of the Royal Statistical Society*, Series B, 1–45

Pain, N. and Westaway, P. F., 1994. 'Housing, Consumption and Borrowing: An Econometric Model of Personal Sector Behaviour', Government Economic Service Working Paper No. 123, HM Treasury, London

1996. 'The demand for domestic output and imports in the UK: a dynamic systems approach', *Manchester School* 64(1), March, 1–21

Palgrave, R. H. I., 1898 (second edition 1926). *Palgrave's Dictionary of Political Economy* edited by H. Higgs, London: Macmillan

Parliamentary Papers (PP), 1817. IV, *Select Committee to Inquire into the Income and Expenditure of the United Kingdom, 6th Report, the Navy* (H.C. 410)

1830. XVIII, *Returns of the Rates of Pay and Allowances to the Officers and Men of the Army in the years 1792 and 1829* (H.C. 580)

1833. VI, *Report from the Select Committee on Manufactures, Commerce and Shipping* (H.C. 690)

1834. XXX-XXXIV, *Report from H. M. Commissioners for Inquiry into the Administration and Practical Operation of the Poor Laws, Appendix B1, Answers to Rural Questions* (H.C.44)

1843. XII, *Reports of Special Assistant Poor Law Commissioner on the Employment of Women and Children in Agriculture* (H.C. 510)

1851. LXXXVIII, Pt. I, 1851 *Census of Population, Occupations*

1859. III, *Select Committee on Lunatics* (H.C. 204)

1871. XXXIX, *Return Showing the Estimated Equivalent Weekly Wage of a Private Soldier* (H.C.192)

1878. XLVII, *Return Showing the Estimated Equivalent Weekly Wage of a Private Soldier* (H.C.182)

1887. LXXXIX, *Returns of Wages Published between 1830 and 1886* (C. 5172)

1892. XIX, *Terms and Conditions of Service in the Army, Report and Minutes of Evidence* (C. 6582)

1893–94. LXXXIII, Pt II, *Rates of Wages paid in the United Kingdom in 1886, General Report [by R Giffen] on the Wages of the Manual Labour Classes in the United Kingdom in 1886* (C. 6889); see also PP, 1889. LXX, *Principal Textile Trades* (C. 5807); PP, 1890. LXVIII, *Minor Textile Trades* (C. 6161); PP, 1890–91. LXXVIII, *Mines and Quarries* (C. 6455); and PP, 1893. LXVIII, *Police, Roads, etc., Gas and Water Works* (C. 6715)

1909. LXXX, *Report of an Enquiry into Earnings and Hours of Workpeople in the United Kingdom in 1906*, Pt.I, *Textile Trades* (Cd. 4545); Pt. II, *Clothing* (Cd. 4844)

1910. LXXXIV, Pt. III, *Building and Woodworking* (Cd. 5086); Pt. IV, *Public Utilities and Services* (Cd. 5196); Pt. V, *Agriculture in 1907* (Cd. 5460)

1911. LXXXVIII, Pt. VI, *Metals, Engineering and Shipbuilding* (Cd. 5814)

1912–13. CVIII, Pt. VII, *Railway Service in 1907* (Cd. 6053); Pt. VIII, *Miscellaneous Trades* (Cd. 6556)

various dates. *Navy Estimates*, issued annually, London: HMSO

Pagan, A., 1995. 'The ET interview: Gregory C. Chow', *Econometric Theory* 11, 597–624

Pearce, D., 1991. 'The role of carbon taxes in adjusting to global warming', *Economic Journal* 101, 938–48

Pearson, P. J. G., 1989. 'Proactive energy-environment policy strategies: a role for input-output analysis?', *Environment and Planning* 21, 1329–48

Peel, C. S., 1926. *A Hundred Wonderful Years*, London: John Lane

1934. 'Homes and habits', in G. M. Young (ed.), *Early Victorian England, 1830–1865*, Oxford: Oxford University Press

Penrose, E. F., 1959. *The Theory of the Growth of the Firm*, Oxford: Blackwell

Perroni, C. and Rutherford, T. F., 1993. 'International trade in carbon emission rights and basic materials: general equilibrium calculations for 2020', *Scandinavian Journal of Economics* 95(3), 257–78

Pesaran, B. and Wright, C., 1992. 'Using and Assessing CBI Data at the Bank of England', Bank of England Discussion Paper (Technical Series) No. 37

Pesaran, M. H., 1984. 'Expectations formations and macro-econometric modelling', in P. Malgrange and P.-A. Muet (eds), *Contemporary Macroeconomic Modelling*, Oxford: Basil Blackwell

1987a. *The Limits to Rational Expectations*, Oxford: Basil Blackwell

1987b. 'Econometrics', in J. Eatwell, M. Milgate and P. Newman (eds), *The New Palgrave Dictionary of Economics*, Vol. II, London and New York: Macmillan

1991. 'The ET Interview: Professor Sir Richard Stone', *Econometric Theory* 7, 85–123

1997. 'The role of economic theory in modelling the long run', *Economic Journal* 107(440), January, 178–91

Pesaran, M. H., Pierse, R. G. and Kumar, M., 1989. 'Econometric analysis of aggregation in the context of linear prediction models', *Econometrica* 57, 861–88

Pesaran, M. H. and Shin, Y., 1995. 'Long-run Structural Modelling', unpublished manuscript, Trinity College and Department of Applied Economics, University of Cambridge

Pesaran, M. H. and Smith, R. J., 1994. 'A generalised R^2 for regression models estimated by the instrumental variables method', *Econometrica* 62, 705–710

Pesaran, M. H. and Smith, R. P., 1992. 'Estimating Long-run Relationships from Dynamic Heterogenous Panels', London Business School Discussion Paper No. DP 17–92

1995a. 'Alternative approaches to estimating long-run energy demand elasticities: an application to Asian developing countries', in T. Barker, P. Ekins and N. Johnstone (eds), *Global Warming and Energy Demand*, London: Routledge

1995b. 'Estimating long-run relationships from dynamic heterogenous panels', *Journal of Econometrics* 68, 79–113

Peterson, A. W. A., 1995. *MREG A Modelling and Regression Program* (MREG version 5.0), Cambridge: Lynxvale

Peterson, A. W. A., Barker, T. S. and Ploeg, F. van de, 1983. 'Software support for multisectoral dynamic models of national economies', *Journal of Economic Dynamics and Control 5*, 109–30

Phillips, P., 1986. 'The ET Interview: T. W. Anderson', *Econometric Theory* 2, 249–88

1988. 'The ET Interview: James Durbin', *Econometric Theory* 4, 125–7

Piggott, J. and Whalley, J. (eds), 1985. *New Developments in Applied General Equilibrium Analysis*, Cambridge: Cambridge University Press

Pinchbeck, I., 1930. *Women Workers in the Industrial Revolution*, London: George Routledge

Porter, G. R., 1847. *The Progress of the Nation*, London: John Murray

Porter, M. E., 1979. 'The structure within industries and companies performance', *Review of Economics and Statistics* 61, May, 214–27

Prais, S. J., 1976. *The Evolution of Giant Firms in the UK*, Cambridge: Cambridge University Press

Prais, S. J. and Houthakker, H. S., 1955. *The Analysis of Family Budgets* (2nd impression 1971), DAE Monograph No 4, Cambridge: Cambridge University Press

Pudney, S. E., 1993. 'Income and wealth inequality and the life cycle. A non-parametric analysis for China', *Journal of Applied Econometrics* 8, 249–76

Pyatt, G., and Round, J. I. (eds), 1985. *Social Account Matrices: A Basis for Planning*, Washington: World Bank

Qin, D., 1993. *The Formation of Econometrics: A Historical Perspective*, Oxford: Clarendon Press

Quah, D., 1993. 'Galton's fallacy and tests of the convergence hypothesis', *Scandinavian Journal of Economics* 95, 427–43

Quesnay, F., 1759. *Tableau économique*, third edition, Paris: Privately printed. Reproduced, edited, and translated by M. Kuczynski and R. L. Meek (1972), *Quesnay's tableau économique*, London: Macmillan

Railway Wages, no date. 'Railway Wages', Public Record Office, LAB 41/25

Ramsey, J. B., 1969. 'Tests for specification errors in classical linear least squares regression analysis', *Journal of the Royal Statistical Society*, Series B, 31, 350–71

Ravenscraft, D. J. and Scherer, F. M., 1987. *Mergers, Sell Offs, and Economic Efficiency*, Washington: Brookings Institution
  1989. 'The profitability of mergers', *International Journal of Industrial Organization* 1(7), March

Reid, S. R., 1968. *Mergers, Managers and the Economy*, New York: McGraw-Hill

Rhoades, S. A., 1983. *Power Empire Building and Mergers*, Lexington MA: Lexington Books

Robinson, P. M., 1988. 'Root-N-consistent semiparametric regression', *Econometrica* 56, 931–54

Rose, M. B., 1986. *The Gregs of Quarry Bank Mill*, Cambridge: Cambridge University Press

Rose, P. S., Andrews, W. T. and Giroux, G. A., 1982. 'Predicting business failure: a macroeconomic perspective', *Journal of Accounting, Auditing and Finance*, 20–31

Rule, J., 1981. *The Experience of Labour in Eighteenth-Century Industry*, London: Croom Helm

Salter, W. E. G., 1960. *Productivity and Technical Change*, DAE Monograph 6, Cambridge: Cambridge University Press

Samuels, J. M., 1965. 'Size and the growth of firms', *Review of Economic Studies* 32, 105–12

Samuels, J. M. and Chesher, A. D., 1972. 'Growth, survival, and the size of companies 1960–69', in K. Cowling (ed.), *Market Structure and Corporate Behaviour*, London: Grey-Mills

Samuelson, P. A., Koopmans, T. C. and Stone, J. R. N., 1954. 'Report of the evaluative committee on Econometrica', *Econometrica* 22, 141–6

Sargent, T. J., 1979. *Macroeconomic Theory*, London and New York: Academic Press

Scarf, H. E., 1967. 'On the computation of equilibrium prices', in W. J. Fellner (ed.), *Ten Economic Studies in the Tradition of Irving Fisher*, New York: Wiley

Scarf, H. E. and Hansen, T., 1973. *The Computation of Economic Equilibria*, New Haven: Yale University Press

Scarf, H. E. and Shoven, J. B. (eds), 1984. *Applied General Equilibrium Analysis*, Cambridge: Cambridge University Press

Schink, G., 1975. 'Ex ante and ex post forecasts', in G. Fromm and L. Klein (eds), *The Brookings Model*, New York: North-Holland

Schmalensee, R., 1989. 'Inter-industry studies of structure and performance', in R. Schmalensee and R. Willig (eds), *Handbook of Industrial Organisation, Vol.2*, Amsterdam: North-Holland

Scott, M. F., 1989. *A New View of Economic Growth*, Oxford: Clarendon Press

Sefton, J. A. and Weale, M. R., 1995. *Reconciliation of National Income and Expenditure: Balanced Estimates of National Income for the United Kingdom, 1920–1990*, Volume 7 of 'Studies in the National Income and Expenditure of the United Kingdom', Cambridge: Cambridge University Press

Shiells, C. R., Stern, R. M. and Deardorff, A. V., 1986. 'Estimates of the elasticities of substitution between imports and home goods for the United States', *Weltwirtschaftliches-Archiv* 122, 497–519

Shoven, J. B. and Whalley J., 1972. 'A general equilibrium calculation of the effects of differential taxation of income from capital in the US', *Journal of Public Economics* 1, 281–321

1984. 'Applied general-equilibrium models of taxation and trade: an introduction and survey', *Journal of Economic Literature* 22, 1007–51

1992. *Applying General Equilibrium*, Cambridge: Cambridge University Press

Silverman, B. W., 1986. *Density Estimation for Statistics and Data Analysis*, London: Chapman and Hall

Sims, C., 1980. 'Macroeconomics and reality', *Econometrica* 48, 1–48

Singh, A., 1971. *Takeovers: Their Relevance to the Stock Market and the Theory of the Firm*, Cambridge: Cambridge University Press

1975. 'Takeovers, economic natural selection and the theory of the firm: evidence from the postwar United Kingdom experience', *Economic Journal* 85, September, 497–515

1992. 'Corporate Takeovers', in J. Eatwell, M. Milgate and P. Newman (eds), *The New Palgrave Dictionary of Money and Finance*, London and New York: Macmillan

1993. 'Regulation of mergers: a new agenda', in R. Sugden (ed.), *Industrial Economic Regulation: A Framework and Exploration*, London: Routledge

Singh, A. and Whittington, G., 1968. *Growth, Profitability and Valuation*, DAE Occasional Paper No 7, Cambridge: Cambridge University Press

1975. 'The size and growth of firms', *Review of Economic Studies* 42, 15–26

Slater, L. J., 1966. *Generalized Hypergeometric Functions*, Cambridge: Cambridge University Press

Smee, W. R., 1846. *The Income Tax*, second edition, London: Pelham Richardson

Smith, R. J., Weale, M. R. and Satchell, S. E., 1997. 'Measurement error with accounting constraints: point and interval estimation for latent data with an application to UK gross domestic product', *Review of Economic Studies*, forthcoming

Snell, K. D. M., 1985. *Annals of the Labouring Poor: Social Change and Agrarian England, 1660–1900*, Cambridge: Cambridge University Press

Soskice, D. and Carlin, W., 1989. 'Medium-run Keynesianism: hysteresis and capital scrapping', in P. Davidson and J. Kregel (eds), *Macroeconomic Problems and Policies of Income Distribution*, Aldershot: Edward Edgar

Soteri, S. and Westaway, P. F., 1993. 'Explaining price inflation in the UK: 1971–1992', *National Institute Economic Review* 144, 85–95

Srinivasan, T. N. and Whalley, J. (eds), 1986. *General Equilibrium Trade Policy Modeling*, Cambridge MA: MIT Press

Stock, J. and Watson, J., 1990. 'New Indices of Co-incident and Leading Economic Indicators', unpublished manuscript, National Bureau for Economic Research, Washington DC

Stone, J. R. N., 1947a. *Measurement of National Income and the Construction of Social Accounts*, Geneva: United Nations

1947b. 'On the interdependence of blocks of transactions', Supplement to the *Journal of the Royal Statistical Society* 11, 1–32

1951. *The Role of Measurement in Economics*, DAE Monograph No 3, Cambridge: Cambridge University Press

1954a. *The Measurement of Consumers Expenditure and Behaviour in the United Kingdom, 1920–1938*, Cambridge: Cambridge University Press

1954b. 'Linear expenditure systems and demand analysis: an application to the pattern of British demand', *Economic Journal* 64, 511–27

1961. 'An econometric model of growth: the British economy in ten years time', *Discovery* 22, 216–219

1962. 'A demonstration model of economic growth', *The Manchester School of Economic and Social Studies* 30(1), 1–14

1978. 'Keynes, political arithmetic and econometrics', *Proceedings of the British Academy* 64, 55–92

1985. 'The disaggregation of the household sector in the national accounts', in G. Pyatt and J. I. Round (eds), *Social Accounting Matrices: A Basis for Planning*, Washington: The World Bank

1986. 'The accounts of society' (Nobel Memorial Lecture 1984), *Journal of Applied Econometrics* 1(1), 5–28

Stone, J. R. N. and Brown, J. A. C., 1962a. 'A long-term growth model for the British economy', in R. C. Geary (ed.), *Europe's Future in Figures*, I, Amsterdam: North-Holland

1962b. *A Computable Model of Economic Growth*, Volume 1 in 'A Programme for Growth', Department of Applied Economics, University of Cambridge, London: Chapman and Hall

Stone, J. R. N., Champernowne, D. A. and Meade, J. E., 1942. 'The precision of national income estimates', *Review of Economic Studies* 9, 111–25

Stone, J. R. N. and Prais, S. J., 1953. 'Forecasting from econometric equations: a further note on derationing', *Economic Journal* 63, 249

Storey, D., Keasey, K., Watson, R. and Wynarczyk, P., 1987. *The Performance of Small Firms*, Routledge: London

Studenski, P., 1958. *The Income of Nations*, New York: New York University Press

Summers, R. and Heston, A., 1991. 'The Penn World Table (Mark 5): an expanded set of international comparisons, 1950–1988', *Quarterly Journal of Economics* 61, May, 327–68

Taffler, R. J., 1982. 'Forecasting company failure in the UK using discriminant analysis and financial ratio data', *Journal of the Royal Statistical Society*, Series A, 145, 342–58

Taylor, J. B., 1980. 'Aggregate dynamics and staggered contracts', *Journal of Political Economy* 88, 1–24

Taylor, L. (ed.), 1990. *Socially Relevant Policy Analysis: Structuralist Computable General Equilibrium Models for the Developing World*, Cambridge MA: MIT Press

Theil, H., 1952. 'On the time-shape of economic microvariables and the Munich business test', *Revue de l'Institut International de Statistique* 20, 105–20

Tintner, G., 1952. *Econometrics*, New York: Wiley

1953. 'The definition of econometrics', *Econometrica* 21(1), January, 31–40

Trade Indemnity, 1993. *Quarterly Business Review*, London: Trade Indemnity plc

Tulloch, A. M., 1863. 'On the pay and income of the British soldier as compared with the rate of agricultural wages', *Journal of the Royal Statistical Society* 26, 168–85

United Nations, 1953. *A System of National Accounts and Supporting Tables*, New York: United Nations

1968. *A System of National Accounts*, New York: United Nations

Unwin, G., 1924. *Samuel Oldknow and the Arkwrights*, Manchester: Manchester University Press

Vercelli, A., 1991. *Methodological Foundations of Macroeconomics*, Cambridge: Cambridge University Press

Wadsworth, A. P. and Mann, J. De Lacy, 1931. *The Cotton Trade and Industrial Lancashire*, Manchester: Manchester University Press

Warden, A. J., 1864. *The Linen Trade, Ancient and Modern*, London: Longman, Green

Weale, M. R., 1992. 'Estimation of data measured with error and subject to linear restrictions', *Journal of Applied Econometrics* 7, 167–74

Weintraub, E. R., 1979. *Microfoundations: The Compatibility of Microeconomics and Macroeconomics*, Cambridge: Cambridge University Press

Westaway, P. F. and Young, G., 1993. 'Capital Structure and Equity Prices in a Macroeconomic Model', paper presented at the ESRC Macroeconomic Modelling Bureau conference, July

Whalley, J., 1986. 'What Have We Learned from General Equilibrium Tax Policy Models?', Working Paper 8625C, University of Western Ontario

1988. 'Lessons from general equilibrium models', in H. J. Arron, H. Galper and J. A. Pechman (eds), *Uneasy Compromise: Problems of a Hybrid Income-Consumption Tax*, Washington: Brookings Institute

1991. 'Applied general equilibrium modelling', in D. Greenaway, M. Bleaney and I. Stewart (eds), *Companion to Contemporary Economic Thought*, London: Routledge

Whittington, G., 1971. *The Prediction of Profitability*, DAE Occasional Paper No. 22, Cambridge: Cambridge University Press

Wickens, M., 1995. 'Real business cycle analysis: a needed revolution in macroeconomics?', *Economic Journal* 105, 1637–48

Williamson, J. G., 1982. 'The structure of pay in Britain, 1710–1911', *Research in Economic History* 7, 1–54

1985. *Did British Capitalism Breed Inequality?*, London: Allen and Unwin

Williamson, O. E., 1975. *Markets and Hierarchies: Analysis and Anti-Trust Implications*, New York: Free Press

Wood, G. H., 1899. 'The course of average wages between 1790 and 1860', *Economic Journal* 9, 588–92

1909a. 'Real wages and the standard of comfort since 1850', *Journal of the Royal Statistical Society* 72, 91–103

1909b. 'Tests of progress applied to the woollen trade', *Huddersfield Technical College, Textile Society Journal*, Sixth Session, 64–77

1910. 'The statistics of wages in the United Kingdom during the Nineteenth Century, Parts XV–XIX, the cotton industry', *Journal of the Royal Statistical Society*, 73, 39–58, 128–63, 283–315, 411–34 and 585–626

Woollen and Worsted Wage Enquiry, 1839–1907. 'Woollen and Worsted Wage Enquiry, 1839–1907', Public Record Office, LAB 41/61, 41/25

Wrigley, E. A. and Schofield, R. S., 1981. *The Population History of England 1541–1871*, London: Arnold

Young, A., 1770. *A Six Months Tour Through the North of England*, London: Strahan

Young, G., 1992. 'Industrial Investment and Economic Policy', in A. J. Britton (ed.), *Industrial Investment as a Policy Objective*, National Institute Report No. 3, London: NIESR

1993. 'Debt deflation and the company sector: the economic effects of balance sheet adjustment', *National Institute Economic Review* 144, 74–84

Yule, G. U., 1926. 'Why do we sometimes get nonsense correlations between time-series? – A study in sampling and the nature of time-series', *Journal of the Royal Statistical Society* 60, 812–54

Index

292   **Index**